ST/CTC/168
Current Studies Series A, No. 27

United Nations Conference on Trade and Development
Programme on Transnational Corporations

THE TRADABILITY OF BANKING SERVICES

Impact and implications

United Nations, Geneva 1994

NOTE

The UNCTAD Programme on Transnational Corporations of the United Nations serves as the focal point within the United Nations Secretariat for all matters related to transnational corporations. In the past, the Programme on Transnational Corporations was carried out by the United Nations Centre on Transnational Corporations (1975-1992) and by the Transnational Corporations and Management Division of the United Nations Department of Economic and Social Development (1992-1993). In 1993 the programme was transferred to the United Nations Conference on Trade and Development. The objectives of the work programme include to further the understanding of the nature of transnational corporations and of their economic, legal, political and social effects on home and host countries and in international relations, particularly between developed and developing countries; to secure effective international arrangements aimed at enhancing the contribution of transnational corporations to national development and world economic growth; and to strengthen the negotiating capacity of host countries, in particular developing countries, in their dealings with transnational corporations.

The term "country" as used in this report also refers, as appropriate, to territories or areas; the designations employed and the presentation of the material do not imply the expression of any opinion whatsoever on the part of the Secretariat of the United Nations concerning the legal status of any boundaries. In addition, the designations of country groups are intended solely for statistical or analytical convenience and do not necessarily express a judgement about the stage of development reached by a particular country or area in the development process.

The following symbols have been used in the tables:

Two dots (..) indicate that data are not available or are not separately reported. Rows in tables have been omitted in those cases where no data are available for any of the elements in the row;

A blank in a table indicates that the item is not applicable;

Reference to "dollars" ($) means United States dollars, unless otherwise indicated.

Annual rates of growth or change, unless otherwise stated, refer to annual compound rates.

Details and percentages in tables do not necessarily add to totals because of rounding.

The material contained in this study may be freely quoted with appropriate acknowledgement

UNCTAD/DTCI/14

UNITED NATIONS PUBLICATION

Sales No. E.94.II.A.12

ISBN 92-1-104-433-2

PREFACE

International trade in goods has expanded rapidly in the post-war period. Trade in services expanded as well; however, due to the limited possibilities for transporting many services between producers and buyers located at a distance from each other, the volume of this trade has remained considerably below that of trade in goods. This has meant not only that the establishment of affiliates was the only way many services could be delivered abroad, but also that it was not possible for transnational corporations to split up their production activities to take advantage of local factor endowments.

New telecommunications and electronic data-processing technologies are, however, increasing the tradability of a number of services. This change is likely to have a significant impact on trade, foreign direct investment and the role of transnational service corporations. The implications are of particular relevance to developing countries that are interested in taking advantage of opportunities for increased trade in services to build up their indigenous service industries, strengthen the competitiveness of their economies and enhance their export prospects.

In light of the above, the UNCTAD Programme on Transnational Corporations (the former UNCTC) has initiated a project aimed at providing a better understanding of the tradability of services and its impact, and assisting countries in formulating policies and programmes that could contribute towards maximizing their benefits from trade and foreign direct investment in services in the context of the increasing tradability of services. The present report, focusing on banking services, is a pilot project funded by the Danish International Development Assistance (DANIDA).

Banks and financial institutions have been at the forefront in the application of new technologies to the delivery of their services. As a result, the world's major financial institutions have undergone a profound transformation over the past few decades. More recently, with the application of information and telecommunications technologies, banks are able to deliver a range of services to customers far removed from the location of the production facility.

The increasing tradability of banking services also permits banks, in principle, to locate intermediate stages of the production of certain services -- e.g., processing tasks -- to countries in the same way as corporations involved in the production of goods can locate labour-intensive stages of their production in countries in which factor costs, especially of labour, are low. This development has significant implications for developing countries. These countries are now, in principle, in a better position to benefit from the siting of a number of export-generating banking services affiliates on their territories. In addition, the increased tradability of banking services will allow them easier access to international credit-intermediation services and provide them a chance to improve the quality of banking services available to producers and others. The provision of efficient banking services is a key component in encouraging investment, both domestic and foreign and in promoting economic growth.

The purpose of this study is to examine the tradability of banking products, particularly as regards its technical feasibility and the implications of this for both banking enterprises and national economies, including, particularly, developing countries. The study also outlines policy options and measures which could allow developing countries to maximize the benefits from these new developments.

The research project on tradability is directed by Karl P. Sauvant. This study is based on a research report prepared by Erik Baark, Morten Falch, Anders Henten and Knud Erik Skouby in collaboration with Olaf Valentin Kjær at Unibank, Copenhagen. The study benefited from technical advice by James C. Grant and from the comments of Cristiano Antonelli, Gert Bundgaard, Robin Mansell and Peter Sørensen. It was prepared for publication by Padma Mallampally and Jörg Weber. The text was typed by Kanayalal Israni and Lilian Mercado. The study was desk-top published by Lars Abrahamsen and Claus Nielsen.

The UNCTAD Programme on Transnational Corporations is grateful to the Danish International Development Assistance for its extra-budgetary assistance to this project.

Carlos Fortin
Deputy to the Secretary-General and
Director-in-Charge
Programme on Transnational Corporations
United Nations Conference on Trade and Development

Geneva, November 1993

INTRODUCTION

The services sector has grown rapidly during the past few decades. Services now account for the largest share of the gross national product and employment in all developed and many developing countries. As a result, increasing importance is being attached to the efficiency and competitiveness of services as a factor determining the economic performance of countries.

Traditionally, services tended to be regarded as useful, but relatively unimportant economic activities.[1] In developing countries, the services sector has suffered from widespread inefficiency and a low priority given to it by policymakers. Traditional and informal modes of organization still tend to prevail in the provision of many essential services. The formal sector has often been split into two components: private service firms based on foreign direct investment on the one hand, and public corporations on the other.

The growing role of services in national economies has led more recently to a recognition of the importance of the services sector for economic analysis and policy formulation. Services are now high on the agenda of international, regional and national policy making. At the national level, deregulation and privatization of several services and the liberalization of international transactions have been implemented by several countries. At the international level, the liberalization of international transactions in services has been one of the key issues addressed in the formulation of a General Agreement on Trade in Services during the Uruguay Round of Multilateral Trade Negotiations.

Due to the limited possibilities for transporting many services between producers and buyers located at a distance from each other, international trade in services did not receive much attention until recently. During the 1980s, the picture changed, as the importance and potential of trade in services became apparent. In the case of the United States, for instance, the share of services in the country's exports (which had declined from 22 per cent to 19 per cent in the 1970s) grew to approximately 26 per cent in 1985 and 29 per cent in 1990. Services now account for 30 per cent of United States exports and approximately 20 per cent of world trade.[2]

In addition, sales of services by foreign affiliates of transnational corporations have become an important source of income for those firms. The sale of services by affiliates of United States firms was $119 billion in 1990, as compared with $138 billion earned in cross-border sales of private services by United States firms.[3] Nevertheless, transnational service corporations have found it difficult to split up their production activities in order to take advantage of local factor endowments, owing to the lack of tradability of services.

The extent and pattern of international transactions in services are likely to change significantly, however, as a result of the increased tradability of many services due to the application of information and telecommunication technologies. This report studies the extent to which these technologies are affecting the tradability of the products of one service industry -- the banking industry -- which plays an important role in both developed and developing countries, the resulting impact on trade and foreign direct investment in banking services and the implications, especially for developing countries. More specifically:

- Chapter I discusses the concept of tradability and its relevance for banking services.

- Chapter II provides an overview of the main characteristics and trends in banking and of the extent to which advanced information and telecommunication technologies have affected the tradability of products currently offered by banks, possible future services, the development of modern banking and its role in development.

- Chapter III contains a detailed technical analysis of the nature of various banking-service products, their production processes and delivery, focusing on their technical tradability or transportability on the basis of information and telecommunication technologies.

The chapter deals with the technological, economic and regulatory barriers that impede the process of delivering banking services abroad at arm's length, although the latter two factors are discussed more fully in chapters V and VI, which consider the prospects and consequences of increased tradability for banking.

- Chapter IV discusses the role of the expansion of international dedicated telecommunications networks for banking services in the reduction of the technological barriers to tradability. It provides a description of the major networks and information services utilized by banks and the role of such networks in facilitating the tradability of banking services.

- Chapter V presents an analysis of how increased tradability affects the structure of international banking, with particular reference to the choice between foreign direct investment or the setting up of affiliates abroad by banks, and trade in banking services across borders, drawing, in part, on the results of a questionnaire survey of major banks in Europe, North America and Japan.

- Chapter VI discusses impacts and implications of the increased tradability of banking-service products for developing and developed countries. More specifically, it considers the kinds of benefits or drawbacks that might emerge from the new opportunities for tradability in the industry.

- Chapter VII outlines policy implications of tradability for both developing and developed countries, including the policy measures that could be considered in order to exploit the new opportunities for, and reduce potential negative impacts of, the tradability of banking services. The primary purpose of the discussion is to identify some policy options for enhancing the opportunities for developing countries to benefit from the tradability of banking services and outline some practical measures that could be initiated through international or bilateral assistance to help developing countries exploit potential opportunities.

● The final chapter contains a summary and the conclusions, including a consideration of the extent to which the conclusions reached with respect to banking services are of relevance to other industries in the services sector.

Karl P. Sauvant
Chief
Research and Policy Analysis Branch
Programme on Transnational Corporations
United Nations Conference on Trade and Development

Geneva, November 1993

Notes

1   For a brief overview of different views on services and the role of technological change in the sector, see UNCTAD, *Technological change in services and international trade competitiveness*, prepared by Ian Miles and Sally Wyatt (UNCTAD/ITP/TEC/29, 1991).

2   "The final frontier", *The Economist*, 20 February 1993, p. 63.

3   John A. Sondheimer and Sylvia E. Bargas, "U.S. international sales and purchases of private services", United States Department of Commerce, *Survey of Current Business* (September 1992), p. 82.

Contents

List of tables

List of boxes

List of figures

Chapter I

INFORMATION TECHNOLOGY, SERVICES AND TRADABILITY

A. The concept of tradability of services: its technological, economic and legal aspects

"Tradability of services" is defined here as the possibility for the cross-border delivery of final services or of individual components (intermediate products) in the services-production chain without the movement of the provider or the customer. This basic definition is conceptualized here at three levels of analysis: the technical, the economic and the political levels. At the *technical* level, tradability refers to the purely technical transportability of intermediate or final products in services. At the *economic* level, it is concerned with the economic feasibility and realization of such technical possibilities. The main considerations at the *political* level involve the legal aspects of trade which, to a considerable extent can define the limitations of realizing the technical and economic possibilities for trade in services. At each of these levels it is possible to identify a range of factors that influence the tradability of service products. Table I.1 identifies some examples of such factors which, although not exhaustive, illustrate the kind of variables that are likely to

be most influential in determining the ultimate scope of tradability.

Table I.1. Examples of key factors influencing tradability

Type of factor	Examples of factors
Technical	- Telecommunications - Data processing
Economic	- Transaction costs - Internationalization af markets - Firm strategies
Political/ cultural	- Liberalization - Authorization procedures - Trust

Clearly, the various factors at the three levels are linked together to determine the actual cross-border trade of a service. For example, trade may be technically feasible, but it may not take place for economic reasons, or the economically viable trade of a service product may be hindered by the existing legal framework. There is a general consensus, however, that technological developments in telecommunications and data processing influence the economic conditions for tradability, which in turn requires new legal or regulatory initiatives.

1

The starting point of the analysis is the technical dimension, i.e., the actual transportability of a service. Transportability, or the technical possibility of delivering a service to a customer located at a distance, is a necessary precondition for trade, and hence the core of the concept of tradability of services. It is, however, not sufficient to ensure trade; for that at least one of the parties to trade must benefit in an economic sense and, moreover, they must be allowed to trade.

Technical tradability covers two distinct aspects. The first aspect, the transportability of *final* products, concerns the delivery of service products over geographical distances to consumers. A good example is the case of transborder transactions where customers use cards to draw local currency from their own accounts by means of an automatic teller machine (ATM) terminal in a foreign country. The second aspect, the transportability of *intermediate* products, concerns possibilities for splitting up the production processes of services (divisibility) and the location of parts of the production in a different geographical area. These possibilities depend on the feasibility of transportation of intermediate products, such as for example conciliation of the address of a recipient of a money-transfer order. Divisibility enhances the transportability of services products. By splitting up the production process into different components with varying degree of transportability, the production of the least transportable components can take place at the location of the customer, while the remaining parts can be produced elsewhere.

The relationship between information and telecommunication technologies on the one hand and the different aspects of tradability on the other is outlined in figure I.1. The introduction of electronic data-processing (EDP) has in-creased the possibilities to divide the process of production into different components.[1] This divisibility of service products affects the actual division of labour in that it increases the possibilities for transporting services or parts thereof. In addition, the diffusion of digital network technologies in public telecommunications networks increasingly facilitates network-based delivery of information. In combination, these technical innovations permit instantaneous, interactive, long-distance processing of transactions. Distance and national borders become much less important factors in access to information and the processing of large quantities of data. This has increased the possibilities for transporting services or parts thereof. As already mentioned, transportability is a necessary precondition for tradability across national borders. However, tradability depends on economic and legal factors as well.

Economic factors influencing tradability, i.e., the economic feasibility of utilizing transportability and divisibility, can be analyzed primarily in terms of the growth of an international market for products and services in general and the potential for outsourcing intermediate service products. The growth of the international market for services and that of foreign direct investment (FDI) by transnational corporations (TNCs) leads to new requirements for financial and other services transactions in relation to both the trade and the foreign affiliates of these firms. Sourcing intermediate products from affiliates or foreign firms is driven primarily by the balance between achieving factor-cost reductions, e.g., a reduction in labour costs for the production of a specific service product (or intermediate product) by placing part of the production process outside the firm --- and the transaction costs associated with this shift in the location of production. Thus, an analysis of the economic factors promoting tradability must look at the trends in international markets which generate demand for a transborder provision of services, as well as the economic feasibility of cross-border trade in final services and subcontracting of intermediate services production. In addition, strategies adopted by firms in the services sector play an important role in determining the extent to which the technical feasibility of tradability will be exploited.

Legal or regulatory factors also affect the tradability of services. For the purpose of the present study, the most important aspect is *liberalization*, which covers various ways to increase the level of competition by means of

deregulation of the markets for services (including, among others, the core area of telecommunications) and opening up markets to foreign equity participation. Also important are the legal requirements that are placed on a firm that intends to conduct business in services within a particular national or international context.

There are also a number of cultural factors that can influence the extent to which services that are tradeable in both a technical and an economic sense will actually be traded. The level of confidence or trust that customers associate with their services transactions is particularly important here. Such considerations are

Figure I.1. Divisibility, transportability and tradability

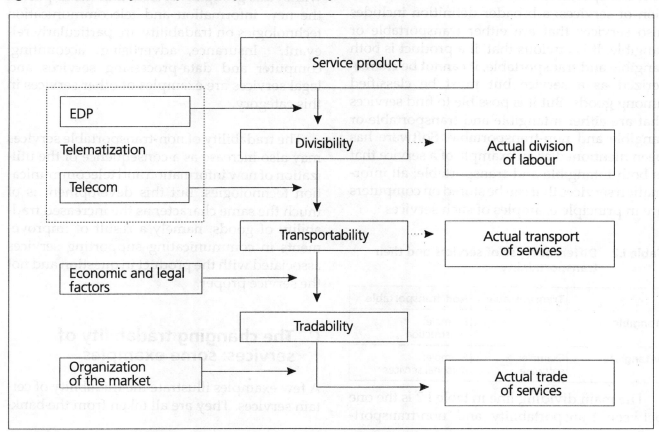

especially important in services such as banking and other financial services.

B. Types of service products and their tradability

Services typically are intangible and non-storable, and hence the possibility of transporting, and trading, many services over a distance has been limited. But these characteristics do not fit all services. Computer software, for instance, is storable.

In order to illustrate such differences among services, table I.2 presents examples of different types of services. As the figure shows, the category of services that is both intangible and non-transportable constitutes a narrow definition of services; a broader definition includes also services that are either transportable or tangible. It is obvious that, if a product is both tangible and transportable, it cannot be characterized as a service but must be classified among goods. But it is possible to find services that are either intangible and transportable or tangible and non-transportable. Software has been mentioned as an example of a service that is both intangible and transportable; all information services that can be stored on computers are in principle examples of such services.

Table I.2. Different types of services and their transportability

	Transportable	Non-transportable
Tangible		Example: construction
Intangible	Example: software	Example: personal services

The main dividing line in table I.2 is the one between transportability and non-transport-

ability. One might argue that information services stored on computers in reality are examples of "immaterial goods" and no longer should be characterized as services. Though such a definitional exercise does not in itself contribute much to the clarification of the new developments and possibilities created by the introduction of information and telecommunication technologies, it indicates that the dividing line between transportability and non-transportability is of crucial importance and that information services no longer have to depend on face-to-face contact between producers and consumers, i.e., that delivery can be separated in time and place from production.

Banking services with a high information content belong to that category of services. It is within this group of services that the impact of the new information and telecommunication technologies on tradability are particularly relevant. Insurance, advertising, accounting, computer and data-processing services and legal services are examples of other services in this category.

The tradability of non-transportable services may also increase as a consequence of the utilization of new information and telecommunication technologies. But this development is of much the same character as the increased tradability of goods, namely a result of improvements in communicating supporting services associated with the product in question and not the service proper.

C. The changing tradability of services: some examples

A few examples illustrate the tradability of certain services. They are all taken from the banking industry. A good example of the instantaneous cross-border delivery of a banking product is the use of an ATM to provide foreign exchange to a customer abroad by means of a debit or a credit card with the equivalent sum being debited from the customer's home country account. Here the service delivered belongs to the sphere of retail banking, which is concerned with the direct interaction of banks with private customers.

Another example concerns what are usually termed back-office processes. In most banks in developed countries, the processing of such transactions increasingly takes place at computing centres in locations far away from the data

---

Box I.1. Moving data processing back to the United States

"Cost-cutting pressures are driving United States banks in London to move their data processing back to the United Sates. J. P. Morgan's United Kingdom subsidiary recently transferred all computing from its London IBM mainframes to its data centre in Delaware. Many other subsidiaries of United States financial outfits have similar plans.

"Towers Perrin, a New York-based company specializing in pay and actuarial-benefits consulting has made major savings by moving its European data processing to Philadelphia. Its United Kingdom and continental European offices were previously linked to the Woking (United Kingdom) data centre. Now they use IBM's information network to connect to the Philadelphia one.... The move helped the Philadelphia computer centre because it had spare capacity, especially at night (day time for European users). "The only difference users notice is that the clock on the system is five hours adrift and in the bottom right-hand corner of the screen it says 'Phila' instead of 'London'."

Source: The Banker, March 1992, p. 17.

---

entry point (which would typically be at the counter of a branch office). The example described in box I.1 shows that some United States banks are using the opportunities offered by data-communications networks to shift back-office data processing back to their home country. The advantage offered by this arrangement is that new economies of scale can be achieved by concentrating major data-processing tasks in computing centres that have spare capacity. For example, due to time differences, the computing centre of a United States bank will have spare capacity for processing during the night which can be utilized by its European branch offices. A similar arrangement has existed for many years with regard to Danish banks operating in Greenland. All back-office processing required by local branch offices of the Danish banks have been conducted at the computing centres of the banks in Copenhagen using satellite communications (box I.2).

One important effect of these new developments is the reduction of foreign direct investment (FDI) in the local subsidiaries of banks operating internationally. The tendency to reduce investment in local affiliates has already appeared among major United States banks operating abroad. For a variety of reasons, the banks that established foreign affiliates in small European countries are now in the process of concentrating their activities in major regional centres from where they serve primarily corporate customers (box I.3).

D. Sub-contracting and facilities management

At the same time that there are signs of relocating data processing to home countries of transnational banks, the increasing tradability and

Box I.2. Remote processing for Danish banks in Greenland

In the mid-1980s, the Danish Savings Bank Bikuben and a number of other Danish banks established special links via satellite from their branch offices in Greenland to computing centres in Copenhagen. As a result, most of the back-office processing has been moved to Copenhagen and the branch offices are primarily serving customers from terminals at the counter. For the bank's customers, there is very little difference between being served at the counter in a branch office in Greenland and being served at a similar counter in one of the branch offices in Copenhagen. Indeed, it has sometimes been observed that the response time for terminals in Greenland is less than for those in the city area of Copenhagen, where telephone traffic density is relatively high.

Source: Information obtained from the Danish Savings Banks Association, Copenhagen.

Box I.3. Closing foreign affiliates

In 1991, Chase Manhattan Bank closed its Danish subsidiary. The reason for this move was that the branch office established in the mid-1980s by Chase Manhattan Bank had primarily served corporate customers from the United States; the services demanded by these customers can now be delivered from the London branch office. (It had apparently not been feasible or interesting to compete for retail customers in Denmark). The case of Chase Manhattan Bank illustrates how the increased tradability of banking services for corporate customers may have reduced FDI in banking among developing countries. However, the move to concentrate activities in a regional centre may also have been prompted by the economic recession and the crisis in the United States banking sector, rather than merely the technological opportunities for tradability.

Source: Børsen (Copenhagen), 3 January 1992, page 18.

the potential for remote processing of major components of service transactions provide new opportunities for exports of services and, eventually, the sub-contracting of some of the data-processing work involved in modern services such as banking. Facilities management and out-sourcing of processing tasks through contracts with independent firms has taken place for many years in the banking sectors of developed countries.[2] Recently, however, there has been a surge of firms which are either spin-offs from large banks or highly specialized providers of data processing or network services which undertake facilities management. Generally, such facilities-management contracts are set up between two firms in the same country. Occasionally, a contract will involve cross-border transactions. For instance, the United States software company TCAM markets County NatWest "integrated settlement system", and the United States-based network supplier EDS (which is owned by General Motors) manages card processing for the Switch card sold by the Midland Bank in the United Kingdom (box I.4).

In Lithuania, a number of Danish banks are involved in a project to modernize the country's banking sector, which in its present state constitutes a major obstacle to economic development. As part of this project, a proposal to conduct on-line processing of back-office transactions and new services in the Lithuanian banks by a data processing centre in Denmark was considered. Although the export of data-processing services appeared technically feasible, the implementation of the proposal was postponed because of cultural and social differences.

There are also cases -- although few at present -- of labour-intensive routine banking tasks

Box I.4. Facilities management

"It is not always easy to draw the line between what makes a bank's information technology unique and what is standard. The facilities management successes of United States network supplier EDS have been showing banks that it is certainly not in data processing. But when it comes to systems development the boundaries blur. Some, like Hong Kong's International Bank of Asia, have been happy to give EDS the job of full system evaluation and development of its own data centre and communications systems. Others, like the United Kingdom's Midland Bank, have passed over their Switch card processing, which includes applications development, but would be unlikely to pull off a similar deal for core banking processing.

"Ronald Bain of EDS believes it is dangerous to lay too much emphasis on the straight machine-processing element. "It's about a delivery service - the machine, the application and the administration. Banks get competitive edge not from systems but from management and marketing". Preferring the term systems management to FM, EDS takes a pragmatic approach to the business. "They buy a unit of service and so get control and cap costs. For an investment house [EDS runs Shearson Lehman's London back office package] we would charge by the trade"."

Source: "Competitive edginess", *The Banker*, June 1991, pp. 38-39.

Box I.5. Exports of intermediate services from developing countries

Increased tradability has already provided possibilities for a few developing countries to export intermediate service products such as remote data entry and processing. A rather well publicized arrangement is the way that the New York Life Insurance Co. has hired 50 claims examiners in Castleisland, Ireland. These examiners receive claims documents shipped by air from New York every day, and process them at terminals linked via a 56-kilobit-per-second optical fibre leased line to a computer centre in Clinton, New Jersey, after which checks or correspondence are sent out.[a]

Similarly, American Airlines tickets are sent from New York to Bridgetown in Barbados and Santo Domingo in the Dominican Republic. There, the information on the tickets is keyed into computers and transmitted by satellite links to American Airlines' computers in Oklahoma for further processing.[b]

A relevant example related to banking is the process of verification of names, addresses etc. of recipients of bank transfers. This is a rather labour-intensive process which requires extensive and time-consuming checks of records, in order to ensure that money is not accidentally transferred to a wrong account. There is a consortium of United States and Canadian banks which has agreed to purchase such services from a firm situated in the Caribbean.

a. "Offices moving offshore", *Communications Week International*, 10 December 1990, p. 19.

b. Ibid.

being undertaken by sub-contractors in developing countries. One of these examples is the verification of addresses etc. for recipients of money transfers between Canadian and foreign banks which is conducted by a firm located in the Caribbean (box I.5).

These examples further illustrate the extent to which tradability of banking services has increased due to the application of information and telecommunications technologies. In all these cases, the production of a service product relies on information processing which takes place in a location away from the place where the service product is consumed. The fact that a service product, or a component of it, can be transported has important implications for trade in such services, and for the nature of the services themselves.[3] Once the actual service product or a component of its production process can be transported over distances, it becomes potentially tradable across national boundaries and -- within economically feasible limits -- deliverable to any place on the world where an appropriate information and telecommunication infrastructure exists.

E. Trade and foreign direct investment in services

The previous section has provided a number of examples of trade in services. However, in comparison with goods, the volume of international trade in services is still limited. Although services, especially in developed economies, constitute by far the largest share of gross domestic product (GDP) (table I.3), international trade in services only makes up about a fifth of total international trade, as shown in table I.4.

The main reason for the relatively low volume and share of trade in services in total trade is non-transportability of many services. The limited tradability of services has been one reason why FDI by major transnational services corporations, which increased substantially during the 1980s, has been more important than trade in the internationalization of the services sector.[4]

Foreign direct investment in services is similar to FDI in goods in terms of the share of services FDI in total FDI as compared with the share of services in GDP. The stock of outward services FDI for the most important industrialized countries ranged between 37 per cent of total outward FDI from the United Kingdomand

Table I.3. Sectoral composition of GDP in developed and developing countries, 1970 and 1987 (Percentage)

Country group	Agriculture		Industry		Services	
	1970	1987	1970	1987	1970	1987
Developed countries	4	3	41	35	55	63
Developing countries	24	15	31	36	45	49

Source: GATT, *International Trade 88-89*, vol. 1, pp. 23-24.

Table I.4. Share of world exports of merchandise and commercial services in total world exports, selected years, 1970 and 1992 (Percentage)

Category	1970	1980	1987	1992
Merchandise	81	83	81	79
Commercial services	19	17	19	21

Source: GATT, *International Trade 88-89*, vol.1, p. 39, and figures from GATT obtained from Seamus Bannon, *Nye markeder - nye muligheder. Det internationale marked for serviceydelser* (New Markets - New Possibilities. The International Market for Services), in *Fremtidsorientering* no. 4, September 1993, pp. 18-22.

67 per cent of total outward FDI from Japan in 1990. The stock of outward services FDI was considerably lower in the 1970s, indicating that the flow of outward services FDI constitutes an increasing share of total flow of outward FDI.[5]

This growth of FDI in services has taken place in spite of the fact that services FDI has faced the obstacle that strategic services (such as banking, insurance, telecommunications) are often protected through restrictions on FDI. Moreover, EDI in services has been constrained by the lack of divisibility of production processes of many services which has curtailed the exploitation of country specific comparative advantages. Unlike in the case of production of goods where labour intensive processes may be located in countries with low labour costs, the most important reason for establishing affiliates abroad in services is to supply services to local markets; a division of labour between countries with different factor endowments is severely limited because of the limited tradability of most services.[6]

The examples presented earlier suggest that these trends are about to change fundamentally. With the merger of telecommunication and computer technologies, it becomes technically feasible to produce a service product in one place and consume it elsewhere. This change emanates from the rapid development and diffusion of a complex set of interacting technologies, including very powerful data processing in large computers and the so-called personal computers which have now become widespread in the developed countries as well as the diffusion of digital network technologies in telecommunications.

Many countries have liberalized the telecommunications markets which were dominated by large public corporations and monopoly firms. This has led to the introduction of new frameworks of regulation at the national level which provided more open markets for service products. The networks that will emerge from this process are likely to change the structure of the telecommunications infrastructure from provision of universal telephone services towards more diversified and specialized networks.

The conditions under which service providers throughout the world, including the developing countries, gain access to such networks becomes an important issue in a future, more liberal environment for international

trade.[7] In this situation, banks in developing countries may face competition from services exported by major international banks based in developed countries. Moreover, the role of foreign bank affiliates could be altered substantially with profound effects on the level, character, and impact of FDI in host countries.

F. The General Agreement on Trade in Services

As mentioned earlier, the increased significance of services for national economies, particularly the changes taking place in developed countries, have led to a growing recognition of the importance of the services sector for economic analysis and policy formulation, and services are now high on the agenda of international, regional and national policy making. For example, the liberalization of international transactions in services has been one of the key issues addressed in the Uruguay Round of Multilateral Trade Negotiations. After several years of discussions, the formulation of a General Agreement on Trade in Services (GATS) (box I.6)[a] has been concluded with specific binding commitments by participating countries to liberalize services transactions. The national schedules containing these commitments complement the articles of the agreement and the annexes, including those dealing with special problems in certain industries such as telecommunications and financial services, by indicating which services a country has agreed to subject to the liberalization rules of GATS, and to what extent.

---

[a] Although this study was completed by November 1993, it was decided to incorporate information on the final results of the GATS negotiations which became available before the study went to press.

G. Tradability of banking services: its significance for development

Although financial services have increasingly been recognized as an important component of economic growth, they have seldom been given adequate attention in the debate on development strategies. As discussed in chapter II below, banks perform important functions in the economies of both developed and developing countries, but there are significant differences between the banking industries in the two groups of countries. Those differences have important implications for the total impact that increased tradability can be expected to have in the short-run and, in particular, in a long-run perspective.

Significant consequences may arise from the divergence between a dynamic and rapidly expanding banking industry in the advanced industrialized countries and a relatively stagnant and inefficient banking industry in developing countries. Advanced technologies being rapidly applied in the banks in developed countries are accelerating this divergence, and accentuate the implications that they may have for the financial services sector in developing countries. The central role played in this process by information and telecommunications technologies and the increased tradability of service products is part of this process. Several studies published in recent years have identified this trend and discussed its impact on developing countries in general terms.[8]

If current trends continue, the banking industry in developing countries will face major difficulties in becoming competitive on the international market. If countries choose to maintain high levels of general protection for domestic banks, and the information and tele-

Box I.6. The GATS multilateral framework

The General Agreement on Trade in Services (GATS) establishes a multilateral framework of rules for trade in services. Under the Agreement, trade in services is defined to include services supplied to a country through (a) cross-border supply by non-resident suppliers; (b) consumption abroad by residents; (c) commercial presence of foreign service suppliers; and (d) the presence of natural persons for the supply of services by foreign service suppliers. The text of the GATS consists of 29 articles and six annexes.[a] The articles incorporate a number of important principles and concepts inspired by the General Agreement on Tariffs and Trade, the framework relating to trade in goods that has been in operation since 1947.

"One such principle is the *most-favoured nation* (MFN) clause which prohibits discrimination between and among parties to the agreement. This principle, which is a cornerstone of the GATT regime governing trade in goods, will be equally essential to the international regime in services.

"Another principle is the requirement for *transparency* with respect to rules, regulations and procedures which affect trade in services. In other words, making the rules and regulations a matter of public knowledge...

"The framework also aims at the *progressive lowering of trade barriers*. The GATS is expected to serve as a vehicle for countries to lower progressively barriers to trade and expand access to markets. The word "progressive" implies a degree of pragmatism and flexibility. It recognizes that participants negotiate from very different starting points...

"The GATT principle of *national treatment* or non-discrimination between foreign and domestic products is another major plank of the services framework."[b]

/..

Box I.6 (continued)

The application of these principles to international trade in services will lead to predictable and transparent trading conditions as well as progressively higher levels of services trade liberalization. Some of the other provisions of the framework relate to institutional arrangements, such as dispute settlements, and safeguards relating to, for example, balance of payments."

---

a. "General Agreement on Trade in Services", in GATT secretariat," Final Act Embodying the Results of the Uruguay Round of Multilateral Trade Negotiations", CMTN/FA, 15 December 1993, (mimeographed).

b. Arthur Dunkel, "Telecom Services and the Uruguay Round, "*Transnational Data and Communications Report*, vol. 15, no. 1 (January/February 1992), pp. 17-19

communication infrastructure does not become available, there is a strong possibility that the banking services available in such countries will remain backward. In that case, developing countries may forego the important contribution that an efficient banking sector can make to economic development. The importance of linkages between financial services and other industries of an economy have become clear during the past two decades.

If, on the other hand, a rapid liberalization takes place across the board for the banking industries in developing countries, it is likely that domestic banks will face serious difficulties in their local markets, particularly if international agreements force these countries to open these markets for services provided directly by foreign competitors. Experience in some countries such as Singapore (see chapter VII) shows that a selective regulation (e.g., the establishment of a "separation fence") and incentives for the introduction of advanced information and telecommunications technologies in the banking industry may be the best option for a majority of developing countries.

H. Conclusions

In view of the structural change towards services, the share of services in world trade should have grown as well. As shown above, this has not been the case. Explanations can be found in regulatory barriers as well as in the characteristics of services production. The regulatory barriers are increasingly being removed as a result of a general liberalization move, formalized, e.g., in the GATS. The characteristics of services production that have made trade in services difficult are increasingly being changed by the development of information and telecommunication technologies. Based on these trends it appears that a large potential for trade in services is emerging. Because of the widespread application of information and telecommunications technologies in the banking industry and the characteristics of banking products, it can be expected that this industry will be at the forefront in this respect. This potential is analyzed in the discussion of the tradability of banking services that follows.

Notes

1   In some discussions, the concept of tradability has explicitly incorporated the role of information and telecommunication technology. See, for instance, Karl P. Sauvant, "The tradability of services", in UNCTC and the World Bank, *The Uruguay Round: Services in the World Economy* (New York and Washington, D.C., 1991), pp. 114-122: "Increased tradability means, first of all, that information-intensive final services (bill payments, insurance policies, software, and so on) can be delivered abroad by way of telecommunication lines. It also means that individual components in the services production chain can become tradable and that specialization can take place, as in manufacturing". In this volume, the definition of tradability does not necessarily imply reliance on telecommunication lines.

2   Facilities management in information-technology services has been defined as the management of a part, or all, of an organization's information-technology services by an external source at agreed service levels, to an agreed cost formula and over an agreed period (*The Banker*, April 1992, p. 16).

3   It should be noted that many service products, for instance in the banking sector, are already delivered to other domestic locations over long distances via telecommunication facilities. From a technical point of view, the capability to deliver services via telecommunications within or outside the borders of a country is more or less the same.

4   Another important reason for the growth of FDI in banking was the introduction of new regulations. Thus, for example, the so-called "Regulation Q" provided United States banks which established affiliates outside the United States with the means to circumvent the requirements for deposits in the Federal Reserve Bank.

5   See United Nations, Transnational Corporations and Management Division, *World Investment Report 1993: Transnational Corporations and Integrated International Production* (United Nations publication, Sales No. E.93.II.A.14), p. 18.

6   See, for example, UNCTC, *Foreign Direct Investment and Transnational Corporations in Services* (United Nations publication, Sales No. E.89.II.A.1), p. 114.

7   See, for instance, United Nations, Transnational Corporations and Management Division, *World Investment Report 1992: Transnational Corporations as Engines of Growth* (United Nations publication, Sales No. E.92.II.A.19).

8   See, for example, OECD, *Trade in Services and Developing Countries* (Paris, OECD, 1989).

Chapter II

BANKING SERVICES, THEIR ROLE AND RECENT DEVELOPMENTS AFFECTING THE INDUSTRY

The previous chapter has provided a number of examples suggesting that some banking services have become more tradable at arm's length across borders. Before proceeding to a more detailed analysis of the tradability of banking services, the industry and its significance for economic development require a closer examination. This chapter provides an overview of the industry, its functions and products, and outlines recent economic, regulatory and technological changes affecting national and international banking.

A. The industry and its functions

A definition and delimitation of the banking industry involves a discussion of three basic aspects of banking: what banking is; what different kinds of banks do according to the internal structure and division of labour in the industry; and how banks function in society (table II.1).

Table II.1. Dimensions of banking

First aspect	• Ex ante: what banking is • Ex post: what banks do
Second aspect	• Retail • Corporate
Third aspect	• Payment-related functions • Intermediation of capital flows

With respect to the first aspect, that is, what banking is, no generally accepted definition exists. The legal definition of a bank and its activities -- banking -- differs between countries. This problem can be dealt with using two different approaches. One approach is to define, ex ante, what banking is; the second is to look ex post, at what banks actually do. The present study takes an ex ante definition of "the traditional bank" as the point of departure, but then utilizes a combination of these two approaches. This implies, for example, that it will not exclude, in advance, financial and other services not traditionally seen as part of banking services.

Using a general delimitation, banks belong to the category of financial intermediaries, i.e., enterprises in the business of buying and selling financial assets. Based on a combination of regulatory rules and the actual division of labour, the following categories of financial intermediaries can be distinguished:

1) central banks;
2) commercial banks and savings banks;
3) building societies;
4) finance houses;
5) insurance companies;
6) pension funds;
7) unit trusts;
8) investment trusts;
9) girobanks;
10) leasing companies;
11) factoring companies.

The above categories are common in most countries, but the exact division of labour, and frameworks regulating it, are very different. There is thus no generally accepted definition to distinguish a traditional bank (category 2 in the list above) from other financial intermediaries. This study defines a bank as an institution that has its liabilities as (mainly) money and performs all of the three following basic functions:

a) permits money to be withdrawn or transferred from one account to another;
b) accepts and safeguards deposits from customers; and
c) lends money to suitable customers who wish to borrow.

These functions are the core activities of banks. The problem of distinguishing banks from other financial intermediaries is, however, made difficult by the fact that boundaries between different parts of the financial sector have increasingly become blurred, particularly over the past few years. So-called financial supermarkets incorporating banking, insurance and

real estate have sprung up, and there is a tendency for different parts of the financial services industry to enter related markets. For instance, some insurance companies and real estate chains possessing considerable capital resources have started to offer credit facilities, loans and other services that have traditionally been the preserve of the banks. This study, however, focuses on services performed by banks connected to the core activities defined above, but including counseling, cash management and liquidity management. It excludes related areas of financial services such as insurance and dealing in real estate.

The second aspect of the definition of banking deals with the "internal" structure of the industry, i.e., what different kinds of banks do: provision of retail services, corporate services etc. This particular relevance to the present study, as there are some differences in the ways that corporate banking and retail banking have utilized information and telecommunications technologies. These technologies have been used in customer-related services in corporate banking for a longer period than in retail banking, although computerization in retail banking services has developed quickly in recent years with the growth, for example, of automatic teller machines (ATMs) and electronic funds transfer positions of sale. On the other hand, back-office functions in retail banking have relied to a larger degree on information and telecommunications technologies since the storing and processing of data have been more widespread in retail banking where vast amounts of uniform and simple transactions take place.

The third aspect concerns the functions that banks perform in the economy. The most basic function of financial intermediation, including by banks, is the provision of services to facilitate the exchange of goods and other services. A very important function in this context is to provide the means of payment and facilitate their use so that financial transactions between buyers and sellers can take place. In addition, in modern economies, there is also a need to facilitate deals that are not contemporaneous exchanges of goods or services, i.e., to extend credits and debits, which is a system to exchange current goods for future claims to payment. This function caters to the needs of the economy with regard to saving and investment. These needs can be divided into those meeting microeconomic objectives and those achieving macroeconomic objectives. The microeconomic objectives include the ability of the system to deal with the effects of risk on savings and the supply of funds to investors and the capacity to innovate and adapt to changing needs. The macroeconomic objectives concern the balance of savings and investment in relation to the level of activity in an economy.

A distinction can thus be made between different functions of a bank. On the one hand are functions that are closely related to payment transactions; on the other hand, there are functions that are related to the intermediation of capital flows, i.e., providing an intermediate link in the savings-investment cycle. In the first case, an efficient banking industry provides services that facilitate activities, such as trade, undertaken by other businesses in general, thereby enhancing their productivity and profitability. The services related to payment transactions are closely related to the withdrawal or transfer of money described above as one of the core functions. In the second case, banks are contributing more directly to the growth of the economy by collecting funds from savers and providing credit facilities for new investment, thereby spreading risks over a larger group.

These services (intermediation) are closely related to deposit taking and lending described above as the second and third core functions.

As a result, the performance of a bank is measured by the proceeds from the provision of payment facilities and from the safeguarding or lending of funds for a period in the form of fees, commissions and interests and not by the sum transferred or loaned.

B. Banking and the development of the economy

Traditionally, the development of a national economy has been closely associated with the development of a national banking system. Indeed, it has been argued that the way a country's financial system is organized can give it an edge over its competitors.[1] Certainly, a properly functioning capital market and system of financial intermediaries are prerequisites for allocating resources generated within the economy effectively and thus promoting economic growth.

In carrying out their role, banks have traditionally established a local presence for essentially three reasons:

- Basic banking services as such are not very complex, i.e., the "production process" performed in banks can be carried out at a very low level of complexity, thus allowing the presence of banks in virtually any economy.

- Trust is a necessary condition for banking, and it has traditionally been linked to a local presence and the knowledge of local customs and business practices.

- The payment services and intermediation links in the savings-investment circuit offered by banks are important for the functioning of any economy. These services have been, and to a certain extent still are, based on an exchange of means of payment or claims presented in a physical form -- coins, notes, paper documents -- that require the local presence of banks. The role assigned to a physical form of the means of payment has largely been a matter of adequacy of information. The only way to minimize risk related to the behaviour of the opposite party in an exchange situation has often been to exchange physical stores of value.

The combination of the liberalization of banking regulations and technological developments in the form of new applications of information and telecommunications technologies influences these three factors. Information and telecommunication technologies create new possibilities for the exchange of information, while liberalization increasingly makes detailed information on business partners available via these technologies. Thus, the rationale for a local presence outlined above is weakened by these trends. In short, technological developments make international trade in banking services possible, whilst liberalization and deregulation increasingly allow such trade to take place.

In addition, with the higher levels of complexity of the advanced industrial economies, the production process in banks that service these economies has become more complex as well. The use of computers to deal with this increasing complexity has in itself been a driving force in the development of information and telecommunication. The ascendancy of microelectronics as a new core technology at the heart of information and telecommunication has thus in a more specific way underlined the central role of the banking sector. Banking in the industrialized countries has become a highly computerized business; in this process the role of banking in the development of the economy has been extended beyond its core role of generating resources or acting as an intermediary. The industry has by its use of the new technology, become a frontrunner for the broader social application of this technology.

The process started when computers began to be used internally for rationalization purposes. In the next phase, computers and telecommunications means were used in customer relations and forced -- or stimulated -- business connections to use them as well, influencing on this way the money-using, credit and saving habits of the population.[3]

One implication of these trends is that small banks can lose some of their competitive advantages, because they have to buy expensive new equipment and software to ensure that they are able to deliver the necessary services. It has been argued that, whereas virtually no economies of scale exist in paper-based banking, there are substantial economics of scale to be reaped in banking based on electronic/digital systems.[4] If that should be the case, it becomes possible for large banks to spread the costs of new systems over a larger customer base, thus reducing the marginal cost of providing additional transactions. In some cases, the marginal costs incurred on expanding such services become very small. The result of this will be to challenge smaller banks, banking systems of smaller economies and, in particular, the banking systems of developing countries. The challenges are not insurmountable, however; for example, small banks can acquire production services from third parties at very competitive prices.

The internationalization of the advanced industrialized economies -- that is, increasing international trade and investment as well as the growth of cultural exchanges and the extension of the mass media -- tends to reduce the importance of trust in banking relations and, hence, the need for a local presence in foreign countries. The personal visit to a branch office and contact with the local staff, that used to be an integral part of customer services and relations with banks, is now increasingly complemented with (occasionally even substituted by) telephone calls answered by computers. As a result, in fact, big international banks are often considered to be more reliable than local banks.

In the future, while the services produced by banks are likely to remain very important for the functioning of economies, the need for a local presence of banks to carry out commercial or personal economic transactions is likely to become less important as a result of the introduction of information and telecommunication technologies. When claims are presented and payments effected electronically, there is no absolute need for the customer and the bank to be present at the same location. This development is already apparent in payment transactions, where procedures giving adequate information for these are well-established. In the provision of credit, the relevant routines are less developed, implying that this business area still demands the presence of the parties involved.

Due to cultural traditions and language barriers, national banking systems are likely to flourish for many years, but technological developments are creating the basis for a new emerging international banking system. In it,

banking services will be traded around the world, eroding the basis for a specifically national banking system based on local presence. The important role of the domestic financial industry in modernizing an economy will, in this respect, be affected by increasing competition from international financial institutions. This development is the price of specialization in all economies, but the impact is more acute in developing countries because of their weaker economic base.

C. Categorization of banking services

Banking services can be categorized in two ways:

- An *activity-based description*, i.e., a description of the various activities connected to each function carried out in a bank.

- A *product description*, i.e., a description of activities connected with each service product that a customer of a bank receives.

A listing of the generally existing computerized systems provides an *activity-based description* of banking services:

- accounting systems;
- administrative systems;
- payment systems;
- funds systems;
- systems for internal transactions;
- systems for interbank clearing;
- systems for international transfer;
- self-service systems;
- information systems;
- office automation systems;
- management systems;

- expert and decision-support systems; and
- other applications.

Such a description can be useful in short-term planning for the use of information and telecommunications technologies in a bank. However, the activity-based description orients itself on existing organizational structures; one of the most important consequences of the introduction of information and telecommunications technologies are the changes it engenders in those structures. The organizational pattern of functional units in banks may well be replaced by cross-functional, independent units whose activities are defined in relation to customer needs rather than specific functions. This tendency makes it difficult, and possibly less useful, to discuss the tradability of banking services merely on the basis of a description of the technological possibilities that are associated with the existing functions. It is necessary to supplement this kind of description with an analysis of emerging new service products and the telematization (i.e., the extent to which a service can be transmitted over telecommunication lines) of the activities related to these new services. New financial products such as SWAPS and Euro products have emerged in recent years. Self-service products like home banking and ATMs were impossible to provide just one decade ago.

The dynamic nature of service-product development thus calls for an operational distinction between existing and future services. The present study distinguishes between three major categories in this respect:

- existing services not using telecommunications (not telematized);

- existing services using telecommunications (telematized); and
- future services.

In addition, the distinction between retail and corporate banking is maintained, even if these two types of banking services are provided by the same bank. This is because the perspectives for telematization of the same kind of service are likely to be quite different for retail and corporate banking.

A *product-based* categorization of banking services should cover services related to both of the two aspects of the basic functions of banking mentioned above. An exhaustive list of services offered by banks in advanced industrialized countries will not be provided here. Banks have developed a great deal from the three basic functions, offering today as many as 250 different retailing products.[5] The main categories and products are listed below, while the products will be discussed in detail in chapter III and in annex 1.

The range of banking services includes:

1. Transactions-of-payments services
Cheques
Payment cards
Bank transfers
Standing orders
Direct bank drafts

2. Liquidity management
Options
Futures
Forward contracts

3. Financing
Bills
Mortgage deeds

Export credits
Consumer loans

4. Deposits and savings
Current/cheque accounts
Deposit/savings accounts including, investment and high interest deposit accounts
Special types of savings accounts, e.g., mortgage deposit, holiday savings
Budget/credit accounts

5. Consulting/specialized advice
Information and services often tailored to suit the needs of specific market segments, such as high income wage-earners, real estate buyers, students, people working abroad.

6. Investment, trust and taxation
Safe deposit
Executor and trustee
Insurance
Life assurance
Pension plans
Tax planning
Investment, e.g., unit trusts, share plans.

The range of services listed above shows that some overlap exists between the two major types of services, i.e., payments transactions (basically groups 1 and 2) and credit intermediation (basically groups 3 and 4). Consulting (groups 5 and 6) could also be added as a third type of service. This study, however, categorizes consulting services as a form of specialized advice (group 5) and an integral part of providing payments transaction and especially credit intermediation services. Investment, trust and taxation are included in consulting, but the part connected to insurance lies outside the scope of this study.

The overlap between the different types of services can be seen as part of the process that is blurring the boundaries between the firms offering these services. The process, reflecting the complexity, sophistication and dynamism in the industry, is shaped by several interrelated factors: global economic instability and slower, uneven economic growth; rapid change in the regulatory structure; and advances in telecommunications and information processing technologies. In order to illustrate the relevance of these changes for the development of tradability of services, an outline of the effects of the economic and regulatory and the technological factors respectively is given in the following section.

D. The role of economic and regulatory factors

As the main theme in this volume is the technical tradability of banking services, the economic and regulatory regimes are not a major focus of the discussion. Nevertheless, two key forces in the "blurring process" mentioned above and influencing the tradability of banking services must be noted. They are disintermediation and securitization.

Disintermediation describes the process that shifts financial intermediation away from banks to non-bank or non-financial intermediaries. In the industrialized economies, the vast majority of financial transactions by individuals and businesses are conducted through third-party intermediaries. A long-term trend can be observed whereby the share of total funds advanced to the non-financial sector mediated by financial institutions declines. More specifically, as table II.2 shows, the share of funds mediated by financial institutions in the United

States rose from 53 per cent in 1950 to 81 per cent in 1983. However, the share of non-depository institutions rose from 20 per cent to 50 per cent, while the banks' share remained relatively constant. The non-depository institutions include pension funds, insurance companies, consumer finance companies, mutual funds, real estate investment trusts and securities brokers and dealers.

Table II.2. Share of total United States credit market funds advanced to non-financial institutions, 1946-1950, 1981-1983 (Per cent)

Period	Total	Banks and savings institutions	Nondepository institutions
1946-1950	19.9	32.4	19.9
1981-1983	81.0	31.5	49.3

Source: Based on Richard McGahey et al., *Financial Services, Financial Centers* (Boulder, Westview, 1990), p. 83.

This growing market share of non-deposit-taking institutions reflects a breaking up of the traditional "banking relationship", i.e., the implicit or explicit agreement between borrowers and the bank, and the bank and its depositors. Traditionally, financial intermediation has involved lending to borrowers by funding loans through liabilities issued against the "full faith and credit" of the lending institution itself. With the increasing economic and financial volatility beginning in the late 1970s, this traditional banking relationship began to erode. To cover costs, banks charged more in fees and cut back on options and services. For borrowers, this made other forms of financial intermediaries look more attractive. This increased the pressure to liberalize the regulatory barriers to entry in banking. As a result, the number and diversity of nonfinancial institutions in the market has grown rapidly, which has in turn eroded the traditional banking relationship.

Securitization is the substitution of tradable securities for traditional bank loans or mortgages. Whereas disintermediation merely replaces banks with non-bank intermediaries as holders of generally identical financial claims, securitization fundamentally alters the forms of financial claims. Traditional lending involves an agreement defining obligations between borrower and lender. Securitization changes this direct contact into market relations where the borrower typically deals with an underwriter who then seeks investors. This process has enhanced disintermediation as borrowers and investors bypass banks and transact business directly.

Thus, the combined social processes of global economic volatility, deregulation of the financial system and the tendencies within the industry towards disintermediation and securitization tend to change the banking industry from a highly regulated industry with special customer relations ("the banking relationship") into a standard market-oriented industry.

E. The role of telecommunication and data services in banking

This section provides an overview of the role of telecommunications and data services in the two main areas of banking:[6] retail and wholesale.

1. Retail banking

In retail banking, information technology was first introduced in the form of mainframe computers which were utilized to automate some back-office functions. Data processing was used to mechanize the routine tasks performed by back-office clerks. Today, information technology has moved into the front-office in the form of network terminals at the counters. Indeed, it has moved beyond the counter and even closer to the customer in the form of ATMs and home-banking services offered via the telephone. This movement of technological innovation from the back-offices to the front-offices, from innovation in the production process to the development of new products, has been termed the reverse product cycle, in contrast to what is seen as the normal cycle for material production (i.e., innovation starting with the development of a new product, to be followed by innovation in production processes). The result of this sequence of diffusion of information and telecommunications technologies in banking has been that the development of new banking products has tended to come *after* the back-office services were automated.

The effects of the new information and telecommunications technologies in retail banking are not confined to the development of new products. The new technologies have also sparked a profound restructuring process along two lines. The introduction of home banking-and audiotext-systems has reduced the need for branches, while the development of advanced ATMs increases further the relevance of fully automated branches. Another development is the introduction of electronic data interchange (EDI). This innovation opens up prospects for a new mode of payment that will grow in importance in the future and rests on a technology that in itself constitutes the means by which banks may deliver tradable services. At the same time, EDI potentially enables the parties involved to settle deals via public or dedicated networks and bypass the banks. Electronic data interchange thus potentially can enhance the disin-termediation process and, in the longer run, even be a stronger restructuring force.

2. Wholesale banking

The use of information technology in wholesale and inter-bank transactions has a much longer history than in retail banking. In the nineteenth century, the telegraph -- in one of its first and most important civilian uses -- was used for transmitting financial information. But before the 1970s, high telecommunication costs nevertheless reinforced the separation of national financial markets. Complexity and costs grew substantially with physical distance. The combination of regulatory changes and technological advancements has drastically reduced the transaction costs of new financial instruments, helping to push the internationalization of financial services.[7] The computerization of financial markets has, in principle, made it possible for traders to participate from remote locations and act in the trading almost as quickly as if they had been physically present. In the past few decades, SWIFT and Reuters have provided banks with an international network based on dedicated network technology. These developments are discussed further in chapter IV.

F. Conclusions

The definition and scope of the banking industry differ from country to country. For the purposes of this study, banks are considered to be institutions that accept and safeguard deposits of money from customers, permit money to be withdrawn or transferred from one account to another and lend money to suitable customers. These functions are of key importance for the functioning of all economies and, in particular, for the process of economic development.

The banking industry is undergoing a profound restructuring propelled by a combination of economic, political and technological developments. The industry is increasingly seeing the entry of new and non-traditional players, and this is accompanied by a trend towards substituting traditional, specific codes of business with a more market-oriented regime.

The diffusion of information and telecommunications technologies through the informatization of existing services changed banking institutions and has facilitated the emer-

gence of a range of new services (e.g., swaps, financial futures and options). At the same time, improved information flows have probably tended to reduce earnings and introduce competition in hitherto protected markets. Both these trends have increased the potential tradability of banking services. On the other hand, regulations and traditions as well as insufficient telecommunication connections outside the electronic "highways" connecting financial centres still limit the actual international tradability of banking services, as will be discussed in the following chapters.

Notes

1 It has been argued that Japan's recent success in the development and use of industrial technology, as compared with that in the United States, can be attributed to differences in the organization of the financial sector in the two countries. The Japanese financial system has ben construed as being highly regulated by the Government, whose financial policies have been seen as being systematically designed to support industrial policy priorities. Interest rates have been kept low and industry has been financed by long-term, low-rate bank loans rather than by equities. These conditions are seen to be favourable to finance the development of technology. See, for example, Sonja Ruehl, "Interest rate policy and credit rationing in Japan", in L. Harris, J. Coakley, M. Croadsdale and T. Evans, eds., *New Perspectives on the Financial System* (London, Croom Helm, 1988); R.W. Goldsmith, *The Financial Development of India, Japan and the United States* (New Haven, Yale University Press, 1983); and M. Morishima, *Why has Japan Succeeded'?* (London, Macmillan Education, 1982).

2 See C.A.E. Goodhart, *Information and Uncertainty* (London, Macmillan, 1975), pp. 6-7.

3 These trends are discussed, for example, in Harris et al., op. cit., and generalized in Amin Rajan, *Services: The Second Industrial Revolution?* (London, Butterworth, 1987).

4 See Dario Baldini, "The banking sector" paper presented to the Conference on New Information Technologies, Brussels, 17-18 October 1991, p. 25; and Ugur Muldur, "Economies of scale and scope in national and global banking markets", in Alfred Steinherr, ed., *The New European Financial Marketplace* (London, Longman, 1992).

5   Will Ollard, "International banking: away from the past", *The Economist*, 25 March 1989, p. 46.

6   Chapter III provides a more detailed description of existing services and their current level of reliance on telematics.

7   It has been estimated that, during 1965-1985, the cost of processing and transmitting international financial information declined by 98 per cent. The exact figure can be questioned, but there is no doubt that it has been drastic. See Bank for International Settlements, *Recent Innovations in International Banking* (Basle, Bank for International Settlements, 1986), p. 195.

Chapter III

TRADABILITY OF BANKING SERVICES: THE POTENTIAL

This chapter focuses mainly on the technical feasibility of trade in banking services, although some economic and legal aspects are also discussed within the context of technical opportunities. The single banking product is chosen as the analytical unit. The central component of the research methodology is to look at the tradability of banking services product by product, production process by production process. The tradability of each banking product is discussed in order to provide an empirical foundation for a later discussion of its implications for developed and developing countries.[1]

A banking product is defined from a bank's point of view. A product is characterized not only by the service delivered but also by *how* the service is delivered. Different products can provide the same kind of service from a customer's point of view. Payment services, for example, can be delivered by a range of different products: cash, checks and payment cards. Each product has its own features with respect to tradability. The prospects for trade in banking services thus depend on the mix of products applied to serve a customer's needs.

The analysis is based on the empirical evidence provided in the technical annex (annex 1), supplemented with information from other sources, including literature on banking and information technologies. The material in the annex is primarily based on an analysis of the banking products from a single bank, which is recognized to be in the forefront in developing new applications for information technology. In this manner, technical information of currently feasible applications at a quite detailed level is provided.

In dealing with the technical aspects of tradability, the discussion focuses on the divisibility of each product into intermediate products or processes, and on the transportability of both final and intermediary products. The following aspects are covered in the analysis:

- Current use of telecommunications and data services in the production of specific financial services.

- Level of currently transported and traded banking services.

• Tradability or the technical transportability of products and components thereof.

• Impact of telecommunications and data services on tradability.

• Banking services likely to be developed in the future and their impact on tradability.

An attempt has been made to make the discussion of each aspect as detailed as possible, and each product is discussed separately. After a short presentation of the function of each product, its divisibility is examined by listing the procedures into which the production process can be divided. Thereafter, transportability and tradability of each procedure and of the final product are discussed.

The products are categorized into groups according to the classification provided in the technical annex (table III.1). A completely clear-cut categorization is impossible to provide. Some products are used in more than one context (e.g., both retail and corporate), other products possess inseparable features belonging to different kinds of services (e.g., credit and payments).

The impact of economic and legal factors is briefly discussed in the subsequent sections. The chapter concludes with an identification of key factors affecting the overall tradability of banking services. Among others, the need for

local presence is discussed from a functional point of view. In other words, which of the present banking functions carried out at the branch level today will continue to require local presence in the future?

A. Tradability of banking services by product and product group

1. Retail banking

(a) Payment-transaction services

Customers' payments can be transacted by means of a wide range of banking products, tailored to different needs and representing different levels of technology (table III.2). Increased reliance on telematics for these services occurs at two levels:

Table III.2. A selection of retail payment delivery methods

- Cash handling/dispensing
- Cheques
- Debit cards
- Credit cards
- Electronic funds transfer point of sales (EFTPoS)
- Bank transfer
  - paper-based
  - electronic
- Homebanking

• Reorganization of work processes, including the processing of a transaction elsewhere in a bank's network.

Table III.1. Categorization of banking products

Type of product		Transactions of payments services	Liquidity management	Financing	Deposit
Retail	Negotiable				
	Non-negotiable				
Corporate	Negotiable				
	Non-negotiable				

- A shift towards automatic payments from terminals outside the bank or electronic funds transfer.

To analyze both these processes, each type of payment-transaction service is described first in terms of the activities involved, step by step, its current level of telematization and possibilities for further telematization. Secondly, the shift from one product to another is discussed. That is, how does the number of transactions in each group develop, what are future perspectives? Thirdly, how will new kinds of payment transactions involving electronic means evolve, and what are the future prospects in that respect?

(i) Cash handling/dispensing

Cash is normally issued only by national central banks. However, handling of cash forms an integral part of commercial banking activities. A product analysis must therefore include the handling of cash.

Cash is the physical expression of money. It is obvious that cash itself cannot be transported by use of telecommunications and information technology. However, some of the functions related to the usage of cash can be automated. Cash can be dispensed in banks at the counter, at ATMs located at the banks premises or elsewhere, or at electronic funds transfer point of sale (EFTPoS) terminals located in shops. In addition, cheques can be cashed in connection with payment transactions in shops. The accounting is often done at front office terminals; day-to-day back-office activities are then largely reduced to the physical transportation of money, although there are a great deal of differences among countries in this respect. Cash dispensing from ATMs involves the same back-office activities, but no front-office activities are involved.

Cash dispensing at EFTPoS terminals or the cashing of cheques in shops is usually not, from a bank's point of view, distinguished from payments by cheques or EFTPoS. Automatic teller machines provide facilities for dispensing of cash from a banking account. Currency exchanges, which can be perceived as a kind of cash dispensing, can also be provided from ATMs.

The introduction of ATMs has made self-service cash dispensing possible. The most immediate consequence of this is the potential for saving labour costs -- the cost of an ATM-transaction is estimated to be a quarter of that of an across-the counter transaction.[2] However, what is more important in this context is that the introduction of ATMs has made it possible to provide cash dispensing at a distance from a bank's premises. However, some local presence is necessary: a network of ATMs must be established, maintained and filled regularly with cash. This activity can be (and often is) separate from the bank, both physically and legally.

Cash dispensing is the most frequent service delivered at the counter in a branch. Therefore, arm's length electronic cash dispensing is the most important precondition for distant retail banking. In some countries, the introduction of ATMs has already decreased the average number of visits per customer in the bank dramatically and thereby reduced the need for an extensive local branch-network.[3]

(ii) Cheques

While payments by cash are made without any involvement of banks, cheques require at least one bank as an intermediary in the process. Table III.3 lists several different kinds of cheques which can be obtained in most banks.

Table III.3. Cheques and related products

- Ordinary personal cheques
- Bank drafts
- Internationally accepted cheques (e.g., eurocheques)
- Travellers cheques
- Postal cheques
- Cheque-guarantee systems
- Cheque-guarantee card

Ordinary personal cheques are, by far, the most common type of cheques. Any debtor using personal cheques as payment must possess a banking account from which the payment can be drawn.

Payment-transaction services provided through an ordinary cheque can be divided into the following procedures:

- Issue by debtor's bank.
- Completion by debtor.
- Acceptance by creditor.
- Redemption by creditor.
- Clearing with debtor's bank.

In contrast to payments involving cash, the physical presence of the cheque is not necessary at all stages in the process. This improves the possibilities for undertaking some of the functions at a distance. Issuing requires some kind of physical interaction, while redemption and clearing technically can be made at a distance by use of telecommunications.

Fraud is a crucial issue. Acceptance of a cheque by a creditor requires either extensive trust in the debtor, possibly obtained by use of a control and identification system, or a guarantee provided by the debtor's bank. In practice, it is very difficult to obtain general acceptance of cheques without a guarantee from the issuing bank. Such a guarantee can be given up to a certain limit, either for all cheques issued by any

person, or for holders of a guarantee card. However, this complicates the issuing of cheques, as a review of the credit-worthiness of debtors becomes necessary. It should be noted that the total financial risk involved per customer is limited both by the maximum amount guaranteed per cheque *and* the number of cheques issued.

Banks issue cheques and provide guarantees without contact with the customer. Cheques are issued and mailed to the customer regularly without any personal communication, once the necessary trust is obtained. Transportability is increased by guarantee systems based on the use of telecommunications providing information on unsatisfactory customers (e.g., Telecredit in the United States).

Creditors are often dispersed and their need for redemption can be quite irregular. This restricts the possibilities for establishing standard procedures for redeeming cheques. Compared with issuing, time is a more critical factor in redemption. Most creditors will demand redemption to be completed overnight or at least in one or two days. The need for the physical transport of the cheque to be redeemed makes it very difficult to trade intermediate services by use of telecommunications. Distant redemption could in theory be made by communication via the telenetwork exclusively and without physical transportation. However, taking the current physical form of cheques into consideration, a high degree of confidence in the creditor is required if physical transportation of the cheque is to be avoided.[4] Today the standard procedure is physical transfer of a cheque to the creditor's bank for redemption.

Trust and fraud are less critical issues for the clearing of cheques, as this involves cheque-issuing institutions (typically, banks) only. In addition, the limited number of players involved makes it more easy to establish standard procedures. Today, inter-bank clearing of cheques can be done electronically; in some countries, cheques are normally not physically brought back to the bank of origin. The use of telecommunications thus makes the clearing of cheques a more tradable service. It can be handled by a third party, e.g., a clearing house.

Bank drafts are very similar as regards transportability to guaranteed personal cheques. The only difference is that the service is used less frequently. Bank drafts are mostly used in corporate banking and discussed further in subsection 2 below.

In retail banking, the use of international cheques is confined to customers travelling abroad. Ordinary personal cheques are seldom readily accepted in foreign countries, and a number of substitutes have been developed, including the following:

- *Eurocheques*, which are guaranteed by the issuing bank, are an attempt to create an internationally accepted uniform cheque. The divisibility of the service into intermediate processes involved and the technical prospects for tradability of these cheques are similar to those of other kinds of personal cheques.

- *Postal cheques* are handled at the post office and not in banks. However, the product and the process involved are basically the same as for Eurocheques.

- *Travellers cheques* can be characterized as a hybrid between cash and cheques. The cheques are issued at a fixed amount usually denominated in a major currency. The cheques are prepaid by the customer; in this way no financial risk is involved for the issuing bank. In contrast to cash, they are personal. The market was dominated by one single issuer (American Express), but Visa's Master Card Cheques has a growing market-share. The issuer does not need to have any information on the customer. Therefore, the question of trust does not limit transportability, which makes travellers cheques more tradable than other cheques. Travellers cheques are traded today in the sense that local banks provide cheques issued by one of the major issuing banks. However, the tradability of traveller cheques does not directly depend on the use of telecommunications.

Until recently, the use of cheques was encouraged by most banks because the money placed on a cheque account provided them with extra liquidity. For this reason, banks in some countries (e.g., France and Denmark) have provided cheques to customers without any additional charge, although processing and clearing of cheques are costly. After the introduction of more efficient payment products -- first of all debit cards -- the same banks try to reduce the number of cheques by imposing a fee on each cheque issued.

Although the application of information and telecommunication technologies has increased the tradability of processing of cheques, the most important impact is the creation of electronic alternatives to cheques, e.g., debit cards. These alternatives have already substituted the usage of cheques in many instances.

(iii) Debit cards

Plastic cards that provide the identification and

entitlement of cardholders when used along with either physical or electronic signatures such as their personal identification number for access to bank accounts are referred to as debit or payment cards. To date, the most familiar use of this debit card is as a means of accessing cash at ATMs or to allow for immediate payment by EFTPoS for goods and services. Thus, debit cards are an integral part of a payment system consisting of three products based on information and telecommunications technologies: the card itself, ATMs and EFTPoS (table III.4.).

Table III.4. Debit cards and related products

- Debit cards
- Automated teller machines (ATM)
- Electronic funds transfer point of sale (EFTPoS)
- Manual funds transfer

While originally introduced in most countries for domestic use, the use of debit cards has been extended internationally with interchange agreements between groups of banks such as Plus Network which allows Asian, United States, Canadian and European customers to access their bank accounts in foreign countries and withdraw cash in local currency. In the not-too-distant future, payments at point of sale are likely to be made in much the same manner. Sophisticated interbank or clearing mechanisms were developed to allow these forms of international payments to take place.

Debit or payment cards can serve as electronic cheques. However, the development of electronic self-service systems adds further facilities to debit cards such as cash dispensing outside banking hours.

The functions involved in the use of this product are:

- Acceptance of customers based on an assessment of creditworthiness.
- Issuing of card.
- Payment or cash withdrawal.
- Redemption of withdrawal by creditor.
- Clearing with the issuing bank if different from creditor's bank.
- Advice of transaction to debtor.

The acceptance of customers is a manual procedure which is combined with the use of databases to identify unreliable ones. Card issuing is a manual routine task as well (in the sense that it involves physical activity). Payments and cash withdrawal are most often made electronically by use of ATMs or EFTPoS. In this case, redemption and clearing are handled electronically in the same process. However, in smaller shops, manual payment methods based on paper are still in use. In this case, manual work is necessarily involved in redemption as well.

(iv) Credit cards

Credit cards combine payments and credit into one product, as the customer's payment is delayed by a certain amount of time after the transaction has taken place. It should be noted that many other kinds of payment services involve the same combination. For both debit cards and most types of cheques, the actual money transfer takes place *after* the transaction. With the introduction of telebased clearing and payment systems, this period has been shortened to one or two days in most cases (a little longer for international transactions). However, in the case of credit cards, the credit lasts for at least two weeks and in most cases longer, although the actual credit period obtained by the use of credit-cards has been shortened during the last few years. In addition to payments and credit, a number of fringe benefits, e.g., travel insurance, are often offered to the card-holders. These benefits seem to become more and more common and have even been introduced for holders of some debit cards as well.

Another important feature is that a credit card can be issued without any reference to a bank account, although a debtor's bank may be asked to confirm the debtor's creditworthiness. Therefore, credit cards are provided by many other institutions than banks, although a credit card by nature is a banking product.

Three kinds of credit cards can be distinguished according to usage and issuing institutions (table III.5). The features of different types of cards are essentially the same. The usage of retail cards is often limited to a specific chain of retail stores, petrol stations or similar establishments. Travel and entertainment cards are becoming more generally accepted for usage outside the travel and entertainment industries. Bank credit cards often provide longer credit than the two other types of cards.

Table III.5. Types of credit cards

- Bank credit cards
- Retail- or store cards
- Travel and entertainment (T & E) cards

The working processes involved are essentially the same as for debit cards. The main difference is that time is a less critical factor due to the longer period of credit. Compared to debit cards, an electronic infrastructure is less important, and products like travel and entertainment cards were already well established for transactions abroad even before electronic

international clearing was commonly introduced. The task of rating creditworthiness is often delegated to the customer's bank.

The combination of credit and payments into one card was thus to a certain extent rooted in the lack of technology for the instant clearing of payments. The paper-based environment in which credit cards were originally introduced had implications for the kind of restrictions put on usage as well: it was not possible to introduce restrictions on the maximum daily or weekly usage. Because of the difficulties to introduce payment restrictions and the longer credit provided, the acceptance of credit-card holders must be more carefully done, which makes this working process in the provision of credit-card services less tradable. On the other hand, other processes such as redemption and clearing are more tradable in the case of credit cards than for debit cards, as time is a less critical factor. Today back-office processing facilities for many United States credit card companies are located in low cost areas outside the traditional financial centres. In the United States, Wilmington, Delaware, is an example of such an area far away from the densely populated metropolis, that has attracted back-office processing facilities.[5]

(v) Electronic funds transfer point of sale

An Electronic Funds Transfer Point of Sale is used when funds transfer is made in connection with a payment, in most cases in a retail store or similar establishment. The procedures for transacting the payment can be divided into the following elements:

- Recognition.
- Authorization.

- Message entry.

First, the debit card and the personal identification number (PIN) code are checked against a central database. Following the recognition of the cardholder, it is checked whether the account currently is open for payment transactions. Then the payment message is entered manually by the cashier, and the message is transferred via the telenetwork to the clearing agent or bank who process the payment. In principle, the transaction is approved electronically by the issuing bank immediately and no risk is involved for the creditor. It is not possible to limit the number of transactions in the same way as with cheques, but a maximum level for daily or weekly payments is often incorporated into the system. However, unless on-line connections from all ATMs and EFTPoSs are established to the same central database, the amount can be exceeded by cashing money from different locations the same day. Still, banks consider the system more safe than cheques due to the electronic control before each transaction.

All the processes involved can be carried out at a distance. However, acceptance of new customers requires exhaustive knowledge about them. In contrast to cheques, debit cards require an infrastructure of terminals (manual or electronic). This makes it very costly for individual banks to develop their own card, unless they can share parts of the infrastructure with other banks. This has forced banks to cooperate on standards so that it becomes possible to use the same terminals. However, so far, only a few countries have one universal debit card operated by all banks cooperating together.

Debit cards are often operated by subsidiaries of banks or independent firms. Most of the production processes related to this product can easily be separated from the other activities of the bank. Moreover, substantial economies of scale can be obtained by the provision of a common card covering a number of banks.

Issuing the card itself and the processing of card transactions are highly tradable products. However, electronic usage demands access to a network of terminals. The establishment of such a network requires substantial foreign direct investment or cooperation with local service providers.

(vi) Bank transfer

A bank transfer involves the following operations:

- Ordering of transfer by debtor.
- Transfer of money from debtor's to creditor's bank.
- Transfer of a statement from the debtor's to the creditor's bank.
- Confirmation or issuing of a receipt to debtor.
- Transfer of a statement from the recipient bank to the client (recipient).

The last two processes mentioned are in some cases optional.

A distinction is sometimes made between two kinds of bank transfer: paper-based and electronic. In fact, most bank transfers are made partly electronically and partly on paper. Transfer of money from one bank to another is in most cases done electronically by the use of national and international financial networks (see chapter IV). However, the transfer can also be made by mailing a bank cheque. Transfer by telex or telefax is a kind of hybrid between an electronic and a paper-based transaction. In principle, the transfer itself is made electronically. However, the manual routines involved at both ends are similar to those involving paper-based transactions.

Transfer of an advice or statement is generally less telematized than the money transfer. This is partly due to lack of standards for electronic documents.[6] Communication between the bank and the debtor is, in the case of retail banking -- apart from use of telephone -- mostly done without any use of electronic communication. If a receipt is needed it will be paper-based and transferred by mail.

The type of communication channel used for communication between the recipient bank and the recipient depends on the kind of recipient. If the recipient is a large business enterprise, a purely electronic communication system can be applied. However, paper-based communication is still by far the most common.

Many banks offer to implement regular payments such as housing rents, gas, electricity etc. without prior notification from the customer (direct debit and standing orders). As communication between the debtor and the debtor's bank is the main step in this process, which is the most difficult to perform electronically, the paper-based part of the transaction is thereby reduced considerably.

(vii) Homebanking

Homebanking is a way of providing banking services via the telenetwork directly at the customer's premises. Thus, homebanking is not really an independent banking product, but rather a means to provide other banking service products, including first, bank transfers and, secondly, informational services.

Homebanking is by nature a purely electronic service, connecting the bank's internal computer system directly to the customer. In principle, homebanking can be introduced in relation to manually handled banking services. However, almost all homebanking systems are developed as an externalization of access to computerized services. Hence, a high degree of automatization of the banking system, together with a reliable telecommunications infrastructure are essential for the introduction of homebanking.

The discussion in this section concentrates on the homebanking systems directed towards the retail market. The overwhelming majority of systems developed for the retail market is either based on voice response or, in countries where videotex has been introduced successfully (notably France), on screen-based systems based on the videotex standard. Personal computer based systems exist as well, but their use is limited by the number of modem-connected personal computers in private homes. Most voice-response systems demand a touch-tone telephone or a tone-pad that can be used in connection with a dialing-device-equipped telephone.

Three kinds of retail-service products can be delivered by homebanking: general information, customer-related information and payment-transaction services. From a technical point of view, general information is the most simple to provide, while transaction-services require proper identification of the user and a credible safety procedure. In retail banking, the top three banking products delivered via homebanking systems are:

1. Information on balances on private banking accounts.

2. Funds transfer between the customers' own accounts (cash- management).

3. Funds transfer to third party (e.g., bill payment).

From the bank's point of view, homebanking is desirable because it reduces the time spent on personal communication with customers. Homebanking will not significantly reduce the average number of visits paid to the local branch. The products delivered via homebanking systems can normally be delivered through telephone communication as well. Therefore, it is primarily the time spent on telephone communication that can be reduced.

As an electronic service, homebanking is a highly tradable banking product. However, the service can only be delivered in combination with other services. Hence, the impact on tradability depends on whether homebanking can contribute to the tradability of other products.

From a purely technical point of view, homebanking will not lead to any remarkable increase in the tradability of banking products, as homebanking will mainly substitute functions that are already carried out at a distance by telephone. However, seen from an economic perspective, the cost of international telecommunications will be a barrier for trade of retail banking products requiring telephone communication. Homebanking can potentially be a way to reduce the costs of international communications. However, with the current design of homebanking systems, no substantial savings in connection time can be obtained, as this will require more equipment at the customer's premises. By using international gateways, videotex can reduce costs considerably compared to international telephone tariffs.

At the national level, homebanking has (in combination with cash dispensers and EFTPoS systems) been used by banks that want to expand beyond their branch networks. A prominent example of this is the Bank of Scotland, which in its attempt to penetrate the English retail market has been in the forefront in using homebanking in the United Kingdom.

In addition to the technical and economic aspects, there is a cultural aspect involved in homebanking. It includes, among others, the language barrier connected to cross-border communication which, however, can be reduced by use of multi-lingual homebanking systems.

In conclusion, homebanking can increase the tradability of retail banking products to a certain degree. However, homebanking demands a relatively sophisticated infrastructure and customers familiar with the use of information-technology- based services. These obstacles are still relevant for homebanking at the national level. Hence, the widespread use of international homebanking at the retail level is unlikely in the near future.[7]

(viii) Future payment products

Smart cards are rather a new technology more than a new banking product. Most debit and credit cards are based on magnetic-stripe technology. However, smart-card-technology is used today in some systems.[8] A smart card or a chip card is defined as a "portable data-storage device equipped with intelligence and provision for identification and security safeguards".[9] The use of smart card-technology for debit and credit cards reduces the risk of fraud, as more complicated identification procedures can be adopted. Furthermore, smart cards are able to keep track of the holder's banking account and other relevant information. In this way, part of the functions currently performed via on-line connection to a central database can be executed by use of information available on the card itself, and the need for interactive communication and a telecommunications infrastructure is reduced.

A smart card can act as a true multipurpose card. Technically, it will be possible to integrate, for instance, a credit card and a prepayment card in the same smart card. Furthermore, the card can be applied at the same time for non-financial purposes as well (medical receipts, travel authorization etc). However, this is unlikely to happen in the near future.

Smart cards are somewhat more expensive to produce than ordinary magnetic-stripe-cards. However, the major obstacle to introducing smart-cards is the need to upgrade the vast number of terminals designed for magnetic-stripe cards, although smart cards can be used in the existing network of terminals. However, if the new opportunities of the card are to be utilized in full, investment in new terminals will be necessary.

Prepayment cards are a new product based on the smart-card technology. Electronic cash has already been introduced in the form of an electronic purse or a prepayment card. A prepayment card contains a certain amount paid in advance. The card is typically introduced as a non-personalized card, and is in this way very similar to cash. The card is mostly used for payment of small amounts, replacing coins and low-value banknotes. Today, the cards are mostly produced for single purpose businesses, e.g., payphones, trains, buses and parking.[10] However, multipurpose prepayment cards are

being introduced for payments of a limited number of different services. Most cards are issued by telephone companies or other non-financial institutions. In Japan, financial institutions have been involved in issuing prepayment cards, e.g., the Nippon Card System Corporation.

Prepayment cards can not be considered as a banking service today. However, if prepayment cards gain general acceptance as a means of payment, they must certainly be considered as a banking-service product -- even if issued by other kinds of institutions. In this case, it will not be the first time a product developed outside the financial sector becomes eventually a financial product. For instance, the first credit cards grew out of the centuries-old practice of retailers granting credit to their customers.[11]

The most ambitious project in this area so far is the Danish project Danmønt (DanCoin).[12] The intention of this project is to establish an universal means of payment supplementing the debit card in the area of small transactions. The card will be issued by telephone companies, banks and public transport companies in cooperation. By purchasing a card, consumers get access to a number of services, offered by service providers that have signed a contract with Danmønt.

Although it is technically feasible to introduce electronic cash, general acceptance lies far in the future even in the most advanced countries. The experiences from the Danmønt project indicate that it can be difficult to pass the threshold for a wider scope of applications. Till now, the small number of applications of the prepayment card has limited the user's interest. At the same time, shops and other businesses have not shown interest in obtaining terminals due to the small number of cardholders.

Technically, the issuing and production of prepayment cards is more tradable than traditional cash handling. In principle, the same card can be applied for more than one currency, in the same way as international credit cards.

Dispensing services through prepayment cards is becoming more tradable by the use of electronic cash. A cash dispenser has to be filled with cash regularly, while it will be possible to load a prepayment card electronically without any physical handling of cash. Hence, it will be easier to operate a purely electronic dispensing system.

A notable legal aspect of this development is the blurring of the boundaries between cash, traditionally issued by central banks and dispensed by commercial banks, and other means of payments such as prepayment cards provided by private, domestic and even foreign institutions.

(b) Liquidity management

Liquidity management is not a very important area in the retail market. Two needs for retail customers can be identified:

- Funds transfer between the customer's personal accounts (cash management).
- Indemnifying against loss due to fluctuations in interest or currency rates.

(i) Funds transfer between own accounts

This kind of services is offered in most home-banking systems. The service is closely connected to deposits, which will be discussed in a subsequent section.

(ii) Forward contract

Insuring against loss due to fluctuations in interest or currency rates can be made by use of a forward contract. For retail customers, this is only relevant when customers need to take positions in the market, for instance in relation to dealing in real estate. Few customers will need a forward contract more than a few times during their lifetime. Forward contracts will be discussed in the context of corporate banking, where the product is more widely used.

(c) Deposit services

The most meaningful definition of trade in this context is that trade occurs when a customer opens an account abroad for the purpose of serving primarily domestic needs, or vice versa. Annex I identifies three distinct groups of products serving the needs for deposits in the retail sector, namely, short deposits, time deposits and pension-scheme savings deposits. In this discussion, however, a slightly different categorization is used: the distinction is made between current accounts and savings accounts instead of short and time deposits. The two categorizations are not very different, as virtually all time deposits are used as savings accounts. However, in recent years it has been more common to establish savings accounts with other restrictions than time restrictions on withdrawal, or with other features that distinguish them from current accounts. Although this distinction is less clear-cut than the one applied in the annex, it is more useful for an analysis of tradability.

In addition to the above types, hybrid accounts could be included in the list. In recent years the boundaries between different types of deposits have become blurred -- especially the distinction between short and time deposits.

There is a tendency to merge more functions into a single account, e.g., savings, credit and payments.

(i) Current accounts

The main purpose of this type of account is to accomplish payments transactions. The different types of accounts can therefore be categorized broadly according to the kind of payment they serve (table III.6).

Table III.6 Types of current acounts by type of payments served

Type of account	Type of payment
Pass book accounts	Cash
Cheque accounts	Cheques
Debit card accounts	Debit cards
Budget accounts (direct debit accounts)	Bank transfer

Budget accounts are accounts on which regular payments are made automatially after agreement with the depositor (direct debit or standing order). Most banks offer more than one payment facility connected to the same account. For all types of accounts, the deposits from the customer are almost always made by bank transfer of pay-rolls from employers (bank giro credit).

The processes involved in the opening and managing of short-term deposits are:

- Opening of a bank account.
- Depositing of funds.
- Dispensing of funds.
- Assigning of interest.

In addition to the above procedures, statements must be sent to the customer.

Technically, an account can be opened from a distance without any problems. In reality though, most customers find it quite complicated to open a private account abroad without assistance from a domestic bank. This is partly due to legal problems, partly because very few banks offer facilities to private customers abroad as a routine service.

Depositing of funds will in most cases be made by bank transfer, which from a technical point of view can easily be made at any distance. Assigning of interest is a fully automated procedure in most banks and there are no technical restrictions on its tradability.

The least tradable procedure, apart from the opening of an account which only takes place once, is the dispensing of funds. Therefore, the tradability of service provided by each type of account is closely related to how dispensing takes place, i.e., which types of payment products are offered in connection with the account.

(ii) Savings accounts

With this kind of account, the depositor's possibilities to withdraw funds are often restricted with respect to time (time deposits). The main use of this kind of deposit is for saving. The interest rate is usually higher than that paid for short deposits.

Time deposits can be made either for general or specific purposes (education, housing etc.). Specific-purpose-accounts are often designed according to specific national regulations regarding bonuses, tax exemptions or similar conditions. They are thus less tradable than general-purpose-accounts.

The procedures involved are the same as for current accounts. In general, transactions -- especially withdrawals -- occur less frequently in the case of savings accounts than in the case of current accounts. This makes savings accounts a more tradable product than current accounts.

Thus, in contrast to current accounts, trade can occur with respect to savings accounts. The main reasons for establishing savings accounts abroad have been to make savings in a different (and more stable) currency or because of higher interest rates or because of a lack of confidence in the domestic banking system. A desire to avoid legal authorities (e.g., tax authorities) can play a role as well.

The parameters for international competition are thus quite different from the ones usually discussed. They comprise a stable convertible currency and discretion in respect of banking transactions, rather than a low interest margin which interests the depositors.

As the technical development and the liberalization of financial markets have made it more easy to establish accounts abroad, some of the incentives to hold an account abroad have disappeared: more countries allow the opening of accounts in foreign currencies and international reporting to tax authorities has become more common (although paying tax is still fairly easy to avoid for people who wish to do so).

(iii) Pension-scheme savings

Pension-scheme (or superannuation scheme) savings are savings held on a very long term basis (10-50 years). Risk aversion is low and related to the real value -- not the nominal value of the assets. The savings are made in deposits as well as portfolios of stocks, securities and other financial and non-financial assets. The portfolio can be maintained either by depositors themselves, on advice from the bank or by the bank alone. Often, a part of the portfolio is placed in unit trusts, investment trusts or similar institutions that reinvest and maintain the portfolio on behalf of the depositors. These trusts may be independent or they may be associated with the bank.

The procedures associated with pension-scheme savings are:

- Opening of an account.
- Depositing of funds.
- Maintenance of portfolio (custodial service).
- Calculation of interests.
- Withdrawal of funds.
- Regular advice to depositor.

Apart from the maintenance of a portfolio, the procedures are identical to those of other types of deposits. The maintenance of the portfolio is basically a manual procedure, although information and communication technologies are applied once the investment decisions are taken. It is thus a procedure that requires highly skilled manpower.

Technically, all services connected to pension schemes can be provided from any location. An economic barrier for trade, however, is that, for reasons of risk aversion, the majority of the portfolio investments in real assets in the home country are normally preferred to investments abroad. Therefore, portfolio management requires intensive knowledge of and communication with the home country. To be attractive as a location for the administration of pension schemes, a healthy economy with ample opportunities for long-term investments and a stable currency is required rather than lower relative costs of operation.

(d) Financing

In retail banking, there are numerous types of loans covering various types of "investment", e.g., loans for cars, boats and other durable consumer goods and loans for students guaranteed by the Government. These products can be grouped into the main products of financing identified in table III.7.

Table III.7. Retail financing products

- Bills
- Mortgage deed
- Housing loan
- Consumer loan
- Credit card
- Overdraft

(i) Bills

The issuance of bills is in most cases related to payment for a purchased good. Traditionally, the drawer used to be the seller and the drawee the buyer of the good purchased. After the issuing, the drawer could sell the bill to a bank. However, it is becoming more common that the bank itself issues the bill directly. The processes involved are:

- Rating of creditworthiness of the drawee.
- Issuing of bill by the drawer.
- Dealings with issued bills.
- Payment from drawee at maturity of the bill.

All the procedures are basically manual, although electronic products are applied in some of the processes. Rating is made partly on basis of personal communication, partly by search in electronic databases on unreliable payers. Pay-

ment can be made by use of any of the payment products discussed above.

The rating requires an exhaustive knowledge of and/or confidence in the debtor. Both the issuing of and dealing with bills require knowledge of the debtor's creditworthiness. The procedures of issuing and receiving of payments do not require a local presence and can easily be made at a distance. However, the need for seizure of a debtor's assets in case of default demands local presence.

(ii) Mortgage deed

A mortgage deed is issued as a security for a loan -- typically a housing loan. Hence mortgage deeds are closely related to housing loans. The deed is often (but not always) processed by the bank providing the loan. Hence, a mortgage deed can be an intermediate as well as a final product. The processes involved are:

- Enquiry from the owner.
- Issuing of deed.
- Recording of deed in a central register (to secure the pledge of the lender).

Enquiry and issuing of the deed are manual procedures. The enquiry demands contact with the owner. As few customers will be involved in the issuing of deeds for more than a few times, it must be assumed that they are unfamiliar with the procedures, and that some advice is needed. This increases the demand for personal communication and restricts the possibilities for introducing electronic procedures that are partly based on self-service. Issuing and registration can, in principle, take place anywhere. Normally, speed is not a critical factor; the main barriers to tradability are language and knowledge of national procedures for registration.

(iii) Housing loans

Housing loans are loans made for the specific purpose of financing real estate. The lender normally deposits a mortgage deed as security for the loan.

The procedures involved are:

- Rating of creditworthiness of debtor.
- Valuation of the underlying assets.
- Issuing of loan document.
- Payment of avails.
- Amortization, setting terms of repayment, calculation of interests etc.

The rating of creditworthiness of retail customers is basically a manual procedure and includes a valuation of the mortgage deed, if the deed is deposited as a security. The rating thus requires both knowledge of and/or confidence in the debtor and knowledge about the local market for real estate.

Housing loans are by far the biggest loans provided in retail banking. Therefore the rating needs to be more carefully done. However, if the deed is considered to be a sufficient security, the personal rating can be done in a cursory fashion. During the long period of high inflation and ever increasing prices of real estate, some creditors were provided housing loans solely based on a valuation of the deed and without any personal credit rating.

Just as in the case of mortgage deeds, most customers will not use the product very often. This limits the possibilities of introducing self-service based on electronic-data-processing (EDP) procedures. On the other hand, in most cases time is not a very critical factor. This improves the potential for tradability.

The issuing of documents and the payment of avails are manual procedures. Determining amortization, setting terms of repayment etc., are EDP-based routines. None of these procedures require direct communication with the debtor and can easily be performed at a distance. Furthermore, mainly routine work is involved. However, in the case of issuing, language may be a barrier for international trade.

(iv) Consumer loans

Consumer loans are a broad category covering numerous types of loans including those for "investments" such as durable goods purchases. Consumer loans are usually loans without any limits for the borrower's possibilities of using the avails. Acceptance is based on the creditworthiness of the borrower alone. Although the loans in general are much smaller than housing loans, more thorough knowledge of the customer is needed, as no deed is deposited as security. The processes involved are the same as for housing loans.

Consumer loans must in general be considered less tradable than housing loans, as greater knowledge of the borrower is needed. However, for some limited groups, e.g., groups with high income, staff employed in a certain corporation or other groups with obvious good creditworthiness, consumer loans are much more tradable.

(v) Overdraft

An overdraft works like a current account with a negative deposit. Within a certain agreed limit, any amount can be withdrawn or deposited on the account. Often, an overdraft is connected to a current account, i.e., the bank accepts both positive and negative balances on the account. Interest calculation is based on the actual balance. Sometimes an additional fee depending on the permitted maximum negative balance is added.

Apart from a personal rating of creditworthiness, the processes involved in an overdraft are the same as for a current account. The importance of a credit rating depends on the size of the overdraft limit. The rating will have a different character than the rating applied for other financing products, as an overdraft often will act as a number of small short-term loans. The rating, therefore, needs to be reviewed periodically.

An overdraft is less tradable than a current account, as more confidence in the debtor is needed. On the other hand, if a bank takes care of all other accounts of the customer, the bank will often possess sufficient knowledge to provide an overdraft without additional rating.

2. Corporate banking

A corporate customer's banking-service needs are basically the same as those of private retail customers: payment transactions, liquidity management, finance and deposits. Most of the products provided in retail banking are offered in corporate banking as well, the differences being the larger size, greater frequency and a more international orientation of transactions. However, many corporate customers have more specialized needs. For this reason a number of products have been developed specifically for corporate customers. It is on those products that this section concentrates.

(a) Payment-transaction services

As shown in the annex, a number of payment products can be identified as specifically tailored to corporate banking. The products are listed in table III.8.

Table III.8. Corporate payment and related products

- Bank drafts
- Letters of credit
- Direct debit
- Electronic data interchange (EDI)
- SWIFT
- Reuters
- Globex
- Dealing 2000

In addition to these products, cheques, bank transfers and office banking (the corporate equivalent of homebanking, but much more complex and sophisticated), discussed above in connection with retail banking, are widely used. In countries with more advanced financial systems, cash is rarely used for corporate payments.

SWIFT, Reuters, Globex and Dealing 2000 are primarily network services offering EDI in support for other banking products. These products are discussed separately in chapter IV.

(i) Bank drafts

The procedures involved in a bank draft, and their divisibility, are basically the same as for a cheque. The only difference is that the cheque is filled in by the bank itself. In contrast to a cheque, a bank draft is issued in the name of the bank, and then bought by the debtor. As a consequence, the acceptance depends solely on the confidence in the issuing bank. Its wider acceptance makes bank drafts more suitable for international payments than ordinary cheques.

Tradability possibilities are good. Issuing can be ordered by the customer by phone, telex or fax and sent directly to the creditor. As the acceptance depends on confidence in the issuing bank, firms in some countries may prefer to buy a bank transfer for international payment in a recognized international bank rather than in a local bank.

(ii) Direct debit

Direct debit allows the creditor to order a bank transfer from the debtor's account, without prior confirmation from the debtor. Direct systems are widely used in relation to regular payments from retail to corporate customers. However, direct debit is also used for payments between corporate customers, including domestic as well as international payments.

The procedures involved are:

- Ordering of bank transfer (or establishment of a standing instruction) by creditor.
- Effectuation of bank transfer.
- Advice of debtor.
- Advice of creditor.

The ordering of a transfer can be made electronically by use of home banking or by telex, telephone or other non-EDP-based forms of communication. The two other procedures are both EDP-based.

Direct debit requires the debtor's confidence in the creditor, and of course confidence in the transferring bank. Direct debit is an electronic transfer that provides good opportunities for trade once an adequate telecommunication infrastructure is established. At the national level, direct debit is often left to a clearing house or a financial computer-processing centre. Technically speaking, these institutions can easily provide their services internationally.

(iii) Debit collecting

In addition to the straightforward payment of amounts due, the transfer of various documents is often involved in a payment transaction. These financial documents can be both statements on the implemented or planned payments as well as invoices, bills of lading, certificates, insurance policies etc.

The transfer of these documents is normally left to the bank that handles the payment transaction. To the extent that these documents are paper-based, this restricts the tradability of this procedure. However, in many cases documents can be faxed or confirmations sent by telex. The original documents can then be forwarded by mail afterwards. Use of electronically based documents is also becoming more and more common for international transactions. This makes it possible to use EDI for an electronic exchange.

Collecting requires more knowledge concerning the local legal conditions than do straightforward payments. Technically, this can make the service less tradable. On the other hand, handling of especially paper-based financial documents involves more manual work than straightforward payments or handling of electronic-based documents. Therefore, the economic incentives to relocate certain functions to a low-cost area are higher.

(iv) Letter of credit

A letter of credit (or documentary credit or bankers credit) involves a short term credit and a guarantee in addition to the payment. Furthermore, an exchange of financial documents is involved in the transaction.

A letter of credit is used in connection with trade in commodities or services. A letter of credit makes it possible for exporters (the sellers) to receive their payment when the goods are delivered for shipment. The importer (the buyer) will then pay the bank when the goods are received. In case of default, the bank bears the risk.

The procedures involved in providing this product are:

- Seller asking for a letter of credit.
- Issuing of letter of credit by buyer's bank.
- Forwarding of letter of credit to seller's bank.
- Shipment of goods and handing over bill of lading to seller's bank by seller.
- Payment of seller by bank.
- Receiving of goods and payment to seller's bank by buyer (bank transfer or similar procedure).
- Closing of letter of credit.

In theory, all of the procedures can be made electronically (except of course the handling of the goods). However, this requires electronic communication systems connecting the forwarding agents and banks at both ends. The demand for electronic infrastructure is thus quite advanced. Therefore, the exchange of documents is typically still carried out manually.

Technically, a letter of credit is a tradable service. However, the exchange of documents constrains the possibilities for now, although the introduction of electronic forms will change this in the future.

Both the seller's and buyer's banks take a financial risk in using a letter of credit. The seller's bank needs to trust the buyer's bank, and the buyer's bank needs to trust the buyer. The seller's bank will prefer a letter of credit issued by an internationally recognized bank. On the other hand, the buyer will often only be able to obtain a guarantee from a local bank. For bigger corporate customers, a letter of credit might be one incentive to seek banking services abroad, because of the more immediate acceptance of letter of credits issued by big banks.

(v) Office banking

Office banking is the corporate equivalent of homebanking, the general concept of which was outlined in the previous section on retail banking. However, the functionality of office banking systems is broader than that of homebanking systems, the use of technology is more sophisticated and, often, the systems are integrated with the clients' administrative systems. The service is almost always screen-based, applying personal computers or mainframe systems at the customer's premises. Communication is quite often channelled through dedicated data-networks or leased lines although the vast majority of small and medium-sized as well as a number of larger-sized companies communicate via the public telephone network. The facilities offered to corporate customers include access to financial information services (exchange rates, major financial events etc.), information on cash and off-sheet balances (including balances in other banks) and any kind of electronic payment services. Trade with stocks and securities can also be done from an office banking system.

It follows that virtually all routine transactions performed in most corporations can be made by use of an office-banking system. Office banking thus increases both the tradability of single products and the tradability of banking as an integrated mix of services.

The major part of office banking cannot be separated from the underlying services. However, general financial information can be produced anywhere, with access to the needed information. The general information is often produced outside the bank, for instance, by a specialized news agency.

(vi) Banking-related electronic data interchange

As stated above, many banking products involve exchange of different types of documents and information, in addition to the actual straightforward payment. While payments made through the banking sector in many ways have been automatized by the use of information and telecommunications technology, transfer of information related to payments is still mostly done on paper. Electronic data interchange offers the opportunity to make electronic transfer of both payments and documents related to a payment transaction.

Electronic data interchange is defined as electronic exchange of structured data. Electronic data interchange is not a specific banking product but can be used for exchange of many different kinds of information. Electronic data interchange is perhaps the technology with the biggest potential to change the way a company operates, the way companies relate to each other and the relations between companies and banks.

At present, though, this potential has not yet fully evolved. One of the major reasons for this is the lack of common standards. The United Nations Economic Commission for Europe has initiated standardization based on the EDI-FACT standard (EDI for Administration, Commerce and Transport). EDIFACT has been adopted as a basic standard by both the United Nations and the International Standards Organization (ISO),[13] and is becoming the most accepted standard. Thus, common sets of standards are emerging, but they are not yet introduced everywhere.

In a few countries, a standard exists for internal communication within the financial sector. In Denmark, the major banking institutions agreed upon a common specification of EDIFACT in 1989. This specification is now used for electronic communications between banks and major customers, although it is not yet widespread. Many corporations use EDI for other communications with non-financial institutions as well.

The banking industry was one of the first to adopt EDI for internal communication within the industry. However, in contrast to what is seen in other areas, the banking industry is not in the frontline of developments with regard to the introduction of EDI. Many of the EDI systems used in the financial sector are developed outside the sector and hosted on private networks owned by other companies such as IBM or GEISCO. However, some banks see EDI as an area for possible market expansion, and for linking their customers closer to the bank by offering EDI systems integrating most of the customer's communication needs. At the same, it should be noted that standardization of formats, protocols etc. will simplify procedures involved in a change of bank connections, making it easier for customers to switch banks. In any event, banks are forced to develop EDI-based systems because they are -- or will become -- a common demand of corporate customers, and banks that do not develop these systems will simply lose competitive ground.

The convenience of telefax machines has undoubtedly further delayed the introduction of the more complicated technology of EDI. However, as the exchange of documents has been the most important barrier against paperless (and therefore more tradable) payment services, the use of EDI is an important step towards more tradable banking services. One of the main barriers to its rapid application will be a lack of technical standards and standardized security systems for the many different types of documents related to payments. Moreover, in order to obtain the benefits of EDI, customers must enable their background systems to read and process electronic messages, reuse data, and construct and send messages out of the company. This requires a substantial investment in hard- and software as well as manpower in the company. Finally, this process will need to be initiated in entire industries or business areas in order for companies to be able to communicate electronically.

(b) Liquidity management

In contrast to private customers, corporate customers often demand services in the area of liquidity management. They are often demanded in relation to risks of changes in interest and currency rates. A large number of instruments have been developed, tailored to different needs. However, the instruments can basically be classified, following the list of products outlined in the annex, into those depicted in table III.9. Most of these instruments are negotiable and some are traded at stock exchanges. They are thus liquid assets which can be bought and sold according to changes in a firm's need for liquidity. The fact that an instrument often can be cancelled simply by buying a reverse risk position adds to its flexibility. Some instruments are, however, not negotiable as they are not standardized -- for example, most foreign exchange forward contracts and currency options reflect a single customer's needs. These are difficult to price; accordingly, the secondary market is quite small.

Table III.9. Liquidity-management products

- Forward contracts
- Futures
- Options
- Swaps

(i) Forward contract

A forward contract is defined as a contract that offers the buyer and seller of foreign exchange or securities the possibility of fixing the price or the exchange rate. In this way interest- and currency-rate risks can be covered. As forward contracts can be made for any asset, other kinds of risks can be covered as well, for instance, risks related to fluctuations in the prices of raw materials.

A forward contract can for instance be used to cover the risk of fluctuations in exchange rates for a firm that has agreed to buy a number of goods at a fixed price in dollars, for payment after three months. The firm can then make a three-month forward contract on a certain amount of dollars at an agreed rate. The firm will in this way be able to avoid a loss if the dollar rate increases. On the other hand it will not benefit if the rate decreases.

A forward contract is normally made with a financial institution as an intermediary guaranteeing claims on buyer and seller. The procedures involved are:

- Enquiring by buyer and seller.
- Evaluation of enquiries and creditworthiness of partners.
- Issuing of contract.
- Making up the contract on maturity.

Issuing of the contract demands knowledge of the creditworthiness of both parties. As the bank itself does not take any position in the market, the financial risk is not related to market conditions. However, market-knowledge is relevant in the setting of conditions in the contract.

Tradability is to some extent restricted by the need for knowledge of the creditworthiness of both parties. However, many larger corporations establish forward lines with foreign banks, and they use them intensively if that is advantageous. In addition, communications between the parties involved are made by manual procedures. Once the contract is made, the contract itself is tradable.

(ii) Futures

Futures are similar to forward contracts and the procedures involved are similar. The main difference is that futures are standardized in every way -- e.g., with respect to type of underlying asset, quality, quantity and expiry date. That makes futures negotiable. Moreover, changes in the contract price (due to fluctuations in the underlying asset) are settled daily. The settlement is normally done through a clearing house. In this way, the risk taken by a financial

institution of guaranteeing the contract is reduced.

Futures are frequently traded before maturity and they are quoted at many of the bigger stock exchanges. Therefore, they are more liquid assets than forward contracts. The market for futures has been rapidly expanding in recent years.

The tradability of futures is high. In principle, a firm of any origin can, through a broker, buy a future at any exchange and thereby cover its financial risk. However, for most corporations, direct trade at foreign exchanges is still far from being a routine business, and both the learning curve and transaction costs are high.

Forward rate agreements are instruments very similar to futures. Instead of referring to an underlying asset, a forward rate agreements refers to an interbank interest rate, e.g., LIBOR (London Interbank Offered Rate). The procedures involved and the prospects are basically the same as for "real" futures. Forward rate agreements are mostly made between two financial institutions. Therefore, they can be perceived as an intermediate rather than a final banking product.

(iii) Options

An option is a contract offering a right (but not an obligation, as futures do) to buy (call-option) or sell (put-option) an asset in a given quantity, at a given time at a given price. Options can relate to different underlying assets, including, for example, currency or interest options, depending on the risk to be covered.

In principle, an option is an agreement between parties with opposite liquidity needs. However, a financial institution is often one of the parties -- or at least acts as an intermediary.

The procedures involved in liquidity management through options are:

- Rating of the creditworthiness of the issuing party.
- Issuing of option.
- Selling/buying of option.
- Payment of the difference between current price and price according to the option to the holder of option.

The last procedure only takes place if holders use their options.

The tradability of an option is similar to that of futures. The difference is that only one party (the seller) needs to be evaluated with respect to creditworthiness.

(iv) Swaps

A swap is "a financial transaction in which two counterparts agree to exchange streams of payments over time according to predetermined rules."[14] The swap is used to change the market exposure related to a loan or similar obligation from one interest base to another.

Swaps can be used to cover interest and exchange rate risks as well as other kinds of financial risks. By issuing a number of swaps, more than two parties can be involved in the same arrangement. Although a swap basically is a liquidity management instrument, swaps can also be used in financing. In this case the exchanged streams of payments will have different time profiles.[15]

A number of hybrid instruments such as swap-option (Swaption) and time-option-swaps (TOS) have been developed in addition to interest and currency swaps. swaps can not be standardized in the same way as futures, as they often include the exchange of a number of different kinds of payments to be made at different points in time.

The procedures involved in a swaps are:

- Mutual rating of the creditworthiness of the two parties.
- Issuing of the swap.
- Rolling over of the swap according to contract.

As standardization of the product is more difficult than in the case of some other liquidity-management instruments, the prospects of full electronic automatization are rather poor, and the product is not really tradable. swaps are mostly used by large corporations and financial institutions that are active worldwide and can go into swaps anywhere. However, a swap issued for a local corporation by an institution situated in a different country will imply more technical difficulties than for most other products.

(c) Deposits

In addition to the current accounts and time deposits discussed in the section on retail banking, services provided in corporate banking include fixed term deposits or wholesale deposits.

A fixed term deposit is a deposit made for a fixed period of time agreed in advance. This type of deposit is generally large and the administration cheap, and thus better rates can be negotiated. A special kind of wholesale deposits are sweeping accounts -- accounts made for an overnight deposit.

Corporate deposits are larger than retail deposits both with regard to the balance and the size of each transaction, and transactions are international to a higher degree. Transaction costs are very important to companies, but a careful trade-off is made taking into account the overall level of interest rates and all the components of transaction costs (fees, loss of value days and currency exchange fees). This implies that they are more tradable to the extent that transaction costs (e.g., communication costs) can be spread out. In addition, an infrastructure of terminals and communication networks is more often accessible to corporate customers. The incentives to move parts of the administrative work to low costs areas are, however, limited.

(d) Financing

The negotiable financing products applied in retail banking (bills and mortgage deeds) are also used in corporate banking. In addition, a number of non-negotiable products have been developed to serve corporate financial needs (table III.10).

Table III.10. Corporate financing products

- Bills
- Mortgage deeds
- Guarantees
- Lending against security to bills
- Mortgage loans
- Financial loans
- Loans for equity
- Leasing
- Export credit loans

Bills and mortgage deeds have been discussed in the section on retail banking, as was the mortgage loan which is identical in nature to the retail product housing loan. Those products are therefore not discussed separately here.

(i) Guarantees

A guarantee is a contract that serves as security for a loan. In case of default, the guarantor is required to fulfil the debtor's obligations. Guarantees are especially relevant if a corporation needs credit from a foreign institution without prior knowledge or confidence in the corporation. Thus guarantees help to make loans more tradable.

The procedures involved in providing guarantees are:

- Rating of creditworthiness of the borrower.
- Issuing of guarantee.
- Repayment of loan by guarantor in case of default.

All these tasks are performed manually. Acceptance and price of a guarantee depend on the confidence in the customer. Exhaustive knowledge of the customer is therefore essential for the guarantor. This limits the tradability of the service, especially for smaller corporations without any international recognition.

(ii) Lending against security to bills

Lending against security to bills is a way in which companies can (temporarily) liquidate bills before maturity. The procedures involved in such lending are:

- Transfer of issued bill(s) to a bank.
- Credit rating of the trade debtors.
- Calculation of the size of the loan (based on the above rating).
- Issuing of loan.

The handling of bills is still done manually. Bills are physically deposited in a bank. The manual handling involved limits tradability. The evaluation of bills based on credit rating is an important element of this banking product. Local knowledge is therefore essential. Thus, while the use of electronic databases can improve the tradability of this service, it is not a very tradable product.

(iii) Financial loans

A financial loan is a loan against security, similar to a mortgage loan, and the procedures involved are basically the same. The difference is that the security is provided in the form of a portfolio of securities instead of real estate. The terms of financial loans are in general shorter than those of mortgage loans.

The technical tradability of financial loans is similar to that of mortgage loans. Many securities are considered not to be as safe as real estate. However, for a foreign bank, securities have the advantage of being more easy to evaluate.

(iv) Loans for procurement of equity

Loans for procurement of equity are loans guaranteed by non-governmental organizations, joint ventures or banks. This type of loan is often used in foreign aid programmes. In the developed world the terms of such loans are similar to those of financial loans and the tradability of this kind of loan is similar to that of financial loans.

(v) Leasing

A leasing agreement offers a company the possibility to rent a piece of equipment instead of buying it. Leasing is a common way of financing new equipment. Leasing can either be a pure financial agreement, where the lessee company itself is responsible for operation, maintenance etc., or part of these functions can be the responsibility of the lessor.

The procedures involved in a pure financial leasing transaction are:

- Rating of the creditworthiness of a company.
- Issuing of contract.
- Payment according to contract.

Other types of leasing may as well include the buying and installation of equipment, maintenance services etc. The tradability of this last type of leasing is limited, as physical interaction is demanded regularly.

Financial leasing, however, is just as tradable as any other type of secured loan, as the leased equipment immediately can be seized in case of payment default.

(vi) Export credit loans

An export credit loan is a loan with security in export orders. The loan serves the same financing purpose as a letter of credit, namely, to provide credit in the period before payment for an exported good has taken place. However, export credits are given to exporters by their own banks without any guarantee from a buyer's bank. The avails can be paid before shipment of goods has taken place.

The procedures involved are:

- Credit rating of the borrower or exporter (and, in some cases, of the buyer or importer).
- Issuing of document.

- Payment of avails.
- Amortization of loan.

The tradability of export credit services is similar to that of other loans with security. In some countries, export credits are issued on the basis of guarantees from export-promoting institutions. Guaranteed loans are more tradable as no credit rating is involved.

(e) Recent innovations

In recent years, more intensive use of information and telecommunication technologies has led to a decline of transaction costs related to the issuing of and trade with commercial papers. In addition, the securitization of financing has become more common in corporate banking. Partly for these reasons, a large number of new types of financial instruments have emerged. The main types of financial innovations are listed in table III.11. These financial instruments are especially used by large firms and by banks and other financial institutions themselves. In general, they are more liquid assets from the creditor's point of view, and therefore cheaper for the debtor. Furthermore, they add flexibility to risk and time profiles.

The new ways of financing do not affect the need for credit-rating. Most of the underlying papers are rated by independent credit-rating institutes such as Standard & Poors. In this way, potential investors can be guided in their investment decisions without having any specific knowledge concerning the debtor. The least transportable process (credit rating) is thus divided from the other processes. Therefore, the new instruments increase the tradability of corporate financing.

Table III.11. Classification of the main financial innovations

Special debt instruments	Variable rate loans Floating rate bonds Note issuance facilities Zero-coupon bonds Junk bonds
Debt-equity instruments	Convertible bonds Bonds with warrants Prêts participatifs
Special equity instruments	Euro-equities Venture capital
Risk-covering instruments	Swaps Futures/forward agreements Options

Source: J. Vinals, "Financial innovation, regulation and investment: international aspects", in A. Steinherr, ed., *The New European Financial Market Place* (London, Longman, 1992).

The separation of credit-rating from issuing and the financial risk, and the possibility of sharing the financial risk between more creditors, make the new instruments more tradable. Even high-risk junk bonds, financing investment projects with a poor credit rating, have proved to be marketable to buyers without any specific knowledge about the investments. The securitization of loans by means of new financial instruments thus increases the tradability of corporate financing.

B. Summary of findings with respect to technical tradability

In the previous section, banking activities have been analyzed product by product and the potential for trade of each product has been discussed. The point of departure has been the technical aspects related to the tradability of each intermediate banking product (transportability). The production of most final banking products can be divided into the production of a number of intermediate products. Transportability has been analyzed for final as well as

Table III.12. The transportability of intermediate and final retail-banking products

Product	Transportability of intermediate product	Transportability of final product	Actual trade in product
Cash handling/dispensing	None	None	-
Cheque	Bookkeeping (ME) and clearing (ME)	Poor	-
Debit cards	Credit rating (S) Clearing (E)	Good	+
Credit cards	Credit rating (S) Clearing (E)	Very good	+
EFTPoS	None	Very good	-
Bank transfer	None	Very good	+
Homebanking	None	Very good	(+)
Prepayment card	None	Fair	-
Current account	Interest calculation (E)	Good	-
Savings account	Interest calculation (E)	Good	+
Pension-scheme savings	Custodial service (S)	Poor	-
Bills	Credit rating (S)	Poor	-
Mortgage deed	Issuing and recording (M)	Poor	-
Housing loan	Credit rating (S)	Fair	-
Consumer loan	Credit rating (S)	Fair	-
Overdraft facility	Interest calculation (E)	Poor	-

Source: Based on annex 1 and other information obtained from a major bank in Denmark.

Notes: M = manual process. E = electronic process; S = process involving skilled labour; +/- indicates whether trade is taking place (+) or not (-).

intermediate products. The analysis shows that tradability very much depends on the kind of service and the products involved in the delivery of the service. Divisibility and tradability are often restrained by product-specific factors. This complicates a comparison of divisibility and tradability among products. Nevertheless, it is useful to summarize the results in order to derive more general conclusions (tables III.12 and III.13).

The first column of tables III.12 and III.13 lists the names of the main products discussed earlier. The second column identifies intermediate transportable products, i.e., work-processes that could be separated from the rest of the production and produced at a distance from a bank. It should be noted that two types of transportability of intermediate products are included. The first, which may be the most obvious, is location of a certain activity -- for instance electronic bookkeeping -- at a distance from both the bank and the customer. The factors promoting this type of division of labour could be either a better utilization of existing capacity or a cost reduction by locating in a low-wage-area. The second type is the location of a certain activity at a distance from a bank but close to the customer. This kind of division typically applies in distant banking for ac-

Table III.13. The transportability of intermediate and final corporate banking products

Product	Transportability of intermediate product	Transportability of final products	Actual trade in product
Bank draft	Bookkeeping (ME) Clearing (ME)	Good	+
Direct debit	Bookkeeping (ME) Clearing (ME)	Good	+
Debit collecting	Document processing (M)	Poor	-
Letter of credit	Document processing (M) Bank transfer (E)	Poor	(+)
Home-banking	None	Very good	+
EDI	None	Very good	+
Forward contract	Credit rating (S)	Good	+
Futures	Credit rating (S)	Good	+
Options	Credit rating (S)	Good	+
Swaps	Credit rating (S)	None	-
Guarantee	Credit rating (S)	Good	+
Financial loan	Credit rating (S) Interest calculation (E) Document processing (M)	Good	-
Loan for procurement of equity	Credit rating (S)	Good	-
Leasing	Credit rating (S)	Poor	-
Financial leasing	Credit rating	Good	+
Export credit loan	Credit rating (S) Interest calculation (E)	Poor	-

Source: Based on annex 1 and other information obtained from a major bank in Denmark.

Notes: M = manual process; E = electronic process; S = process involving skilled labour; +/- indicate whether trade is taking place (+) or not (-).

tivities that require some kind of local presence. The division of activities enhances, in this way, the tradability of the final product. The most typical example is perhaps credit rating. For many products, trust in the customer is essential and the main barrier against tradability. Once trust can be established, e.g., by use of a local institution, a number of products can be provided at a distance and thus traded across borders.

The third column assesses the transportability of each final product. This assessment is based on the assumption that intermediate products are outsourced if such a division improves transportability. It should be noted that the transportability in question relates to the service and not the physical product which may be involved in the provision of the service. For instance, a letter of credit is mainly used in relation to international trade, and the letter is transported between the parties involved in the transaction. However, the transportability of the service of issuing a letter of credit is limited by the need for extensive knowledge of the debtor's creditworthiness.

The fourth column indicates whether actual trade, according to available information, takes place today. In the case of retail home-banking and corporate letters of credit, the the brackets around the entries indicate that only very limited trade takes place today.

It should be noted that the products approach to banking activities adopted in this discussion does not reflect all functions carried out in a bank. A number of functions are not directly related to any of the products delivered. This is the case with managerial and some supporting functions. The preparation of the general ledger, payroll, training of personnel and management of physical facilities are all functions that are not covered in the preceding analysis. However, none of these functions are very relevant for the present discussion because they are not banking-specific products.

More important are different sorts of facilities management, e.g., the provision of software or computer-capacity. These are tradable intermediary services, difficult to relate to specific products. Facilities management will be discussed further in chapter V.

C. Overall tradability in banking

1. Retail banking

In retail banking, the need for a local presence has always been closely related to the need to be close to the customer through an extensive branch network. Tradability is thus very much dependent on the functions carried out in branch-offices. Hence, an analysis of these functions can supplement the product-wise analysis in the discussion of tradability. A look at the list of tasks performed in branch-offices (table III.14) demonstrates that all functions are, at least in some banks, based on an intensive use of information and telecommunications technologies. In principle, all functions can today be performed without customers visiting a branch-office.[16] By using existing electronic products, it is today technically possible to provide all services relevant for retail banking without face-to-face contact with the customer. Some banks have used this opportunity to provide what can be termed "branchless banking services". In return, the banks offer a more narrow spread on their interest rates. Communication between private customers and their banks is in this case made by a combination of three different communication channels:

- Electronic data-transfer (EFTPoS, cash-dispensing by ATMs and homebanking).
- Postal services (mailing of statements on payments and balances and cheque-books).
- Telephone (advice on payments, portfolio-management etc.).

It can be foreseen that the use of these communication channels will gradually be rationalized by a further switch to electronic communication: increased use of homebanking will reduce the need for ordinary telephone communication; and debit and credit cards will replace payments by cheques and cash. Smart cards will replace magnetic-stripe-cards and reduce the need for on-line communication from EFTPoS terminals. Later on, screen-based homebanking will be able to reduce the need for paper-based statements.

Table III.14. Tasks performed in retail branch-offices of banks

1. Cashing cheques
2. Withdrawing money
3. Depositing cheques
4. Transferring funds
5. Till-related bookkeeping/filing
6. Balancing till
7. Tracing/correcting balancing errors
8. Answering account enquiries
9. Securing missing customer information
10. Currency exchange
11. Opening/closing current accounts
12. Opening/closing savings accounts
13. Authorizing minor overdrafts
14. Contracting personal loans
15. Contracting time deposits
16. Dealing with standing orders
17. Delivering statements of account
18. Ordering cheques/cheque cards
19. Buying/selling investments
20. Answering non-account-related enquiries

Most banks use their network of branches as a competitive weapon, but the increasing use of information and telecommunications technologies -- especially electronic payment services -- does diminish the frequency of customers' personal visits to their bank; thus the distance to the closest branch becomes less important. The immediate implication of this in the developed countries has been a reduction in the number of local branches and, in some countries, a wider national coverage of certain banks.

The introduction of information and telecommunications technologies allows that more functions can be located in the back office. Furthermore, back-office functions can be carried out at any distance from the front office. Many banks have utilized this opportunity to establish computer centres in low-cost areas, providing a large part of the back-office functions.

While both transportability and divisibility of all retail banking services have proven to be technically feasible, international trade in retail services is still limited to a few specialized areas. Even if it is technically possible, only a few retail customers choose to hand over their banking business to a foreign bank, unless the bank is established in the country with a local representation. It has not been possible to find examples of foreign banks that have been able to penetrate significantly the retail market without establishing their own branch network. However, increased divisibility will make room for a growing crossborder delivery of intermediate products and supporting functions.

This indicates that there are other barriers to trade than the purely technical aspects of the delivery of banking products to the customer. One reason is that retail customers normally prefer to communicate with only one bank, one that is able to serve all their banking needs. Therefore, the least tradable services determine, to a certain extent, the opportunities for trade.

Looking at specific services, financing is the one least tradable. This is primarily due to the rating of creditworthiness involved. However, in retail banking the information needed for rating is mostly standard information such as earnings, wealth, regular expenditures, debt or other financial obligations. Most of this information is, in a society in which most major payments in some way are directed through the financial system, already available within the banking system. This information can be supplemented with access to databases on unreliable payers. For the majority of customers (excluding the least creditworthy and those with special financial needs), this implies that credit can be obtained at a distance without personal communication with banking personnel. Banks can, in principle, approve loans without seeing the customer.

While it is technically possible to transport information needed for distant creditassessment via the telecommunication network, legal barriers can be a severe restriction. Especially with regard to transport across borders, there are strict limitations on the kinds of personal data that can be exchanged. The legal framework for data protection can thus be a key issue in the development of international retail banking.

Another way to overcome the problem of rating is the abovementioned outsourcing of the credit-rating process. This approach is applied in the credit-card business, where international credit-card companies often accept new customers on the basis of evaluations made by local banks.

Retail capital intermediation is thus technically possible. However it must be noted that this product has to be competitive compared to wholesale trade with credit. If financing can be obtained at better terms from another country, any domestic bank can (unless legal restrictions prevent it) provide retail loans financed by foreign credit.

It is well known that the introduction of information and telecommunications technologies has played an important role in the blurring of the boundaries between different kinds of financial institutions. The integration of different kinds of financial services tends to reduce tradability. Customers become less mobile, as the transaction costs related to a shift to another bank, insurance company or similar institution increase. At the same time, the blurring of boundaries has led to disintegration as well. In retail banking, this is most visible in payment services. Credit-card companies and giro banks have both successfully created their own niches in the payment market.

While giro banks are nationally-based institutions, credit-card companies are internationally oriented and will probably be among the first to utilize the technical opportunities for an international distribution of retail banking services. Credit-card companies have already been in the forefront of allocating labour intensive activities to low-cost areas in the United States.

Technically, the tradability of credit cards is not very different from that of debit cards. Speed is less essential for credit cards. However, if data are transferred electronically, this difference is not important. The work processes involved are also very similar. More important is that debit cards are connected to a banking account and that banking accounts are connected to finance. Therefore, payments by debit cards are less divisible from other banking products, and the existing market structures, with a dominating market share held by domestic banks, are therefore more rigid. In the area of credit cards, with a market dominated by a few international companies, the market structure is more fit for an international division of labour.

Technically, all banking products directed towards the retail market are tradable. The technical opportunities for a division of final products and the transport of intermediary products are already applied today at the national level. However, international trade on a larger scale has not yet emerged due largely to non-technical factors.

2. Corporate banking

Corporate banking is, by nature, more internationally oriented than retail banking. First of all, corporate banking involves a large number of international transactions. Secondly, big transnational corporations have always used banks in many different countries. However, internationalization itself does not automatically involve trade in financial services, although it can be difficult to distinguish between the two.[17]

Looking at tables III.12 and III.13, it seems that corporate banking is more tradable than retail banking. However, a comparison product by product does not give the full picture. Although the individual products are tradable, customers may prefer to concentrate most of their activities in a single bank, with which they are able to maintain close relations. Therefore, customers may prefer the core of their banking business to be handled by a local bank.

Another aspect is that corporate banking (compared to retail banking) is less standardized and not based to the same degree on mass transactions. Specific knowledge about a single customer is more essential. In addition, the needs of single customers vary often considerably, and these needs are usually also more sophisticated than those of retail customers. Altogether, the skills required in corporate banking are more sophisticated and more specific.

Differences in customer needs require that different kinds of corporate customer groups are distinguished. Those include:

(1) Large transnational corporations.
(2) Medium-scale enterprises.
(3) Small-scale enterprises.

Large transnational corporations have the most advanced needs for financial service. Most of them are already today internationally oriented in their use of banking services. Usually they have their own financing departments acting on international financial markets. They are known and rated by international credit institutions and are able to make use of banking facilities in several countries at the same time. Thus, international trade is taking place already today. However, most corporations still choose a domestic bank as their primary banking connection.

Medium-scale enterprises in many respects have the same needs as large corporations. However, their ability to shop around the world for the most favourable service is much more limited. In their international transactions they usually rely on a domestic bank and its foreign affiliates (supplemented by the foreign banking connections of the domestic bank). Medium-scale enterprises are therefore today dependent on the existence of a domestically advanced banking system.

Small-scale enterprises often have needs very similar to those of retail customers. With respect to tradability, the most important difference is that credit rating of small enterprises is much more complicated and requires more local knowledge than rating of private retail customers. These enterprises will therefore have difficulties in obtaining financing from institutions without any kind of local presence.

It follows that, although a product-by-product analysis reveals that corporate banking products are even more tradable than retail banking products, the corporate sector will in the short to mid-term future tend to remain more dependent on the existence of a local domestic banking industry. This holds true especially for medium scale enterprises.

3. Technology-dependent barriers to tradability

An analysis of each banking product has shown that, technically, virtually all services can be provided by tradable banking products. However, with the exception of credit cards and services provided to larger corporations, trade in financial services is quite limited.

Transport and geographic distribution of the production of banking services are much more common at the national level. This is due to a combination of technical, economic and cultural factors. The required telecommunication infrastructure is not yet established in all parts of the world and not even in all industrialized countries; hence, the lack of infrastructure still constrains the use of telecommunications.[18] The above product analysis indicates a number of technology-dependent barriers to international trade:

- Lack of knowledge of customer's creditworthiness.
- Speed of transactions.
- Communication costs related to the transport of services.
- Language.

These barriers can be termed technology-dependent barriers, because technical solutions are emerging. Better communication facilities and a more international use of databases -- even on information about smaller enterprises and maybe retail customers -- will make financing more tradable. The transportability of this kind of databases has contributed to an institutional separation of credit rating and financing in the handling of an increasing range of financial products.

The speed of international data flows among developed countries will increase dramatically in the near future, and the cost of international communication will probably decline. A wider diffusion of screen-based homebanking systems will, in combination with international standards for EDI, provide a way to overcome communication problems related to differences in culture and language. Electronic data interchange can also in some ways help to reduce the problems due to variations in legal rules and traditions.

4. Potential directions of trade

This chapter has shown that there is an undoubted technical potential for trade in financial services. Furthermore, some of the economic and cultural barriers against trade can be overcome by a further upgrading of the infrastructure for information and telecommunications technologies.

Looking at the types of transportable processes of production in tables III.12 and III.13, it appears that most processes are related to computer-processing or skilled manpower. A transfer of back-office functions from developing to developed countries seems in these cases to be the most likely possibility.

A few processes of production require manpower without highly specialized knowledge. These functions are mostly related to document processing and clearing. Both are areas in which the level of activities is likely to decline with the introduction of EDI and a more widespread use of purely electronic means of payments. Therefore it can be expected that banks will choose to automatize rather than transfer these back-office functions to a developing country.

These issues are discussed in greater detail in chapter VI.

Notes

1   The description in this chapter is based primarily on the Danish experience. Banks in Denmark have generally been advanced in the utilization of information and telecommunications technologies. Concrete Danish experience is used to illustrate the various types of service products and the extent to which they are based on the use of information and telecommunications technologies. The point is, however, only to illustrate some advanced cases, not to endorse a particular way of applying technology.

2   Selfi Report No. 4, "Bærbar bank" (Mobile bank), (Roskilde, Roskilde University Centre, 1987), p. 13.

3   P. Entwistle, "Telecommunication, customer service and Lloyds Bank". Speech delivered at the conference on *Telecommunications and Economic Opportunities for Europe*, Newcastle, September 1988.

4   It is possible to transfer an image of the cheque through the telenetwork. However, this solution is rather expensive and requires the use of advanced compression techniques or the use of a high speed data-network.

5   R. McGahey, *Financial Services, Financial Centers* (Boulder, Westview Press, 1990), p. 303.

6   This will be discussed in more detail in the section on electronic data interchange below in this chapter.

7   The Nottingham Building Society makes transborder use of homebanking. Its homebanking system "Homelink" serves a number of overseas customers in Hong Kong (See Patrick Frazer, *Plastic and Electronic Money* (Cambridge, Woodhead-Faulkner, 1985), p. 294. However, this example must be seen in the context of the very specific status of Hong Kong, and the desire of some Hong Kong citizens to immigrate to the United Kingdom.

8   A number of examples are given in J. McCrindle, *Smart Cards* (Bedford, IFS Ltd., 1990).

9   R. Bright, *Smart Cards: Principles, Practice, Applications* (London, Ellis Horwood Ltd., 1988), p. 161.

10 An overview of prepayment card systems is given in Peter Harrop, *Prepayment Cards: The Electronic Purse Becomes Big Business* (London, Financial Times Business Information, 1991), p. 131.

11 Frazer, op. cit.

12 Harrop, op. cit.

13 European Commission, *Making Payments in the Internal Market*, Discussion Paper COM(90) 447 (final).

14 Bank for International Settlements, *Recent Innovations in International Banking* (Basle, Bank for International Settlements, 1986), p. 268.

15 See J. Vinals, "Financial innovation, regulation and investment: international aspects", in A. Steinherr, *The New European Financial Market Place* (London, Longman, 1992), pp. 166-191.

16 For example, cheques can either be cashed in a retail store or the function can be replaced by cashing with a debit card at an ATM terminal.

17 This will be discussed in more detail in chapter V.

18 This issue will be discussed in more detail in chapter IV.

Chapter IV

REALIZING THE POTENTIAL: NETWORKS AND ACCESS TO NETWORKS

Since the late 1980s, interest in the economic role of "networks" has been growing. This is largely due to three factors:[1]

- The fast and generalized introduction of new information and communication technologies.
- The growing importance of telecommunication networks as providers of essential inputs to the economic system.
- The growing awareness of the role of externalities.

Telecommunications networks are increasingly becoming the basic infrastructure of a modern economy, and each national network must be seen as part of the worldwide telecommunications network. This chapter examines three aspects of telecommunications networks that are relevant to international transactions in banking services:

- Private networks, serving a closed community of users.
- Value-added network services, i.e., applications making the networks function.
- Public networks.

A. Networks and the end of geography in international financial transactions

International networks are essential for the provision of services based on information and telecommunications technologies. This is particularly true in banking. The internationalization of banking has gone further and deeper than the internationalization of goods and other services. This has been a result of developments both in the general economy and inside banking. With the internationalization of economic activities, banks have been under particular pressure to provide quick and comprehensive information from worldwide sources and to facilitate the rapid international transfer of funds. As financial centres are located in different time zones, there is a demand for these services to be available on a 24-hour basis. New telecommunication technologies have offered these services so efficiently that it has inspired an author to suggest that "the end of geography" has arrived in the area of international financial relations.[2] The two main driving forces in this development have been deregulation of controls on capital movements and technology. Both of these forces have underlined to banks the importance of a world-wide network in which operations and functions that previously were impossible can be performed. But the two forces have also opened up the way for new competition. An important development was the tendency, already apparent in the late 1960s, towards non-bank financial firms using electronic communication to create financial instruments. The banks were already then bypassed, as money-market mutual funds were internationally invested in short-term government securities that pay higher interest rates than banks would offer.[3]

The abandonment of controls on capital movements in the developed countries has increased the funds available for international investment and contributed for the explosive growth in cross-border investment since the mid-1980s and fuelled trade in foreign exchange. The growth in cross border activities, which is changing the nature of the financial market place, has been made possible by new technologies that are themselves transforming the financial market-place. The transformation has consequences for states, banks and consumers of financial services. The nation state is increasingly unable to perform its traditional role as regulator of the financial market as large amounts of funds move through the networks. Banks can operate wherever the market and factors of production happen to be, provided an adequate telecommunications infrastructure is available; but the technology also opens the way for increasing competition from non-banks. The consumer can increasingly choose among a wider range of services than those that are provided by local banks.

"Global" has been the watchword in the financial world since the late 1980s. Since then, there has seemed to be no real alternative to banks, as financial service companies, than to choose among three strategies for their actions in the new financial market place:

(1) Banks can build their own private systems and use them as competitive tools. This is only a viable strategy for the largest and best capitalized banks.

(2) Bigger banks and other institutions can build systems (value-added network services) that can be sold to institutions too small to build their own systems.

(3) Banks can buy into systems established by others or share systems based on public networks with other banks.

B. The private international financial services networks

1. Private networks of banks

Citibank of New York is a prominent example of a bank adopting the first option mentioned above. In the beginning of the 1970s, in response to the competition from non-bank financial enterprises, the strategy of Citibank was redefined as that of an "international financial service company". Citibank developed a nationwide network of automatic teller machines (ATMs) and electronics-based services and grew to be the largest United States bank measured by domestic balances. Today it offers a full range of financial services around the world based on a number of private networks built during the 1970s. To sustain these services, Citibank in 1992 began to combine its 100 separate private networks in 92 countries into one global information network. The plan is that the network will include voice, video and data capabilities and support, e.g., electronic data interchange (EDI). This consolidation is expected to save $100 million per year.[4]

Other big United States banks -- such as Bank of America, Chase Manhattan, Manufacturers Hanover (now merged with Chemical Bank), have used private packet-switched networks run by different telecommunications operators. Outside the United States, the Sumitomo Bank of Japan, for example, has operated for a number of years a proprietary packet switched network able to transmit simultaneously data, facsimile and voice.[5]

2. Provision of financial network systems by banks and other organizations

Chemical Bank is an example of a bank adopting the second option mentioned above. It operates a private international network for its own intra-bank services; at the same time, it outsources all telecommunications related to its proprietary system for customer cash-management services to General Electric Information System (GEIS). Chemical Bank's system for cash management is franchised to other banks world-wide, including Barclays in the United Kingdom. Barclays has used the system as a basis for its own, customized system.

The most important examples in this category are, however, the systems built by non-banking organizations. This market can be divided into three broad categories: a) general financial services; b) quotes and sale prices for exchange-traded instruments; and c) quotes and prices for over-the-counter instruments. The market is internationally dominated by five companies: Reuter Holdings PLC (Reuters), Quotron Systems, Inc. (owned by Citicorp), Automatic Data Processing, Inc. (ADP), Knight-Ridder, Inc. and Telerate Inc. (owned by Dow Jones & Co., Inc.).[6] Quotron and ADB have long dominated the market for United States stock-market data, whereas Telerate has had a near monopoly in the market for United States Government security prices (this is likely to change with the increased use of electronics in the market in 1993). Reuters has dominated the market outside the United States and created a market for real-time foreign exchange data in 1973. As early as 1850, the founder of Reuters, Paul Julius Reuter, entered the market for international financial information services, using carrier pigeons to fly stock-market quotations between Brussels and Aachen. The company turned to more advanced modes of communication when the first underwater telegraph cable connecting Dover and Calais was opened the following year and it developed into a global news agency.

Reuters was revitalized in 1973 when an electronically based service for foreign exchange markets was introduced; it is now one of the most important providers of financial networks. Although Reuters is much more than a network provider, the network is an indispensable part of its services as the world's biggest company for real-time financial information. Reuters' main product is financial information distributed on one of the world's biggest private telecommunications networks and received on dedicated terminals. This product was distributed in 1992 to 218 countries and territories connecting approximately 215,000 terminals. The financial information and the terminals accounted for 65 per cent of Reuters' 1992 turnover of 1,567 million pounds sterling.

Other services are being developed in connection with Reuters' information services. It has been estimated that approximately 30 per cent of the world market transactions in foreign exchange, worth $300 billion per day, is traded via Reuters. The company is trying to sustain this position, e.g., via the establishment of *Dealing 2000*, an automated trading system that is being introduced to foreign exchange dealers. This service will show the dealers an updated screen with the best available rates for any relevant type of foreign exchange.

A similar service is *Globex*, which is the world's biggest marketplace for futures and options. It was launched in cooperation with the Chicago Board of Trade, but is planned for use also at the Chicago Mercantile Exchange, the New York Mercantile Exchange, MATIF in Paris and the Sydney Futures Exchange. This coverage implies that approximately 70 per cent of the actual world trade in futures and options will be conducted over this system. All of the participants will be connected to a central computer with the same priorities and rights.

C. The cooperative international financial services networks

The alternatives left to the banks unable to develop their own networks is to buy from other companies that build systems for sale, as discussed in section B, or to participate in one of the collaborative or cooperative network arrangements. A number of collaborative initiatives have been undertaken, including an initiative to specify international conditions for terminals to be used in cashless shopping, EFTPoS Ltd. This initiative, like many others, encountered difficulties when banks thought that they would lose the opportunity to compete with one another by joining the system.[7]

Most banks do however use a number of shared and third-party private networks such as the Society for World-wide Interbank Finan-

cial Telecommunication (SWIFT), VISA International, MasterCard International and ATM networks. The majority of the ATM networks are not owned by card organizations but by banks or network operators.

At least two cooperative systems have, however, been developed with success; the SWIFT and VISA systems. They are systems with very different characteristics, but both count among their members big banks. These systems are value-added-network services (VANS). Like the other networks mentioned above, they transmit data and add value in the sense that they, e.g., format and process data, perform various operations and facilitate the sending of data. A third cooperative network was established in 1990, EUFISERV.

The Society for World-Wide Interbank Financial Telecommunication (SWIFT). This is the oldest and biggest of the international financial networks. It was established in 1973 on an European basis by a group of 239 banks, largely as a response to what were seen as discriminatory rules favouring United States banks in the two credit-transfer systems based in the United States, Fedwire and Clearing House Interbank Payment System (CHIPS). By the end of 1992, SWIFT was owned by more than 2,000 user banks and linked more than 3,500 institutions in 90 countries, including all of the world's major financial centres.[8]

The system is technically a message system. It has two principal functions: the processing of messages and their transmission. These functions in principle only allow banks to automate their data-transmission procedures and eliminate problems of language and interpretation. In principle, it does not have the legal authority of, e.g., CHIPS and Fedwire to settle a final payment. However, in practice, SWIFT is considered a system for final payment for many purposes, as its messages are accepted by banks as authentic and authoritative.

Two operating centres, in the United States and the Netherlands respectively, carry out security procedures such as the authentication of a message's origin, its encryption and decryption plus verification of its integrity as it passes through the system. The backbone of the system is an X.25 transport network installed in 1989 as part of a project to create a much-debated new generation network, "SWIFT II", with a modular structure to resolve future capacity problems. The modules to be implemented from 1993 onwards include EDI-services, netting services for banks trading in ECU and the automatic matching of foreign exchange and money-market transactions (ACCORD).

The success of SWIFT and its growing role in increasing trade in banking services is indicated by data on the number of transactions in SWIFT over time (table IV.1).

VISA International. The credit-card provider VISA (which originated from the BankAmericard pioneered by Bank of America) is now cooperatively owned by a number of banks and has a worldwide telecommunication network. Like the other big international card organizations, Eurocard/Mastercard, Eurocheck and American Express, VISA's network allows its customers to access ATMs in a multitude of countries. Most of the ATMs are not owned by the card organizations, but made available to their subscribers by an agreement with the owners of the ATMs (usually banks or network operators). The networks provide standards and procedures for international withdrawals.

This includes both the telecommunication side regarding routing and switching of authorizations and the banking side regarding international clearing and settlement matters.

Table IV.1. Number of transactions in SWIFT, 1977-1992

Year	Total transactions (Thousands)	Peak day transactions (Number)
1978	21 409	..
1979	34 531	..
1980	46 981	..
1981	62 576	..
1982	79 802	..
1983	104 075	..
1984	129 184	610
1985	156 469	733
1986	191 126	868
1987	221 348	1 004
1988	254 072	1 149
1989	294 922	1 317
1990	331 687	1 460
1991	363 741	1 646
1992	404 518	1 810

Source: Data obtained from SWIFT.

When a VISA card is used in an ATM, an authorization call is placed, including a check for lost and stolen cards and a verification of credit limit and expiration date. Usually, this is performed in less than 2 seconds, for a marginal cost of less than $.001. This demands well-functioning access to the international telecommunications network. More than 95 per cent of the 112,000 VISA-ATMs are located in Western Europe and North America, and less than 1,000 in Africa (predominantly in South Africa).[9] The card can also be used for a purchase in countries without direct access to the international telecommunications network; but issuance statistics for cards reflect a similar pattern, with, for example, 60 million VISA cards issued in Europe and 50,000 in Africa outside South Africa. The growth in the number of VISA cards in Europe (with a similar development for the other major cards -- see table IV.2.) is an indication of the increasing transportability of banking services, as it implies use of banking services at a distance.

Table IV.2. International payment cards in Europe, selected years, 1980-1991 (Thousands)

Card	1980	1985	1990	1991
VISA	10 878	22 615	51 730	59 054
Eurocard/ Mastercard	5 976	11 586	21 686	25 045
Eurocheck	20 812	28 758	40 304	47 276
Total	37 666	62 959	113 720	131 375

Source: EFMA Card Statistics.

EUFISERV. European saving banks have established the European Savings Banks Financial Services Company (EUFISERV) as an alternative to the existing dominant international ATM networks of VISA and the conglomerate MasterCard/Eurocard/Eurocheck. The goal of EUFISERV is twofold: to establish appropriate mechanisms for cross-border cooperation between savings banks, and to promote a new corporate identity for them at the European level.[10] The shareholders of the company consist of 13 European savings banks associations. By mid-1992, 16,000 ATMs were included in the network; it is planned to have 27,000 on-line machines connected by the end of 1993. The plan is to develop a high volume international funds transfer service for members, using the same infrastructure. EUFISERV routes authorization, clearing and settlement on-line and in real time for its members.

D. The telecommunications networks

In principle, the existence of private financial services networks does not preclude the use of public switched networks. In reality, however, the internationally operating banks have preferred to use private, leased lines. Two main reasons for banks to develop such private networks during the 1970s and 1980s can be distinguished:

- The enhanced data-services demanded by the banks were not generally available on public networks. This included problems with connecting LANs over public networks and frequent difficulties of getting needed services across national borders.

- The tariff structure in the public networks made it advantageous for the banks to lease lines for high-volume use.

These conditions seem to be changing in the 1990s. On the one hand, new technologies are reducing the costs of private networks, and the European PTTs are cutting the price of leased lines. But, at the same time, public switched facilities are becoming more attractive to financial institutions for two main reasons. Network operators have begun offering virtual private networks (VPNs), where lines are allocated dynamically according to the need of the customer. This has proved a reliable and cost effective solution for many big customers. The second reason for migrating to the public network is that there is a growing need for the banks to be linked directly with the customers. The banks have to participate in EDI systems in order to retain traditional customers and avoid being bypassed. The EDI systems are often industry-specific solutions connecting the vertical production chain in order to automate orders, confirmations and invoices. These systems clearly have the potential to be used also to settle payments, and that is why the banks need to join in. Technically, the systems are often run by a VANS operator on the public networks; as there are still technical and regulatory problems with direct connections between private and public networks, the banks increasingly are looking to public networks.

E. Access to networks

As suggested above, there is no doubt that, with the exception of very locally operating banks, it is necessary for any modern bank to be electronically connected to the international financial system. Practically all banks in the industrialized countries have access to an international network using one of the options in the categories mentioned. Whereas the option of establishing their own networks is reserved for the very big banks, the option of leasing or purchasing network services from others or participating in collaborative network arrangements, in principle, is open to any bank. Firms like Reuters offer their services on a commercial basis to any financial institution willing and able to pay. SWIFT used to be accessible only to banks. In recent years, however, new categories of institutions such as securities exchanges, brokers and dealers have been allowed to participate in SWIFT.

For banks in developing countries, however, there are two kinds of barriers to international connections. One barrier is the costs associated with the connections. Installation and start-up for a very basic version of systems like Reuters and SWIFT can cost in the region of $225,000. Yearly subscriptions of approximately $65,000 in the case of Reuters and one tenth of that for SWIFT -- which offers a very different service -- have to be added. These costs do not include transaction costs and telecommunications costs. The costs are prohibitive for many banks in developing countries, as evidenced, for example, by the fact that only 10 countries in Africa were actually connected to SWIFT in 1992: Algeria, Botswana, Côte d'Ivoire, Ghana, Lesotho, Madagascar, Morocco, Namibia, South Africa and Tunisia.

Another kind of barrier to connection for developing countries has been the poor state of their telecommunication networks. This barrier may be a more serious barrier to entry in the international economy than the financial barrier where special arrangements are conceivable. With the increasing tendency to use public switched telecommunication networks as the basis for the banking networks, banks in developing countries may, paradoxically, find it more difficult to access these networks. This is due to the fact that whereas dedicated networks can be supplied conditioned "only" by payment, the necessary specific upgrading of the public network might be impeded by a policy allowing only general upgrading of the network.

Notes

1   C. Antonelli, "The economic theory of information networks", in C. Antonelli, ed., *The Economics of Information Networks* (Amsterdam, North Holland, 1992), p. 5.

2   Richard O'Brien, *Global Financial Integration: The End of Geography* (London, Royal Institute of International Affairs, 1992).

3   "International banking", *Financial Times*, 9 May 1990, p. VI.

4   United States, Office of Technology Assessment, *U.S.Banks and International Telecommunications* (Washington, D.C., Government Printing Office, 1992), p. 8.

5   "World banking", *Financial Times*, Supplement, 8 May 1987, p. III.

6   United States, Office of Technology Assessment, *Trading Around the Clock: Global Securities Markets and Information Technology* (Washington, D.C., Government Printing Office, 1990), p. 14.

7   "World banking", *Financial Times*, op.cit.

8   Eric Chilton, Chairperson of SWIFT, speech at The Networked Economy Conference, Paris, March 1993.

9   1991 figures obtained from VISA.

10 *Banking Automation Bulletin for Europe*, No. 112 (April 1992), p. 7.

Chapter V

THE IMPACT OF INCREASED TRADABILITY ON THE STRUCTURE OF INTERNATIONAL TRANSACTIONS IN BANKING SERVICES

A basic proposition in this report is that the advent of new information and tele- communication technologies will in- crease the tradability of banking services. These technologies provide for the technical pos- sibility of transmitting a growing range of ser- vices over distances, and they reduce the trans- action costs, both in the sense that the costs of obtaining relevant market information are being reduced and -- in relation to information intensive services -- in the sense that the costs of transacting the service itself become lower.

This should, *ceteris paribus*, lead to an in- crease in international trade in banking services as compared with banking services provided through foreign affiliates, as a major reason for establishing affiliates instead of trade relations -- according to the theory of transaction costs -- is to reduce these transaction costs. Information technology offers new possibilities for reducing transaction costs.

There are indications that this is indeed, tak- ing place. The number of banking institutions using SWIFT and their use of this network has

shown a marked increase, as has the use of international payment cards (see chapter IV). Especially in domestic use, information and telecommunications technologies have changed the structure of the production process in the industry as a result of the dramatic in- crease in the number of electronically delivered transactions, which replace payment orders and the use of coins, notes and cheques. As an illustration, the development in the number of cards and transactions in the Danish "Dankort" system of the Pengeinstutternes Betalings Sys- temer (PBS), the payment system of Danish banks, is shown in table V.1; "Dankort" is owned and used by all Danish banks.

The question of what effects information and telecommunication technologies will have on trade and foreign direct investment (FDI) in banking services can not be answered on a purely theoretical level.[1] Apart from the prob- lems of economic and regulatory barriers men- tioned earlier, considerations relating to the choice between competing modes of delivery of services need to be taken into account.

Table V.1: Number of cards and transactions in the Danish Dankort system, 1985 - 1992

Year	Cards (Thousands)	Transactions (Thousands)
1985	363	2 053
1986	685	6 627
1987	957	18 131
1988	1 320	40 485
1989	1 610	70 485
1990	1 870	97 119
1991	2 104	125 900
1992	2 299	156 449

Source: Pengeinstitutternes Betalings Systemer (PBS).

A. Modes of delivery

In general, three major categories or modes of delivery are commonly mentioned in the discussions of international transactions in services, including in the banking industry:[2] foreign direct investment (FDI), trade[3] and labour movement. In the case of banking services, labour movement is not an important category, although the upper echelons of management in foreign-owned banks may be dominated by expatriates from the home country of a particular bank, and although smaller foreign affiliates of banks located in financial centres often are manned by expatriates. The absolute majority of employees in foreign-owned banks are residents of the countries in which the banks are located.

Foreign direct investment and trade are, therefore, the two major modes of delivery of banking services abroad. The provision of services through the establishment of branches, subsidiaries, associates or representative offices -- in brief, foreign affiliates -- constitutes FDI, while the provision of financial services by an institution in one country to a consumer or user of those services in another country (that is, provision of services across borders) constitutes trade. It should be added that, although trade and the sale of services by foreign affiliates are alternative modes of delivery, they do not necessarily exclude each other. Banks may utilize a mixture of both methods, and FDI may well constitute a basis for extended trade relations.

1. Types of foreign direct investment in banking

There are four main types of establishment or representation by banks providing services through FDI or other forms of presence in foreign countries:

● Representative offices.

● Branches.

● Subsidiaries and associates.

● Correspondents.

These four types of local representation (and their subcategories) as well as additional categories, are described below. The first three are forms of FDI, involving control by a transnational corporation through equity ownership or a non-equity arrangement, while correspondent banks involve no FDI. The FDI forms may, in turn be classified into:

● legal entities of the home country (e.g., representative offices and branches); and

● legal entities of the host country.

(a) Legal entities of the home country

Representative offices serve as a point of contact for providing marketing information and establishing business connections, as well as acting as intermediaries between the parent banks and their customers, without, as a rule, serving as booking locations.[4]

Branches are legal extensions of the parent bank in a foreign country and are not separately constituted locally chartered corporations. Hence, branches are an integral part of the parent bank, without a separate legal identity, and, as such, are subject to home country control and regulation. Branches may make loans and take deposits and will typically be backed by the larger capital base of the parent.[5]

Agencies are entities that are allowed to lend funds but cannot accept deposits (other than credit balances) from the general public.

"Shell" branches are booking offices located in foreign countries; they do not administer the business carried on their books and have no contact with the local market.

(b) Legal entities of the host country

Subsidiaries are local institutions, incorporated under host country law, in which the bank has a direct or indirect control.

Associates are local institutions incorporated under host country law in which a foreign bank holds a minority interest. From a technical point of view, the distinction between an "associate" and a "subsidiary" is based on the extent to which the parent institution holds a controlling interest in the associated company. The definition of "controlling" interest varies, in turn, greatly from country to country and is not necessarily equivalent to the concept of "majority" participation.

Consortium banks are made up of groups of banks pooling resources and know-how, usually for handling large-scale business of an international nature.

Joint banking ventures are associations set up for the purpose of carrying out specific business of common interest to the participating banks.

2. Non-foreign-direct-investment modes of delivery

Correspondent banking covers all facets of "bank-to-bank-business" and, more specifically, any service offered by a bank to another financial institution.[6] This allows a bank to conduct its business in a foreign country without having any presence other than a direct connection or friendly service relation with another bank.

Direct trade is the other category covering banks doing their business in foreign countries without any physical presence, not even a connection with a correspondent bank.

3. Nature of relationships

Foreign-direct-investment enterprises consisting of legal entities of the home country or of the host country and the non-FDI modes consisting of arm's length trade relations may be illustrated in the following figure where the level of closeness between a parent bank and its foreign affiliates or other relationships is graduated in the case of the two FDI-groups, from representative offices to consortiums/joint ventures:

Figure V.1.Foreign-direct-investment and non-foreign-direct-investment types of organization of the international delivery of banking services

Foreign-direct-investment types of organisation								Non-foreign-direct-investment types of organisation	
Legal entities of home country				Legal entities of host country				Cor	DT
RO	SB	Ag	Br	Sub	As	Con	JBV		

Legend:

RO	=	Representative office
SB	=	"Shell" branches
AG	=	Agencies
Br	=	Branches
Sub	=	Subsidiaries
As	=	Associates
Con	=	Consortium banking
JBV	=	Joint bank ventures
Cor	=	Correspondent banking
DT	=	Direct trade

This categorization does not imply that the two first groups do not involve any arm's length trade. This point is obvious when dealing with representative offices, but it is also the case for other forms of FDI that may help bring about business relations based on trade between a bank in one country and a customer in another country. It is, therefore, not certain that the emergence of new information and telecommunications technologies will diminish the number of different FDI forms, even if the hypothesis that information and telecommunications technologies will strengthen non-FDI forms of delivery is correct and has a decisive impact on the empirically measurable developments.

This situation is reflected in figure V.2, which illustrates the hypothesis that the increasing use of new information and telecommunication services could lead to a greater emphasis on the modes of delivery that entail a greater portion of arm's length trade, including both non-FDI forms of penetrating foreign markets and forms of FDI that lead to the establishment of trade relations. An illustrative figure appears by bending the ends of the straight line in figure

V.1 to form a circle. In the upper half of the circle, banking services are being traded at arm's length across borders, either totally (through direct trade, correspondent relations), or partly (through representative offices or "shell" branches or agencies). In the lower part of the circle, banking services are delivered only nationally by means of FDI, either totally (branches, subsidiaries or associates) or partly (consortiums and joint ventures).

The point of this figure is not whether one is dealing with forms of FDI or non-FDI forms of international transactions. The point is the extent of trade relations and the effects of increased transportability of banking services. Direct trade and trade via correspondent banking are obviously pure forms of trade. Representative offices, likewise, lead to pure forms of trade: the purpose of a representative office is to act as an intermediary between the parent bank in the home country and customers of the host country. In the case of "shell" branches, the purpose of setting up such organizations is to by-pass regulations in the home country. But formally, a trade relation between a customer of the home country and the "shell" branch of the host country is being established. In the case of agencies, a mixture of foreign trade relations and international business relations in the host country will occur. Another mixture will certainly take place in the cases of consortium banks and joint banking ventures, while business via branches, subsidiaries and associates predominantly will rely on intra-national business relations. But this does not exclude these

Figure V.2. Affiliate types and modes of delivery

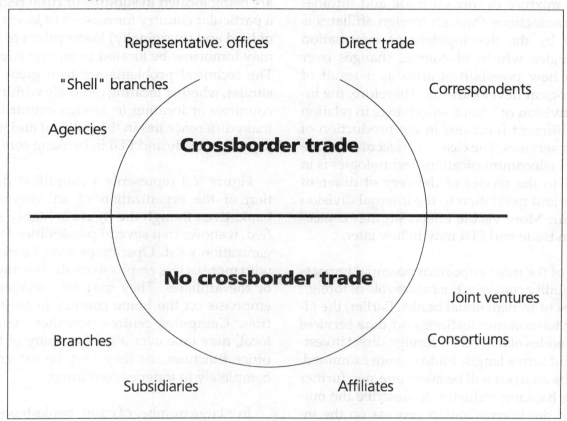

national relations being supplemented by some arm's length trade.

B. Technology and the organization of banking operations

It is impossible to conclude on a theoretical level whether the expansion of information and telecommunications technologies will lead to a greater emphasis on trade or FDI, because the extended use of information technology may both improve the internal communication in a

transnational bank and, at the same time, reduce the transaction costs in relation to banking services, which, *ceteris paribus*, will improve trade relations.

To obtain a fuller picture of the relationship between information and telecommunications technologies and the organizational structures of banks, one has to go one step further than counterposing trade and FDI. There are many forms of FDI, and trade and FDI do not necessarily exclude one another. They often complement each other, as is obvious in the case of representative offices that act as intermediaries between their local customers and the parent bank in another country.

That mixture of foreign trade and intranational transactions through foreign affiliates is affected by the development of information technologies which, of course, changes over time as new possibilities arise as a result of technological developments. Therefore, the internal division of labour will change in relation to the different functions in the production of banking services. The clearest effect of information and telecommunications technologies is in relation to the modes of delivery of different services and in relation to the internal division of labour. More visible effects on the "choice" between trade and FDI may follow later.

One of the most important potential impacts of tradability concerns the future role of foreign affiliates of transnational banks. Earlier, the effects of telecommunications and data services on the modes of delivery -- foreign direct investment and arm's length trade -- were examined. Here, the analysis will be taken one step further into the banking industry, to describe the outcome of the telematization process on the internal organization of banking operations and the division of labour between different levels in the banking industry, e.g., head offices and affiliates.

Three aspects of the reorganization will be analyzed: the relationship between head offices and foreign affiliates (centralization and/or decentralization); the prospects for outsourcing the production of certain banking services; and the specialization taking place in the banking industry. These questions will not only be taken up in relation to the international organization of banks, but also in relation to the organization at national levels, as developments currently taking place inside the borders of a nation may become a feasible possibility in future in international relations. Production sites that today are being located in suburbs or rural regions of a particular country for reasons of lower prices of land and (marginally) lower prices of labour may tomorrow be located in foreign countries. The technical problems are to a great extent similar, whether locating remotely within home countries or locating in foreign countries. The main difference lies in the political and judicial aspects of trade and FDI in banking services.

Figure V.3 represents a simplified description of the organization of an international bank. Even though the figure is highly simplified, it shows that several possibilities for reorganization exist. Operations may be executed with more or less emphasis on the headquarters or the affiliates. They may be executed with emphasis on the home country or host countries. Computer centres, whether central or local, may take over a greater share of branch office functions, or they may be externalized completely to independent firms.

In a large number of cases, banks have established divisions to take care of back-office functions. These divisions have sometimes been located outside city centres or have even been moved -- but only very rarely -- to foreign countries. This kind of division of labour builds upon the increasing divisibility of banking products and the competitive advantage of lower factor costs.

Figure V.3. Typical organization of an international bank

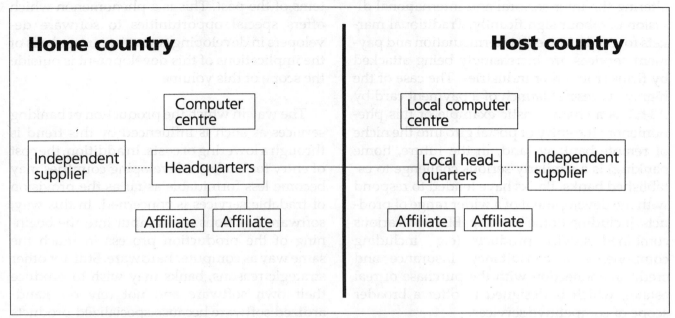

But the opposite development -- a development towards greater centralization of the production of services -- takes place as well. This centralization process takes shape both in the form of the withdrawal of affiliates from foreign markets and in the form of local head offices being closed down and communications being established directly between the home country head office and affiliates in foreign countries.

C. Outsourcing

1. Intermediate products

The question of the international organization of banks mainly concerns transnational banks and the internal division of labour between different parts of the same corporation. But when discussing the possibilities for outsourcing and splitting up and relocating certain intermediate products, the question is also extended to external or independent firms. External firms may become producers of inputs into the production process of banking services by a given bank.

Until recently, outsourcing in banking from external firms located abroad has only taken place on a very limited scale. Although signs of new patterns of internal and external divisions of labour have appeared in other service industries, such as the airline industry and insurance, banking-service firms have so far been relatively slow to use new opportunities. Especially if compared with the production of material goods, where foreign outsourcing of intermediate products has taken place for decades, services still seem to have a long way to go. The question remains whether it will ever become possible to split up the production process in services in a manner fully comparable to material goods.

On the other hand, the changes that are taking place within the banking industry and in its relationship to other services such as insurance, retail trade and telecommunications may be altering the inter-sectoral and international division of labour significantly. Traditional markets for banks in credit intermediation and payment services are increasingly being attacked by firms from other industries. The case of the highly successful launch of a payment card by AT&T is a characteristic example of this phenomenon; the entry of postal giro into the niche of remote banking (and, in the future, home banking) is a similarly serious challenge to established banks. Banks have tended to respond with the development of a wider range of products, including home banking, EDI and various combined service products (e.g., including components of consultancy, insurance and credit in connection with the purchase of real estate), which is designed to offer a broader scope of competitive services.

The telematization of information-intensive service industries surely enhances the purely technical possibilities for new divisions of labour and outsourcing. Nevertheless, other factors related to economic structure and political/judicial systems tend to impede the realization of such processes. Furthermore, banks may not pursue a development of outsourcing for strategic reasons. Banking is a business that heavily relies on trust and confidentiality, and banks may not allow the processing of intermediate services outside the banking entity itself.

This is not the case with the software necessary for running banking operations. To a growing extent, such software is produced outside the banks themselves by external software firms. At the same time, such software producers tend to offer standardized components or systems that may be customized to the specific needs of banks, but which are far less expensive to develop than the large banking systems of the past. This is a phenomenon which offers special opportunities to software developers in developing countries; an analysis of the implications of this development is outside the scope of this volume.

The way in which the production of banking services as such is influenced by this trend is through a lowering of costs. In addition, the cost of entry for banks in developing countries may become less formidable as far as the provision of tradable services is concerned. In this way, software functions as an input into the beginning of the production process in much the same way as computer hardware. Still, for other strategic reasons, banks may wish to produce their own software and not rely on standardized software because specialized products may become parameters of competitiveness.

2. Facilities management

The most prevalent form, presently, of outsourcing in the banking industry is related to so-called facilities management and third-party maintenance of data-processing operations. Another area of interest at the present stage of development is the transmission/networking part of banking services. In both cases, the external service provider may be either a data or telecommunications division of another bank, or a provider from a different business or industry.

Electronic Data Systems (EDS) is a pioneering example of a firm selling facilities management to financial institutions. EDS manages computer developments across the world and takes over all aspects of computer operations if required. The firm offers both third-party maintenance where it assumes control of existing staff and "full blown" facilities management where it draws in their own staff. [7]

Facilities management may also be marketed by data divisions of large banks. Data divisions have been operating inside banks for years resulting in what may be termed "in-house outsourcing". At a certain point, data divisions feel strong enough to enter the external market place. A recent example is County NatWest, which reached an agreement with the United States software company TCAM to market the bank's "integrated settlement system". Another example is Barclays Computer Operations, which has been turned into an independent business selling services to outside customers, but is also forced to compete with other suppliers for contracts with its own parent, Barclays Bank. [8]

Some international banks have opted for facilities management as an alternative to moving their data processing back home as in the case of J.P. Morgan discussed earlier. Three major Canadian banks -- Royal Bank of Canada, Bank of Montreal and Canadian Imperial Bank of Commerce -- have chosen this option for cutting costs instead of closing down their United Kingdom data-processing centres. They have contracted out the running of their computer centres to outside third parties.[9]

The advantages of outsourcing to facilities-management firms are primarily, first, a reduction of fixed costs and secondly, freedom to concentrate on the core business. The possibilities of knowing the costs of data-processing operations in advance depends, of course, on the terms of the contract between the bank and the facilities manager; but possibilities for fixed costs are improved. As regards the second aspect, banks may want to leave what is sometimes termed as the "donkey work" of data processing to data-processing specialists and concentrate on banking. But this, at the same time, touches upon some of the central problems concerning outsourcing of data processing.

These problems are related to the position of information as a strategic resource. If banks leave the management of this strategic resource to external firms, they risk loosing control of the foundation of their banking operations. And this is not the only area of problems connected to outsourcing. Loss of expertise and loss of security are additional potential problematic aspects.

3. Networking

Another important area of outsourcing is, as mentioned earlier, the networking aspect of banking. Often, big transnational banks run their own international telecommunications networks, but, to a growing extent, networking services are and will become externalized. External firms selling networking services may come from both the banking industries itself and from international value-added network services (IVANS) operators.

A recent example of a bank putting up a banking IVANS is Deutsche Bank's Deutsche Gesellschaft für Netzwerkdienste that began operating in autumn 1992. Deutsche Bank has pooled its banking, software and networking expertise into a separate company, positioned to become one of Europe's most powerful providers of financial network services.[10] An example of an IVANS operator selling banking network services is GEISCO. GEISCO does not only provide data-processing support for foreign banking affiliates; the company also provides for example, cash-management services for a number of banks.

D. Specialization

Outsourcing is a specific case of specialization in which external firms provide replacements for services that hitherto had been produced inside the company in question. But specialization takes many other forms; for instance, financial institutions may specialize in certain segments of the market for financial services without trying to provide a broader range of services. This is, for example, the case with State Street Boston which has spun off all traditional banking services. State Street Boston has limited itself to the marketing of custodial services and today the company has approximately 10 per cent of world securities under custody (in value terms).[11]

Specialization is seen by some observers as a necessary consequence of the growing use of the new information and telecommunications technologies. By making computer power mobile, telecommunications technologies have lead to an extension of the market for financial services and therefore enabled data-processing firms or banks to specialize in certain data-processing-intensive banking services.[12] This argument is based on the theory of the relationship between the extent of the market and the division of labour. But although many examples may be cited to illustrate such a development, just as many examples of the opposite development may be found. Specialization is taking place, but, at the same time, a development of so-called financial supermarkets can be observed. Apparently, both developments are occuring simultaneously.[13]

E. Implications of tradability for trade and foreign direct investment in banking

The developments outlined in the previous chapters should, *ceteris paribus*, lead to an increase in trade in financial services by banks in relation to financial business conducted through foreign affiliates, since a major reason for establishing affiliates (instead of trade relations), according to the theory of transaction costs, is to reduce transaction costs. Information technology offers new possibilities for reducing transaction costs.

But information and telecommunications technologies may also contribute to improved communication between head offices and affiliates and may, therefore, result in better performance by the affiliate structure. A clear and strong correlation has been noted between the use of communication technologies in different banks and their physical presence in international markets.[14] Banks with an extensive use of communication technology have a higher physical presence in international markets, which shows that communication technology is an essential factor in the management of international networks of affiliates. As in most other correlation analyses, it is not possible to establish any causal relationship between these two factors -- in this case, information technology and presence in international markets.

The question as to whether information and telecommunications technologies will favour trade or FDI in the internationalization of services can not be solved on a purely theoretical level. Both developments are theoretically possible and may take place simultaneously. Empirical evidence is, unfortunately, rather weak in this area and, therefore, not conclusive.

Before discussing actual developments by examining available evidence, it is, however, necessary briefly to discuss two additional conceptual problems.[15]

The first problem has to do with the fact that the products traded are financial means by themselves. The value of the exportation of a loan, for instance, cannot be equated with the value of the sum transferred. It must be equated with the value of the transfer of the sum. The second problem is closely related to this issue. Although foreign earnings of the factors of production, labour and capital, are normally not included in the trade concept, it must be correct, in banking services, to include interest rates on loans to non-residents as banks traditionally have included the "pricing" of their loan service in the interest rate. The measurement of foreign trade in banking services, therefore, must include fees and commissions and interest rates on loans, while income from direct investment abroad must be excluded, as in all other business areas.[16]

F. Empirical evidence

1. Some examples at the company level

In the past few years, a certain retreat in the physical presence of banks in foreign markets has occured. An example of this phenomenon is the closure of the Chase Manhattan affiliate in Copenhagen in 1992 and the transfer of its business to London, cited earlier (see box I.3.) This does not mean that Chase Manhattan will not continue to service its customers in Copenhagen. Its Danish business will in the future be conducted directly from London via telecommunications links. A similar example is that of the Citibank affiliate in Copenhagen. During

the past few years, the total manpower employed in this affiliate office has been reduced, but at the same time the office has increased the number of employees with direct contact to customers. It is thus the administrative functions that have been rearranged. Another example is the retreat of some back office functions of J.P. Morgan from London to Delaware, United States. The specific reason for this withdrawal is that the IBM mainframe computer of J.P. Morgan in London was due to be replaced at a time when there was spare capacity on the main-frame computers in Delaware. These examples point to the fact that banking operations can be executed from abroad and that telecommunication and data services have enhanced the tradability of banking services.

Anecdotal evidence in the form of these and other cases suggests that North American banks retreated in the 1980s somewhat from foreign markets. But it is not very likely that technology was the decisive factor for this development. The major reason has to do with economic problems. Transnational banks have not been able to acquire a sufficient share of the markets in foreign countries. In this situation, technology offers a kind of solution or tool for a defensive strategy. It is possible to uphold a presence via telecommunication links and, in this way, service large corporate customers.

Economic developments in the Japanese banking industry suggest that a similar development may take place there in the 1990s. The rate of exchange of banking shares have recently dropped in Japan, which limits the possibilities for an expansionist strategy. And, furthermore, total outflows of Japanese FDI in all economic sectors have decreased.[17] As stated earlier, the internationalization of banking normally follows the internationalization of other industries quite closely. Therefore, Japanese banks may retreat somewhat in the coming years, although this is not the opinion of Japanese banking experts, according to the results from the questionnaire survey presented below.

2. Results of a questionnaire survey

This section is based on the results from a questionnaire survey addressed to a number of top banking managers: three from North America, eight from Europe and four from Japan. The questionnaire and a more comprehensive discussion of the results are included in annex 2.

(a) Number of affiliates

The panel of banking experts was asked whether the number of affiliates of banks has increased or decreased in the past 10 years. Although this question is related to events in the past, answers from respondents were quite diverse, largely reflecting the nationality of respondents. According to the Japanese experts, the number of affiliates, both in the home countries of the banks and abroad, has increased, while the North American experts indicated a decrease in the number of affiliates.

The experts were also consulted on the possible development in the number of affiliates in the next 5-10 years. Answers to that question were even more uncertain than those to the previous question. There was no agreement among respondents as to whether the number of affiliates will increase or decrease in home countries and abroad. There was a clear majority, though, in favour of the opinion that the number of affiliates in developing countries will increase. The answers to a great extent also reflected the nationality of respondents. The Japanese banking experts were not only in a

position to look back on an expanding network of Japanese banks; they were also confident that this development will continue in the future. The North American and European experts, on the other hand, were more cautious. Generally, expectations were that banks would concentrate on their home markets, with less emphasis on foreign markets.

(b) Effects of the new technologies

The majority of the panel of banking experts provided a negative response to the question as to whether new information and telecommunication technologies will affect the choice between trade and FDI. This result reflects their opinion that factors other than technology have a greater impact on the tradability of services. In retail banking, cultural aspects, such as trust, were considered more important and, in corporate banking, economic aspects ranked highest. It should be noted, however, that, according to the American experts, information and telecommunication technologies *will* affect the choice between trade and FDI, while the Japanese experts were of the opposite opinion. An explanation for this is probably that Japanese banks, until recently, were very expansive and that technology played only a secondary role in this process. The American banks, on the other hand, have faced a difficult economic situation for some time and have had to minimize their physical presence on foreign markets. Information and telecommunications technologies, in this situation, offer an opportunity for decreasing physical pressure while still servicing the market: a presence in foreign markets -- formerly maintained by means of branches or other types of affiliates -- can be upheld through trade relations improved by new information technologies.

A conclusion could not, therefore, be drawn that the responses to the survey imply that information and telecommunications technologies do not play a role in the international expansion of banks. But, from the answers of the North American banking experts on the one hand and the Japanese experts on the other, it seems that the utilization of these technologies is all a matter, at least at this stage, of the economic pressures banks experience.

(c) Trends in organization

All respondents indicated that efforts to provide better services to international customer were the most important reasons for establishing affiliates abroad in the area of corporate banking; this is very much in line with prevailing explanations in the literature on the internationalization of banking.[18] Another explanation indicated by a majority of respondents, is concerned "strategic positioning", covering issues such as physical presence for the purpose of assessing profitable possibilities, and the establishment of a critical mass as an international bank. Other reasons may be added, such as the execution of activities that are not allowed in the home country, or avoiding taxes by locating in a tax haven. A growing part of bank loans taken by Danish citizens or institutions, for instance, are made by affiliates of Danish banks in foreign countries.

The banking experts were also consulted about reasons for the establishment of retail affiliates; only few answers were forthcoming here. This reflects the fact that the internationalization of banking is predominantly related to corporate customers. Banks that have tried to capture retail customers in foreign markets in developed economies have generally had no success. Retail customers have, so far, proved very loyal to their national banks.

With respect to the reasons for closing affiliates, the most striking conclusion from the answers of the panel of experts is that only a minority of the respondents indicated the possibility of servicing foreign customers by means of telecommunications. This is, once again, a clear statement of the lack of importance that many banking experts attach to information and communication technologies in relation to the international organization of banking operations.

Summarizing their opinion concerning the predominant development in relation to trade and FDI in international banking, a clear majority of the banking experts expressed the view that FDI will prevail. This is the case with both retail and corporate banking, though one third of the respondents believed that cross-border trade will prevail in corporate banking.

Attention should be drawn, however, to the fact that the answer to the question whether trade or FDI will prevail, depended to a large extent on the kinds of banking services involved. Some of the services that *can* be provided cross-border, *will* be provided cross-border. For other services that cannot be provided cross-border, FDI will prevail where profitable, while intermediate solutions may be applied where FDI is not profitable.

When asked whether, in the future, affiliates will increasingly report directly to the head office, eliminating intermediate regional or country headquarters as a result of telecommunications, the answer of the great majority of respondents was that that, indeed, would be the case. To the question whether the relationship between head offices and affiliates will tend towards centralization or decentralization in the production of services as a consequence of new information and telecommunications technologies, two thirds of the experts answered that the relationship will tend towards centralization in corporate banking, while decentralization was believed to be the future for retail banking.

With regard to the production process, a majority of the respondents indicated that, with the new information and telecommunications technologies and the greater possibilities for splitting up the production process of financial services, they saw a potential for independent firms and affiliates of transnational corporations to take part in the production process of financial services.

3. Statistical evidence

(a) Number of affiliates

One of the most important potential impacts of tradability concerns the future role and number of affiliates of transnational banks. Available data on transnational banks indicate a certain retreat from foreign markets in the case of some European and North American banks and an expansion, though not vast, of Japanese banks in other developed countries (tables V.2 - V.4). In this sense, therefore, the data corroborate the answers from the banking experts consulted in the questionnaire survey.

A closer examination of tables V.2 - V.4 shows that the retreat of European banks from foreign markets is almost entirely due to the retrenchment of Barclays while in North America it is mostly because BankAmerica, the Royal Bank of Canada and J.P. Morgan reduced their foreign presence in the form of foreign affiliates.

(b) Trade in banking services

Sales by United States banking affiliates abroad dropped from $87 billion in 1982 to $76 billion in 1989,[19] while financial services provided to non-residents from United States resident banks (exports) increased from $33 billion in 1987 to $54 billion in 1989.[20] For the year 1989, exports of banking services from the United States thus contributed 42 per cent of total foreign banking revenues. In table V.5, this figure is compared with similar figures for other information-intensive services.

Table V.5 shows that there are considerable differences in exports/sales ratios among different selected services. These differences reflect the diverse nature of services and the variety of environments (technological, economic and political) in which they operate. United States external sales and exports of education, for instance, are almost entirely dominated by exports because education of non-residents mostly takes place in the United States through travel by consumers and, therefore, by definition is classified under exports. Tourism services, which are not included in table V.5, are made up entirely of exports according to the same definition. Advertising, on the other hand, relies very much on sales from affiliates abroad, a strong reason being that most advertisements must be adapted to local market traditions if they are to be effective.

Banking has a relatively high percentage of exports (42 per cent) compared with, for instance, insurance (14 per cent). One of the major reasons for this difference is the longstanding role of banking in trade financing. Another reason is that insurance companies often have been legally obliged by host countries to establish local offices if they wanted to conduct business.

The share of service exports from the United States in relation to total United States foreign service revenues does not show any increase in the late 1980s (table V.6). In insurance, advertising and computer and data processing, the share of exports in relation to total foreign revenues from the sale of those services has even shown a decreasing trend. The data sug- gest that the increased tradability of information-intensive services has not been translated into an increase in actual trade, as a share of total foreign sales of services. Explanations may vary from service to service, especially in relation to cultural and political aspects. But on the technical side, it seems that new communication technologies have as much enchanced the

Table V.2. Number of foreign affiliates for a selection of ten European banks, 1986, 1989 and 1991[a]

Bank/host region	1986			1989			1991		
	OECD	Others	Total	OECD	Others	Total	OECD	Others	Total
Crédit Lyonnais	52	63	115	87	55	142	59	43	102
Commerzbank	31	25	56	34	24	58	35	28	63
Crédit Suisse	23	24	47	26	23	49	42	27	69
Union Bank of Switzerland	35	20	55	25	19	44	41	22	63
Deutsche Bank	36	32	68	36	21	57	48	22	70
National Westminster Bank	20	9	29	29	15	44	29	14	43
Banque Nationale de Paris	65	62	127	76	56	132	70	58	128
Robobank	13	6	19	11	8	19	17	10	27
Lloyds Bank	9	4	13	8	4	12	3	1	4
Barclays	170	91	261	114	87	201	85	82	167
Total, above	454	336	790	446	312	758	429	307	736

Source: calculated from Financial Times Business Information, *Who Owns What in World Banking*, 1986, 1989 and 1991.
a/ The data include affiliated companies and major participations in banks and financial companies and foreign offices.

Table V.3. Number of foreign affiliates for a selection of seven North American banks, 1986, 1989 and 1991

Bank/host region	1986			1989			1991		
	OECD	Others	Total	OECD	Others	Total	OECD	Others	Total
Citicorp	74	165	239	75	165	240	77	161	238
BankAmerica Corporation	53	63	116	31	46	77	31	46	77
Royal Bank of Canada	55	76	131	61	38	99	45	36	81
J.P. Morgan	36	48	84	na	na	na	31	22	53
Chase Manhattan	40	66	106	57	63	120	50	57	107
Bank of Nova Scotia	30	38	68	39	39	78	31	39	70
Manufacturers Hanover	36	30	66	..	..	..	33	27	60
Total, above	324	486	810	..	..	..	298	399	686

Source: calculated from Financial Times Business Information, *Who Owns What in World Banking*, 1986, 1989 and 1991.

Table V.4. Number of foreign affiliates for a selection of seven Japanese banks, 1986, 1989 and 1991

Bank/host region	1986			1989			1991		
	OECD	Others	Total	OECD	Others	Total	OECD	Others	Total
Sumitomo Bank	35	28	63	36	27	63	39	27	66
Dai-Ichi Bank									
Kangyo Bank	28	27	55	32	31	63	31	30	61
Mitsubishi Bank	22	26	48	24	24	48	44	32	76
Tokai Bank	19	19	38	24	23	47	28	24	52
Long-term Credit Bank of Japan	20	27	47	na	na	na	23	27	50
Bank of Tokyo	42	45	87	43	41	84	49	62	111
Daiwa Bank	14	15	29	15	16	31	31	19	50
Total, above	180	187	367	..	..	..	245	221	466

Source: Calculated from Financial Times Business Information, *Who Owns What in World Banking*, 1986, 1989 and 1991.

Table V.5. Foreign revenues from the sale of selected services and the share of exports, United States, 1989 [a/]
(Millions of dollars)

Industry	Foreign revenues	Exports as percentage of foreign revenues
Advertising	4 309	3
Computer and data-processing service	8 161	12
Financial services, excluding banking	37 927	13
Insurance	36 811	14
Accounting	443	28
Banking	130 853	42
Research and development and tests	694	54
Legal services	669	59
Education	4 857	94

Sources: Calculated on the basis of United States, Department of Commerce, *Survey of Current Business*, September 1992; United States, Department of Commerce, *U.S. Direct Investment Abroad, Final Results*, Benchmark Survey 1992 (Washington, D.C., United States, Government Printing Office, 1992); OECD, *Financial Market Trends*, No. 52, June 1992.

a/ The United States Office of Technology Assessment made a similar calculation in 1986. But the figures are not entirely comparable because OTA used estimated exports and sales figures. See, United States, Office of Technology Assessment, *Trade in Services, Exports and Foreign Revenues* (Washington, D.C., Government Printing Office, 1992), pp. 41-53.

Table V.6. Exports in relation to total foreign revenues, selected services, United States, 1986-1990[a/]
(Percentage)

Industry	1986	1987	1988	1989	1990
Insurance	22	20	19	22	22
Advertising	5	4	4	4	3
Computer and data processing	20	11	17	15	11

Source: calculated on the basis of data in United States, Department of Commerce, *Survey of Current Business*, September 1990 and September 1992.

a/ The figures in this table are not comparable with those in table V.5 because only majority-owned foreign affiliates are included here, while affiliates included in table V.5 are all foreign affiliates that are owned or controlled to the extent of 10 per cent or more of the voting securities for an incorporated business enterprise or the equivalent for an uncorporated business enterprise.

possibilities for managing an international network of affiliates as they have promoted trade in services.

(c) Foreign direct investment in banking services

Financial services including banking are one of the industries attracting the largest shares of outward as well as inward FDI in services of developed countries: the investment stock in financial services in developed host countries increased at an average annual rate of 21 per cent during 1980-1990(table V.7), compared to an annual rate of 13.5 per cent for the stock of foreign services as a whole.[21] In the developing countries, the picture is mixed. The rate of FDI growth in financial services increased slightly, but was less than that of services FDI taken as a whole.[22] Consequently, the share of financial services in total FDI in services declined during 1980-1990(table V.7). It is not possible to separate the trends in FDI in *banking* services from those of FDI in financial services in general. But

Table V.7. Foreign-direct-investment stock in financial services, including banking, 1980-1990
(Billions of dollars and percentage)

Year/region	Value	Share in total stock in services	Average annual rate of growth
A. **Outward stock**			
Developed countries [a/]			
1980	63.0	35.3	
1985	116.2	43.4	
1990	356.0	49.0	
1980-1990			18.9
B. **Inward stock**			
Developed countries [b/]			
1980	28.4	27.9	
1985	60.7	32.3	
1990	187.1	37.6	
1980-1990			20.8
Developing countries [c/]			
1980	3.4	32.6	
1985	4.6	25.0	
1990	6.8	22.5	
1980-1990			7.5

Source: United Nations, "Transnational corporations in services, including banking: Issues related to the liberalization of foreign direct investment in services", Report of the Secretary-General, E/C.10/1993/6. p. 11.

a/ Ten major home countries.
b/ Ten major host countries.
c/ Ten major host countries.

recent United States data suggest that growth of outward FDI in financial services from the United States was concentrated in areas other than banking (table V.8).

As discussed earlier, technological and political factors are determinants of trade in services. But for actual transactions to take place, the economic factors must be conducive to

Table V.8. Composition of United States outward foreign-direct-investment stock in financial services, by category, 1987-1991
(Billions of dollars)

Category	1987	1988	1989	1990	1991
Banking	18.0	19.1	19.1	19.8	18.8
Insurance	11.6	13.2	14.2	16.1	16.3
Finance, excluding banking	5.0	10.8	23.5	29.4	28.6
Holding companies	34.5	37.5	57.1	65.0	70.1
Total, above	69.1	80.6	113.9	130.3	133.8

Source: United States, Department of Commerce, *Survey of Current Business*, August 1989 and August 1992.

trade. However, the analysis in this volume of the development in banking shows that telematization could, at least partly reduce the incentive for an international division of labour in the production of services. While telematization in a purely technical sense increases the divisibility of services, the same process reduces the actual need for a division of labour. When the production process of a service consists of a series of manual routines, there may be room for outsourcing some of these routines. But

when the production of a service can be performed entirely by a computer, the economic rationale for subcontracting parts of the production process to low labour cost areas disappears and other factors, such as reliability, increase in importance.

This situation is illustrated in table V.9 which shows that employee compensation in United States banking affiliates in Latin America and Africa is much higher than that in affiliates in both manufacturing and other services. While employee compensation in banking in Africa is about half that of employee compensation in United States parent firm, in manufacuturing that figure is less than one fifth and in services less than one fourth. Compared with the overall average compensation of labour in Africa in banking, the figure for affiliates shows that labour in United States banking affiliates in Africa consists of relatively highly skilled personnel.

Employee compensation in United States banking affiliates is very high in both Canada and Europe, compared with employee compen-

Table V.9. Employee compensation in United States foreign affiliates by industry of affiliates and region, compared with employee compensation in United States parent firms, 1989
(Average compensation per employee, in thousand dollars)

Industry	United States	Canada	Europe	Latin America	Africa	Middle East	Asia and the Pacific
All	35.5	29.6	33.9	10.0	8.8	36.2	20.8
Petroleum	48.8	44.6	47.3	21.9	17.1	47.1	36.2
Manufacturing	38.9	35.1	33.4	9.8	7.5	23.5	21.5
Wholesale trade	32.2	32.4	41.1	16.5	14.9	33.5	34.1
Banking	36.4	63.3	56.6	22.3	19.2	47.1	24.6
Finance a/	42.3	35.8	44.9	16.9	..	..	32.1
Other services	24.4	19.8	29.4	9.4	5.6	24.8	26.5

Source: calculated from United States, Department of Commerce, *U.S. Direct Investment Abroad* (United States, Government Printing Office, 1990), pp. 13, 15, 105 and 301.

a/ Excluding banking.

sation in United States parents. This is an indication of the type of banking activities that United States banks are mostly involved in abroad. United States banking affiliates in Canada and Europe are almost entirely engaged in corporate banking which requires highly skilled personnel. This also applies to United States banking affiliates in other areas of the world, which suggests that the primary reason for setting up banking affiliates abroad is not an internal corporate division of labour but an effort to retain and gain corporate customers throughout the world.

G. Conclusion

The main conclusion of this chapter is that information and telecommunication technologies contribute, on the one hand, to the tradability of especially information-intensive banking services, but, on the other hand, reduce the incentives for dividing up production processes in services. If, therefore, the objective is to identify possibilities for developing countries to take part in the international production of services, the lesson from banking is that the services most suitable for a division of labour are the services whose production processes consist of manual routines and that are also divisible.

When looking for such services, one needs to conduct detailed studies of the different prod-

ucts and production processes in the various service industries as it is impossible to determine possibilities for a division of labour at a generalized industry or sectoral level. Not only does the variety of products included in each service category require such an approach but also the ever changing composition of products and production processes in most services. The services included in data processing, for instance, have most certainly changed during the past decade.

A kind of cyclical development appears to take place in the outsourcing and insourcing of intermediate production processes depending on technical innovations in both products and production processes in the various business sectors. If countries pursue policies for increasing their involvement in the international division of labour, it is important to be aware of these technical development stages in order to take initiatives at the right moment. The long-term purpose of such a policy of participating in the international division of labour cannot, of course, be to trace constantly new possibilities for setting up companies involved in intermediate production processes. The perspective must be to establish enterprises involved in these intermediate production processes on a more permanent basis and thereby broaden the range of productive activities.

Notes

1   The theories that are relevant are mainly theories concerning comparative and competitive advantage and theories concerning institutional economics; see, e.g., Ronald Coase, "The nature of the firm", *Economica*, 4, no. 16, (1937), pp. 386-405, and Oliver Williamson, *Markets and Hierarchies* (Cambridge, Massachusetts, 1975).

2   For a conceptual and empirical discussion of the different modes of supply of services, see UNCTAD, Programme on Transnational Corporations and The World Bank, *Liberalizing International Transactions in Services* (1993, forthcoming), chapter I.

3   Trade may, furthermore, be subdivided into two modes of delivery: the mode of delivery where services cross borders; and the mode of delivery where foreign consumers cross borders. Tourism and education are by definition examples of this second kind of trade in the services area. The movement of consumers may be viewed as a fourth mode of delivery of services, especially for considering policies affecting international transactions in services.

4   Unless otherwise stated, the definitions are taken from R.M. Pecchioli, *The Internationalization of Banking* (Paris, OECD, 1983), p. 57-66.

5   Definition according to United States, Office of Technology Assessment, *Trade in Services* (Washington, D.C., Government Printing Office, 1986), p. 55.

6   This definition is taken from Howard Palmer, *Correspondent Banking* (London, Euromoney Publications, 1990), p. 1.

7   *The Banker*, April 1992, p. 16.

8   Ibid.

9   *The Banker*, March 1992.

10 *CommunicationsWeek*, No. 92, 21 September 1992, p. 1.

11 Bernhard Wieland,"Telecommunications and the disintegration of the banking industry", paper prepared for the 9th ITS Conference, Sophia Antipolis, June 1992, p. 6.

12 Ibid.

13 The question of specialization and/or financial supermarkets is taken up again in chapter VI, section 1.

14 Brigitte Preissl, *Telekommunikation und das Auslandsgeschäft von Banken und Versicherungen*, Diskussionsbeiträge zur Telekommunikationsforschung, Nr. 36, WIK, Bad Honnef, 1988.

15 A broader range of conceptual problems are described in different articles in an anthology by Geoffrey Jones, ed., *Multinational and International Banking* (Aldershot, Edward Elgar Publishing Limited, 1992).

16 In *Financial Market Trends* no. 52, OECD has an even broader definition:
    - income on direct investment, received or paid;

- income on other investment (interest or divident received or paid) see OECD, *Financial Market Trends*, No. 52 (Paris, OECD, June 1992), p. 39.

17 OECD, *Financial Market Trends*, No. 52 (Paris, OECD, 1992), p. 14.

18 See, for instance, Silvia Sagari, "Foreign direct investment in banking", in Karl P. Sauvant and Padma Mallampally, eds., *Transnational Corporations in Services*, United Nations Library on Transnational Corporations, volume no. 12(London and New York, Routledge, published for and on behalf of the United Nations, 1993), pp. 115-140.

19 United States, Department of Commerce, *U.S. Direct Investment Abroad* (Washington, D.C., Government Printing Office 1982 and 1992).

20 OECD, *Financial Market Trends*, No. 52 (June 1992), op. cit., p. 46.

21 United Nations, "*Transnational corporations in services, including banking: Issues related to the liberalisation of foreign direct investment in services*", Report of the Secretary-General, E/C.10/1993/6, p. 8

22 Ibid.

Chapter VI

IMPLICATIONS OF TRADABILITY IN BANKING SERVICES

A. Implications for banks

Information and telecommunications technologies allow markets for banking services to expand and make greater specialization in the provision of banking services possible. Although, as discussed in the previous chapters, this is not yet happening on a large scale internationally, it *is* taking place in national markets and internationally in some areas such as corporate banking. Banks are increasingly becoming technologically sophisticated international operators; the resulting changes in the organizational structure, efficiency and competitiveness of banking have important implications for the industry and for the economies of developed and developing countries.

In chapter V, the effects of an increased tradability of banking services on the relationship between FDI and trade and on the organization of banking services were analyzed. This chapter focuses on issues related to raising efficiency and effectiveness in the production of banking services, the improvement of existing products and the development of new services, and on the implications of these changes, combined with increasing tradability of banking services, for developed and developing countries.

1. Efficiency and competitiveness

The convergence between telecommunications and information technologies is the basis for increasing the technical tradability (transportability) of many services, especially the information intensive services. There is no doubt that this technological convergence will have a profound impact on the banking industry in terms of its efficiency and competitiveness.

The centralization process described in the previous chapter obviously takes place for cost-reducing reasons. Telematization is the technical prerequisite for this reorganization to take place; when the price of telecommunications has fallen sufficiently, the transaction costs of running back-office data processing in more remotely located areas reach a competitive level.

A historical review shows that information technology was first introduced in the form of mainframe computers which were utilized to automate back-office functions, primarily in retail banking, because of the vast amount of data to be processed in this area. Data processing was used to mechanize the routines performed by back-office clerks. Today, however, information technology has moved into the front offices in the form of network terminals at the counters. Actually, it has moved beyond the counter and even closer to the customers in the form of automated teller machines (ATMs) and home-banking services via the telephone network.

This development of technological innovation from the back-offices to the front-office, from innovation in the production processes to the development of new products, has been termed the reverse product cycle,[1] in contrast to what is seen as the normal cycle observed in material production (i.e., innovation starting with the development of a new product, to be followed by innovation in production processes). The result of this sequence of diffusion of information and telecommunications technologies in banking has been that the development of new banking products has tended to come after the back-office services have been automated.

The process of telematization has made it possible for banks to reach a higher level of efficiency and productivity and to rationalize their production processes. When the informatization only affected back-office functions, rationalization did not lead to redundancies in the banking industry because banking was an expanding industry. But the effects today are so strong that redundancies are widespread in the developed countries. Local branches in many countries are being closed down because they do no longer play the same role in the retail market as in the past. In Denmark, for example, retail customers are offered lower-cost loans and higher interest rates on saving accounts in

so called direct banking where the customers are only in contact with their banks by means of remote communications, primarily telecommunications.

2. Improvement and development of banking products

When looking at improvements of existing products and the development of new services, it is obvious that these products and services are based upon the telematization of existing services and new forms of combinations of information. Automated teller machines may be conceived as a new form of getting an old product, cash. It may also be conceived as a totally new service product: the possibility of cash dispensing around the clock. Another retail product, EFTPoS, has reached a level in some countries where a vast amount of cash transactions becomes redundant. In Denmark, for example, banking customers seldom visit their banks any more for traditional payment services. Payroll systems are automated, transactions are executed by means of EFTPoS services and account information is retrieved over the telephone by means of computerized voice-response systems. Screen-based home-banking systems have still not taken hold in the retail market, but these systems are widespread in the corporate market.

New banking products are being developed when different types of information are combined in new ways. A case in point, and a very important future area for banks, is electronic data interchange (EDI). Instead of just effecting a payment, banks may offer the service of setting up electronic ordering and invoicing. When banks enter these areas, they add value to the products that they already offer. At the same time they enter areas in which they will meet competition from non-bank firms. Providers of value-added network services (VANS) also compete in these markets. The United States' telecommunications company, AT&T, provides an illustration with its entry into the credit-card market.

In the international financial markets, banks, for a number of years, have had to deal with non-bank entreprises. Reuters and Telerate, for example, play a major role in the provision of financial information and international financial trading. The background for the emergence of these players in the financial field is obviously the development of telecommunications and data services. Though international financial markets have a century-long history, these markets have only become truly international with the technological developments in the past decade.

For banks, the development of new products is necessary for improving business in the future. The spread between interest rates for savings and loans is likely to remain the prime source of income for many banks, but additional sources of income have to be developed. Telecommunications and data services are, therefore, not only more efficient means of transportation for traditional banking. They constitute new areas of business for banks in the future.

3. Specialization and/or financial supermarkets

The discussion concerning the effects of telecommunications and data services on the financial industry contains two apparently opposite views on the subject. The first view emphasizes the development of financial supermarkets, i.e., financial institutions offering a broad range of financial services, including, for example, banking, insurance and real-estate financing services.[2] The other view highlights the specializa-

tion tendencies in the financial industry, i.e., the tendency to specialize in a specific segment of the industry, e.g., custodial services.[3] The two views are based on different theoretical and empirical arguments. In the first case, it is argued that the telematization of services leads to a convergence between different financial services, and that this tendency can furthermore be empirically substantiated. In the second case, the argument is that the widespread use of telecommunications will lead to expanded markets for financial services which traditionally entail specialization. This tendency can also be shown empirically.

In actual fact, it is impossible at present to conclude whether specialization or financial supermarkets will prevail. The financial markets are in a state of flux, and developments in the market will not only, even primarily, be decided by technological innovations, but first and foremost by economic and political parameters. It is very likely that both specialization and the development of financial supermarkets will evolve simultaneously. Specialization may take place in international markets while financial supermarkets may be mostly nationally based.

B. Implications for developed and developing countries

1. Comparative advantage and the division of labour

Telecommunications and data services are instruments for achieving a competitive advantage in banking. The possibility for comparative advantage to play a role in the international division of labour in the banking industry has been discussed in the previous chapter, and the conclusion was that *at present* traditional comparative advantages of low cost labour do not seem to have any great impact. One might say that competitive advantages, reflecting productivity, are more important in the industry than comparative advantages reflecting resource endowments.

Telematization in banking is substituting for exactly the labour intensive functions that low-cost developing countries might be able to provide in the context of increasing technical tradability and expanding international markets. Compared, therefore with the production of material goods, banking affiliates are only seldom set up for the purpose of taking advantage of lower factor costs in the international division of labour. Affiliates are mostly put up for the purpose of servicing a market, not for utilizing the possibilities of an internal division of labour within a banking corporation. There are, however, examples of such a division of labour, e.g., in the case of American banks having routine functions performed in the Caribbean.[4]

A division of labour, though, may take place in quite another sense. Indigenous banks in developing countries will not generally develop their use of telematic services as fast as banks based in developed countries and their affiliates in developing countries. In Ghana, for instance, Barclays Bank and Standard Chartered Bank are ahead of their indigenous competitors with respect to introducing new technology. While computers in other banks are solely used for back-office functions, the two United Kingdom based banks have started building up communication systems, using leased lines for data communications.[5]

Although there may be some positive effects in the form of technology transfer from transnational banks to indigenous banks, such a devel-

opment might also result in a segmentation of the market for banking services in the host developing country. The transnational bank affiliate is likely to take over all customers with international financial relations and the majority of customers with more advanced banking needs, while the indigenous banks will be left with customers requiring less advanced services and rural customers. These customers often are of no interest to transnational banks; indigenous banks with more profound knowledge about the local market may, moreover be the best at servicing these customers. However, the host country might find it unsatisfactory to have to leave the bigger customers to the affiliates of transnational banks. In that case, special efforts and technical assistance programmes would be required to strengthen the capabilities of indigenous banks (see chapter VIII).

Summing up, the implications of increased tradability of banking services for banks in both developed and developing countries are indeed already extensive and will surely become even more widespread in the future. But the implications do not at present seem to approach what has happened in the case of material goods. Banks are not to any great extent taking advantage -- at least, as yet -- of locating parts of their production processes in low-factor-cost countries. Among the developed countries, however, banks may increase their internal division of labour. So far, however, this has largely meant taking advantage of the technological possibilities for centralizing certain functions in the production chain of banking.

2. Implications for developing countries

In most developing economies, banks have an important position as mediators between national economic development policies and actual economic development. The evaluation by banks of the creditworthiness of industrial and other projects is obviously essential. With the reduction of the role assigned to the State in the economies of a number of developing countries[6] and the loosening of protectionism, this important position has been further strengthened because banks are increasingly resuming their capital-allocating role.

Increased tradability of banking services, accompanied by the internal and external liberalization of banking, may imply an increasing role for foreign banks, either through the establishment of foreign affiliates or through arm's length trade. The efficiency and productivity gains resulting from the implementation of new information and telecommunications technologies may, therefore, be strengthened through the activities of foreign banks in developing countries.

Traditionally, banking has been one of the more protected areas in both developed and developing countries. Furthermore, as in other economic sectors, many developing countries have focused more on the potential disadvantages than on the potential benefits of hosting foreign affiliates, though this policy has changed considerably in the past decade. Those disadvantages and benefits must be made explicit to allow an informed policy in relation to the question of trade and FDI in banking. Table VI.1 lists some of the potential benefits and disadvantages of increased tradability through its effects on trade and FDI.

Table VI.1 Potential benefits and disadvantages of the increased tradability of banking services

Potential benefits	Wider scope of services offered by way of imports into the national economy
	More efficient services offered at competitive prices, providing reduced costs and externalities in the economy
	Accumulation of sufficient capital for investment
	Possibility for export of final or intermediate services
Potential disadvantages	Employment in local service firms foregone
	Dependence on foreign service providers
	Local firms less freestanding
	Development of two distinct banking sectors

(a) Benefits

On the benefits side of participating in a liberalized international system of banking with scope for expansion of trade as well as FDI, four aspects deserve to be mentioned.

● The first aspect relates to the variety of services offered in developing countries. Whether banking services are offered by foreign banking affiliates or by means of telecommunications links by foreign banks, there is no doubt that this forms a basis for both a wider scope of services and for more efficient services to be offered, with favourable effects on the cost-structure and growth of the economies of developing countries.

● Secondly, to the extent that FDI is involved, the higher efficiency of transnational banks is likely to make the banking system of host countries more competitive and efficient, owing to a transfer of technology and managerial expertise.[7]

● A third aspect deals with the question of accumulating sufficient capital for investment. In many developing countries, savings are not large enough to provide the necessary capital for investment, and these countries therefore have to take loans from inter-State development banks, foreign national development organizations or foreign banks. If foreign banks are active in a country through FDI or trade, the possibilities for additional resources for investment will grow.[8] These means are not primarily provided by local deposits. It is not unusual for foreign banks that credits largely exceed deposits. To finance this spread, it is necessary to take loans, normally from the parent bank or other affiliates of the parent bank in other countries. As described in the previous section, most foreign banks are not especially interested in the retail market. They are mostly interested in their international customers and the larger local customers. Their main business lies in wholesale banking and trade financing. These activities may not only benefit other transnational business corporations, but also local exporters that may get easier access to export credits.

● A fourth aspect revolves around the possibilities for splitting up the production process of banking services and of locating intermediate production processes in developing countries. As shown in previous sections, this possibility is limited at present, the technological reason being that the informatiza-

tion of banking services, which could lead to increasing trade in banking services, also substitutes the labour-intensive processes that developing countries could aspire to attract. However, this does not mean that the electronic transfer of intermediate banking services is not increasing. But, at present, intermediate services are only rarely produced in developing countries and then transferred to developed countries. It is rather the other way round: intermediate services are being processed in developed countries and thereafter transferred to less developed regions. As discussed above, this is likely to result in more efficient banking services, with benefits for overall efficiency and costs of production. There may also be disadvantages, however, to participating in an international banking system principally as an importer rather than as a participant on both sides of the international exchange of banking services.

(b) Disadvantages

One negative aspect of the growing technical possibilities for delivering banking products over long distances is that it may lead to the closing of domestic banks in developing countries, whether these are affiliates of transnational banks or locally-owned entities. At present, however, this scenario does not seem to be developing to any significant extent. In most instances, affiliates on the spot are necessary. But what is more likely is that back-office functions will be drawn back to a greater extent to the home countries of transnational banks.

In this connection, it is essential for developing economies to build a national economic structure that is as robust as possible, comprising all vital elements of a coherent economy. Specialization has advantages and disadvantages, but the dangers of specialization may be more acute in developing countries because of their weaker economic structure. It is important therefore to secure the basis for indigenous banks, and ensure their survival in the face of the potential competition mentioned above as well as prudential regulation of the industry. In particular, since they have the best knowledge about the local market and, therefore, in this respect are the more competitive, the survival of the indigenous banking industry is an important consideration.

Furthermore, there is no evidence that the apparent comparative advantages of developing countries in relation to low cost labour and land will have any strong impact on the location of banking production sites. As mentioned, competitive advantages on the basis of technological innovations are of far greater importance in the banking industry than traditional comparative advantages.

Another potentially negative aspect relates to the above-mentioned question of outsourcing intermediate products. The positive aspects have been noted, but there are negative sides to it also. Insofar as intermediate production processes are actually located in lesser developed regions, one must be aware of the risks of distorted development. Ireland and some of the Caribbean islands are example of countries where intermediate service production processes are located. The problem is that most of the jobs in these enterprises are low-skilled data-entry assignments, and often the production processes are not connected with other areas of economic activity in the country. This partly has to do with the character of the production processes and partly with the ownership relation, since these production sites are only rarely owned by local citizens.

A final problematic aspect is that the introduction of information and especially telecommunications technologies in banks will require an extensive technological infrastructure throughout the country in question. In most developing countries, lack of a telecommunications infrastructure imposes a barrier for the successful transfer of systems known from the developed countries. This holds particularly true for retail payment systems such as electronic payment cards and EFTPoS systems. Therefore, the usage of the new technologies is likely to be concentrated in corporate banking. This may induce the development of two distinct banking sectors: modern corporate banking sector dominated by international banks and a less technologically advanced retail banking sector dominated by domestic banks serving non-corporate customers and small and medium scale enterprises mainly in the rural areas.

(c) Off-shore banking centres

A specific case of the implications of tradability of banking services for developing countries is the creation of off-shore financial centres. This case is briefly discussed here as the establishment of such centres is conditioned by tradability and telecommunications. Off-shore centres are primarily located according to tax-rules, not because of any connection to the given country's economy.

The creation of off-shore financial centres in developing countries is clearly connected to the appearance of the Eurodollar market and the growth of an international financial market after the collapse of the Bretton Woods system of fixed exchange rates. Examples of off-shore centres are some of the Caribbean islands, Malaysia, Singapore and Bahrain. Off-shore banking activities involve transactions in foreign currencies among non-resident individuals or legal entities of whom one or more is a foreign bank or a domestic bank with a special authorization to operate off-shore.[9]

There are both negative and positive consequences related to the establishment of off-shore centres. Disadvantages derive from a situation where a dynamic off-shore banking system might divert resources and hinder the overall development of the country's banking system. These must be weighed against the advantages derived from off-shore centres, including the following:[10]

- Integration with the national capital market, encouraging mobilization and allocation of resources on a regional basis.

- Provision of a transitional substitute for a capital market until a local capital market is developed.

- Positive effects on local employment.

- Additional tax revenues to host countries in form of personal income tax on local employees.

- Foreign investment funds as well as flows of valuable financial, commercial and industrial intelligence from all over the world.

- Location of non-bank TNCs.

A sustainable outcome of this list of positive effects, though, very much depends on the extent of the actual process of integration of the activities in the off-shore centres in the national economies.

(d) Liberalization, tradability and developing countries

In the Uruguay Round negotiations on services, the point of departure for many developing countries was to question the benefits of liberalization for development. But this point of view no longer the dominates. In both developed and several developing countries, a process of liberalization has taken place which also affects banking services. This liberalization is likely to open opportunities for the implications of technological tradability to unfold. Until now, only a fraction of the future possibilities in this regard has materialized; it would appear, therefore, that there is significant scope for an expansion of, and changes in, the composition of international transactions in banking services. From the discussion of positive and negative effects above, it is clear that benefits and disadvantages cannot entirely be separated. The final outcome, therefore, depends considerably on the specific circumstances and the ability of developing-country Governments to develop the advantageous aspects of the changes in trade and FDI.

3. Implications for developed countries

The implications of increasing tradability of banking services for developed countries are somewhat different from those for developing countries, for the obvious reason that it is in the developed countries that the technical, economic and legal aspects of tradability are evolving at the fastest pace. It is in these countries that a telematized infrastructure for banking products is being built; it is also there that the economic (e.g., internationalization) and political (e.g., liberalization) aspects of tradability are advancing. Developments inside the European Common Market and the North American

Free Trade Agreement are examples to that effect.

As previously stated, the risks for developed countries associated with a parcelling out to developing countries of intermediate banking products are small, mainly for the reason that such a development is marginal. Furthermore, there is no prospect at present that foreign banks will have any significant share of the retail banking market in developed countries. This partly goes for the corporate market, too. But apart from the banking crisis in several developed countries, other dramatic changes are taking place in the banking industry -- both technologically and politically -- affecting both national and international banking in developed countries.

Technologically, a telematized infrastructure is being built, enhancing the transportability of banking services and contributing to a restructuring of the financial sector. At the national level, telematized financial services require less and less face-to-face contact between customers and financial institutions. At the international level, the possibilities for trading financial products around the clock have vastly increased. Politically, the liberalization of the financial industry at national and international levels is leading to major changes involving both a blurring of the boundaries between different segments of the financial sector and the development of an international market for financial services.

In this section, two questions will be examined: first, the creation of a new telematized system for transactions of financial services at primarily the national level; and, secondly, the process of liberalization and its consequences for the restructuring of national banking sectors and the development of an international market place for financial transactions.

(a) A telematized infrastructure

Financial systems in developed countries are moving towards a situation where physical money to a greater extent than ever before disappears and is substituted by electronic information. This is the case both in retail and in corporate banking. The case of banking in Denmark is illustrative because it has been possible there to develop electronic financial systems of a generalized nature. The market for securities is entirely electronic. So is the stock exchange. There is an integrated system for debit cards, covering all banks, including ATM-services and EFTPoS. And a small coin prepayment card with a broad range of applications -- a smart card -- is being tested.[11] All this means that fewer and fewer retail banking customers visit their banks, providing an important basis for rationalizations in the banking industry.

These rationalizations have had an impact on the employment in banks. As more and more services become telematized, the need for employees at the counter decreases, which is surely a much more important background for redundancies in the banking sector than the splitting up and locating of intermediate production processes in foreign countries.

Generalized systems are not under all circumstances the optimal solution for large banks. Even in Denmark where a generalized payment card system has been in place for a number of years, the two biggest banks, Den Danske Bank and Unibank -- created through mergers in 1990 -- aim at building up their own systems. The reason for this is that technology has become a parameter of competitiveness in relation to banking customers. Therefore, there will be a continuous struggle between these two tendencies in the coming years: one towards generalized systems, the other towards specialized systems.

Another tendency has to do with the convergence between different parts of the financial sector and the development of new financial services. Sub-section 2 of this section described how banks are improving existing products and developing new ones by combining different sorts of information in new ways electronically. Banks are entering new business areas and, on the other hand, other businesses are entering banking. This development primarily has to do with liberalization in financial regulations, but telecommunications and information technologies are important prereqisites for allowing such a development to take place. In the end, this may lead to the development of new financial institutions comprising a broader range of financial services -- so-called financial supermarkets.

These developments may lead to a restructuring of the financial sector. In banking today, it seems that smaller and medium sized banks are squeezed and that they may, therefore, be closed or may have to merge with bigger banks. But at the same time, new types of specialized electronic low-cost banks are appearing. These electronic banks rely very heavily on access to more generalized transmission systems -- but not necessarily on centralized systems. Even in a situation in which bigger banks develop their own specialized systems, there will be room for smaller low-cost niche banks.

An important aspect of the widespread usage of telecommunications and data services in the banking industry relates to the effects that this has on the surrounding community. One obvious effect of greater efficiency and effectiveness in banking is cost-saving in other industries. But another and just as important effect is that the usage of information technology will spread to other sectors in society. When banking services become telematized, other sectors being serviced by banks also will become users of telecommunications and information technologies. Banking was one of the first industries to implement the new technologies, and when these extend beyond the front-offices, customers will have to engage in electronic trading relationships with their banks.

This development touches first of all the developed countries with a well functioning telecommunications infrastructure. But as this infrastructure improves in developing countries, the effects will very quickly spread. That is already happening, but the trajectory in developing countries is far more unequal than in developed countries.

(b) Liberalization and trade in financial services

The major reasons for liberalizing banking nationally and internationally were described in the previous section dealing with developing countries. Those reasons also have a bearing on developed countries. Increased competitiveness is likely to result from a loosening of protective measures.

In preparation for the increased competitive environment, banks have lately been highly committed to strategic positioning by engaging in mergers with other banks or with financial institutions from other parts of the financial sector. This merger activity is justified by the expectation that only bigger financial corporations will be able to survive in a larger unprotected market.

Likewise, it has been anticipated by banks that they would have to have the means to open new affiliates on the enlarged market. But this optimistic expectation has not been fulfilled. On the contrary, in a number of cases, banks have been forced to close down affiliates abroad as has been documented in chapter V. An internationalization of banking of this kind has therefore not until now been the outcome of liberalization. However, trade of financial services has increased considerably, (see table VI.2)

As table VI.2 shows, the trade of major developed countries in financial services has approximately doubled during 1987-1990. It should be noted, however, that around 90 per cent of the international financial transactions

shown could be considered to be of a purely speculative character. In the framework of the present volume, this does not constitute a problem as the focus is primarily on tradability as such and not on the purposes of any financial transactions. But it could be an indication of the lack of "real" economic activity behind a majority of international financial transactions which, for the countries involved, raises some serious questions. International financial markets to a large extent tend to live a separate life in relation to productive economic activities in society. However, the impact of international financial transactions is very much felt in societies and productive sectors. A recent grave example of this were the speculations against European currencies in 1992-1993.

Table VI.2. Financial services provided to or received from non-residents by resident banks, selected countries, 1987-1990 (Millions of dollars)

Country	Item	1987	1988	1989	1990
France	Receipts	..	22 157	32 076	42 132
	Expenditures	..	21 709	32 913	45 400
Germany	Receipts	12 967	13 621	18 670	28 118
	Expenditures	9 664	10 027	13 760	20 567
Netherlands	Receipts	9 006	8 591	13 133	17 107
	Expenditures	7 334	7 414	11 468	14 321
Switzerland	Receipts	13 199	11 275	13 659	17 036
	Expenditures	5 854	5 251	7 733	11 179
United Kingdom	Receipts	17 267	20 508	30 390	27 651
	Expenditures	16 674	20 140	31 227	28 604
United States	Receipts	33 082	41 942	54 388	49 087
	Expenditures	27 659	36 247	47 225	45 198

Source: OECD, *Financial Market Trends 52*, June 1992 (Paris, OECD), pp. 45-46.

Note: The table measures trade in financial services by the conventional measure that includes three types of flows of receipts or expenditures by banks providing or receiving such services: income on direct investment received or paid; income on other investment (interest or dividends received or paid); and commissions and fees received or paid. Income on other investment constitutes approximately 9/10 of total receipts and expenditures in most countries, while income from direct investment constitutes approximately 2-3 per cent and commissions and fees the rest. It should be noted that the OECD has not previously published these figures and that some uncertainty, therefore, may be attached to them. The figures are based entirely on

In spite of the disconnected character of the highly telematized international trade in stocks, currencies and hedging products, a continuous struggle takes place among developed countries to acquire a leading position in international financial markets. To become a financial centre, it is important to offer efficient telecommunications connections and liberalized conditions both in relation to telecommunications regulation and the regulation of financial affairs. But there seems to be an inherent contradiction in the liberalization of financial markets: on the one hand, increased competitiveness is obtained; on the other hand, a certain destabilization may take place.

C. Conclusions

The primary focus of this chapter was on the implications of increasing tradability of banking services for banks and developing and developed countries, against the background of the interrelated aspects of building a tele- matized infrastructure for trade in financial services on the one hand, and liberalization measures on the other. In developed countries, both aspects are evolving at a much faster pace than in developing countries; some results of the process can, therefore, be described. A telematized infrastructure at the national level allows for a larger number of transactions to be performed without any face- to-face contact between banks and their customers. At an international level, a telematized infrastructure has vastly improved the possibilities for operating in a truly international financial market.

The liberalization process is a prerequisite for the potential of technical tradability of banking services to unfold. On the other hand, technological changes also form a part of the reasons for political changes. Increasing competitiveness is expected as one of the benefits of liberalizing banking. But, at the same time, it has contributed to some destabilization of national financial systems.

Notes

1   See Richard Barras, "Towards a theory of innovation in services", *Research Policy*, 15, no.4 (1986), pp. 161 - 174.

2   See, for instance, OECD, *Financial Market Trends,* no. 52, (Paris, June 1992), p. 32.

3   For a good example, see Bernhard Wieland, "Telecommunications and the disintegration of the banking industry". Paper presented at the Ninth ITS Conference, Cannes, June 1992.

4   Judith Perera, "Off-shore labour on the cheap", *South*, May 1991, p. 21.

5   Morten Falch and Knud Erik Skouby, *Human Resources, Education and Development in Ghana: A Feasibility Study on the Banking Sector* (Lyngby, Technical University of Denmark, 1991), p. 20.

6   Many post-colonial nations followed a strategy in which the economic base for growth was to be secured by allocating resources from the primary sector to the manufacturing sector and in which the State was to obtain control of these resources through different state and parastatal bodies. See, for instance, D. Rothchild and Naomi Chazan, eds., *The Precarious Balance: State and Society in Africa* (Boulder, Colorado, Westview, 1989).

7   See, e.g., Jayshree Sengupta, "Internationalization of banking and the relationship between foreign and domestic banks in developing countries", *International Journal of Development Banking*, Vol. 6, 1 (1988), pp. 25 - 50.

8   An OECD survey revealed that, in the vast majority of cases in developing countries, the percentage of deposits to credits accounted for by foreign banks was very low, indicating an inflow of means for investment. See Dimitri Germidis and M. Michalet, *International Banks and Financial Markets in Developing Countries* (Paris, OECD, 1984).

9   Sengupta, op. cit. p. 38.

10 Ibid. p. 39-40.

11 See chapter III.A.

Chapter VII

POLICY AND TECHNICAL ASSISTANCE IMPLICATIONS: BENEFITING FROM TRADABILITY

The analysis presented in the preceding chapters shows that the technological developments occurring in information and telecommunications technologies will enhance the tradability of banking services, affecting both developed and developing countries. This chapter draws policy conclusions for developing countries based on the evidence and analysis presented in the preceding chapters. The discussion is based on three propositions:

- Almost all banking services are transportable, making a global competitive market -- as in the case of commodity markets -- possible.

- The economic benefits involved allow the creation and expansion of an international market for tradable banking services.

- However, not very much is actually happening as yet, inspite of the increased transportability of banking services.

There is, nevertheless, hardly any doubt that a new situation is developing and that it demands a review of the policy issues and options available to countries, especially developing countries.

A. International trends and overall policy implications

In the present report, evidence has been presented that indicates that the international trends in technological development fostering the transportability of an increasing range of products are beginning to have a strong impact on the banking industry in developed countries. Nevertheless, these trends interact with economic and legal aspects, so that the outcome in terms of opportunities and threats generated by tradability is still fairly uncertain. The technical possibilities for a greater tradability of banking products that have been identified in chapter III will therefore be restrained by at least four general factors:

- The accelerating but piecemeal diffusion of information and telecommunications technologies in the developing countries.

- The uncertainties related to the implementation of the international framework regulating trade in services, in terms of country offers and the extent and degree of liberalization they would represent (GATS).

- The slow speed of the structural transformation of the banking industry in developing countries.

- The tendency to maintain national regulation regimes that limit or constrain foreign participation on account of the problems experienced in financial markets during recent years, particularly as a result of fluctuations caused by speculation against exchange rates.

The diffusion of information and telecommunications technologies has been very rapid in banking, and a transition to services delivered via dedicated or public networks is gradually taking place in most developed countries. The speed at which this transition is taking place often tends to be overestimated, but the growth of networks related to special areas such as foreign exchange dealing illustrates how quickly information and telecommunications technologies may become essential to financial services.

Developing countries have relatively little influence on this process of diffusion, but, as mentioned in chapter I, the Uruguay Round of Multilateral Trade Negotiations has led to the formulation of new principles for international trade in services, incorporated in GATS. The GATS Annex on Financial Services appears to follow the scope and intent of regulations already adopted within the cooperation framework among OECD countries quite closely. While the precise extent and degree of liberalization are still to be determined through further negotiations after entry into force of the agree-

ments negotiated in the Uruguay Round, all of the developed country participants and a fair proportion of developing country participants had made commitments in the Uruguay Round for liberalization of financial services. More liberal regulatory regimes in various developed countries will allow the most competitive banks to expand and specialize in the delivery of services across borders. This will probably lead to political and economic pressures for changing the conditions of access of foreign banks to domestic markets in developing countries.

Structural change in the banking sector of developing countries is also an area where innovations have been moving rather slowly, exhibiting little fundamental change for more than a decade. In the vast majority of developing countries, banks have maintained their basic functions and service levels at the same stage for many years, lagging far behind the developments that have characterized banks in developed countries. It seems likely that the structural economic reforms that are carried out in many developing countries will create requirements for new services and functions, but for most banks in developing countries this would necessitate key changes in the organization and performance of establishments delivering services. The static nature of banking services in developing countries certainly tends to slow down the rate at which the tradability of services will become effective in the domestic banking sector.

Finally, the volatile nature of financial markets which are increasingly mediated via fast telecommunication links, and the effects of currency speculation generate a situation where many developing countries will be eager to maintain some kind of "separation fence" between domestic and international financial markets. The controls on international financial transactions resulting from a "separation fence" would vary from one particular country to the next, but there seems to be little doubt that such controls will affect the delivery of tradable financial services. The case of Singapore described below illustrates, however, that it is possible to combine the objective of fostering an internationally competitive financial sector with the aim of shielding the domestic economy from extreme fluctuations in the international financial market.

The increased tradability of services that this volume has ascertained leads to a situation in which banks in developing as well as developed countries will need to consider new defensive or offensive strategies. In addition, however, policy makers will have to examine a range of aspects that should determine the strategy and policy approach to adopt in the particular situation that a country faces. The policy options can be conveniently analyzed in terms of three dimensions, as follows:

- The overall requirements of a country.
- The available infrastructure.
- The regulatory framework.

In the discussions of policy implications for developing and developed countries below, these dimensions will be the starting points to outline possible courses of action.

B. Policy implications for developing countries

The consequences of tradability of banking services for developing countries depend, to a considerable extent, on the requirements of these countries. These requirements are, of course,

contingent on the particular country in question, but some general aspects may be identified as particularly important to developing countries as a group. One of these aspects is that the domestic financial system in developing countries usually involves a fairly large segment based on providing informally mobilized means of investment resources, while the formal segment primarily hinges on limited capital resources made available through domestic banks.

This means, on the one hand, that banks generally occupy a far more dominant role in the formal component of the financial systems of developing countries than they do in many developed countries, a situation that makes domestic banks both highly vulnerable and very difficult to reorganize in the short-term. On the other hand, any efficiency and effectiveness that can be achieved in the banking system is likely to have major effects for the economic system as a whole.

1. Requirements for new banking services

The role that banks thus play in the development process gives rise to a number of specific considerations. The domestic requirements are dominated by the need to facilitate investment in the development process, including commercial banking services for small and medium-sized firms. There is currently less demand for the advanced retail banking services offered to a select group of individual customers in most developing countries, and competition in the provision of new and improved services for this group of customers is not visible. An example is provided in table VII.1 which shows a very general assessment of the services offered by the financial sector in Sub-Saharan Africa. The types and number of banking products typically offered by local banks in the markets in these countries represent only a limited selection of those offered by banks in most developed countries.

Table VII.1. The availability of banking products in Africa, 1993

Widely offered	Very occasionally offered	Not offered
Cash	Payment card	EFTPoS
Cheque	Credit card	Pension scheme
Bank transfers	Prepayment card	savings
Bills	SWIFT	Homebanking
Mortgage deed		Prepayment card
Consumer loan		Forward contracts
Housing loan		Direct debit
Lending against		Dealing 2000
security to bills		Reuters
Financial loans		Globex
Loans for equity		EDI
Current account		Options
Short deposit		Futures
Time deposit		Financial leasing
Bank draft		
Letter of credit		
Guarantee		

Source: Based on an assessment received from ACT Kindle, Ireland. The table excludes South Africa, where banks offer most of the services listed.

The drive to introduce information and telecommunication technologies in the banks in developed countries has been closely connected with the need to save on costly labour input and the need for these new services. Most of these needs are not yet manifest in the developing countries and thus the drive for information and telecommunications technologies is not felt in these countries. Nevertheless, the majority of banks in developing countries have an objective need to improve the performance of back-office processing and make services more effective for their customers, even if the customers often belong to the category of small or medium-sized commercial businesses. The new information and telecommunication technologies offer the possibility to substitute scarce qualified labour power with technology and reduce faults and mistakes in the processing procedures.

Even if the possibility of introducing new technologies is out of reach for the management of a single bank, it is likely to be advantageous for many countries. In view of this, policymakers have to consider the possibility of creating an environment that encourages domestic banks to seek cooperation with foreign partners. Such foreign partners may be able, with the increased tradability of banking services, to supply new products or to provide systems for the remote processing of back-office transactions. This would imply that banks in developing countries will have to consider the option of purchasing tradable intermediate services such as assistance in back-office processing, or the software for new products, from transnational banks.

One option is to buy a "suitcase bank" -- a software-system that can be installed on a personal computer, providing the basic banking services. This option makes it possible for persons without adequate formal training in banking procedures to keep records according to (international) standards and to answer (simple) questions with updated information. The "suitcase bank" opens up at the same time a possibility to bridge the gap between the formal and the informal segments of the banking sector, if the informal segment is provided with "suitcase banks".

With improved telecommunication services, an obvious enhancement of the "suitcase bank" would be to establish on-line connections between the "suitcases" and the headquarters of the bank and, if necessary, also with a cooperation partner in developed countries. At the same time, this approach, which can raise the efficiency of both the formal and the informal segments of the domestic banking sector, is not likely to result in a "hollowing out" of these banks in the long run. The latter is an immanent problem with many other assistance programmes to the banking sector.

The immediate course of action suggested by these considerations is to initiate an investigation of the local requirements for new banking services that could benefit from the introduction of "suitcase banks". The emphasis could be placed on the specific needs of the different segments and on the need to bridge the gap between the formal and informal segments.

A second area of initiative that policy makers from developing countries will have to consider is to study the need for technological upgrading of back-office processing in local banks, or other aspects that can benefit considerably from the introduction of tradable intermediate services. This kind of survey may encourage local banks to cooperate in order to establish joint service providers that can deliver such services, or purchase them from vendors abroad.

2. International cooperation and local competition

The area where the effects of tradability may be most clearly felt will be related to international financial transactions. In this area, the majority of developing countries is characterized by a strong position of transnational banks, often in the form of affiliates. Most of the activities of transnational banks are directly connected to investments and manufacturing activities of transnational corporations based in the home countries of the banks

involved.[2] This implies that these banks will be predominantly interested in providing services to these corporate customers. They will do this increasingly on the basis of tradable service products or intermediate services.

The consequence is that policy makers in developing countries face a major dilemma. On the one hand, transnational banks that have started operations in developing countries during the investment boom of the 1970s may increasingly find it technically feasible to serve their corporate customers in host countries via information-and-telecommunication technologies-mediated services. This would encourage these banks to close foreign affiliates, as they have done in several developed countries. This tendency may become particularly important on account of the problems that many transnational banks may face due to the competition among banks in developed countries.

On the other hand, the tradability of banking services has tended to be combined with a continuing need to have some kind of physical presence in host countries where major customers such as transnational corporations are active. This need may increasingly lead to opportunities for cooperation with domestic banks in developing countries.

The new prospects of profitable business based on the delivery of tradable banking services or the provision of intermediate services can thus lead to both competition and cooperation among foreign and domestic banks in a large number of developing countries. It is likely that domestic banks that enter into alliances with transnational banks will benefit considerably from the technology that is transferred in connection with setting up systems that service customers via co-operating bank offices.

The development of local technological capabilities should be an important objective for many banks in developing countries, but the acquisition of such capabilities through co-operation with foreign banks can take many forms. On the one hand, affiliates of foreign banks will often lead the introduction of services that are based on the application of information and telecommunication technologies. On the other hand, locally owned banks may seek alliances with major banks abroad and thus take advantage of the tradability of intermediate products through the application of information and telecommunication technologies. In some cases, there may be a conflict between these two forms, and policy makers in developing countries will often stress the need to support technological development in locally-owned banks.

3. Risks of dependence on transnational banks

The need for technology transfer is, however, also associated with risk for the receiving country. As mentioned in chapter II, inherent in the positive effects through the transfer of technology from foreign-based banks to indigenous banks is the risk of segmentation of the market for banking services. The foreign-based international banks tend to take over customers with international financial relations as well as the more advanced national customers, while the indigenous banks tend to concentrate on the less advanced and rural customers. These customers do not tend to elicit the interest of international banks, and indigenous banks with a profound knowledge about the local market may even be the best at servicing these customers. But host developing countries might find it unsatisfactory to leave the

bigger customers to foreign-based transnational banks in the long-term.

This is, therefore, an area where technical assistance programmes are needed. Such programmes could include funding of the purchase of computers and communications systems and educational activities in the uses of new information technologies in the banking sector. A specific example of possible assistance is the "suitcase bank" discussed above.

This does not necessarily lead to a change of focus from small and less advanced customers to bigger and more advanced customers. Telematic systems may also lead to an improved interconnection between the formal and informal part of the financial system in developing countries. An example of this is the establishment of Caisse Commune d'Epargne et d'Investissement in Cameroon in 1987 aiming at using new technology to create a hybrid between the formal French-dominated banking system and the traditional informal credit operatives, called Tontines.[3]

Summing up, the implications of increased tradability of banking services for banks in both developed and developing countries are indeed already extensive and will surely become even more pronounced in the future. But the implications do not at present seem to reproduce what has happened in the case of material goods. Banks do not, to any great extent, take advantage of locating parts of their production processes in low-factor-cost countries. Among the developed countries, however, banks may increase their internal division of labour. But this is a result of the technological possibilities for centralizing certain production functions.

4. Provision of infrastructure for information and telecommunication technologies

A very important area of policy intervention related to the tradability of banking services is the improvement of information technology and the telecommunications infrastructure. The preceding analysis has clearly demonstrated the extent to which modern banking is dependent on the use of information and telecommunication technologies. A look at the tables in annex A will also show that, for the vast majority of banking-service products, access to advanced information and telecommunication technologies infrastructure is a necessary condition for the delivery of tradable services. For many developing countries, this fact has the implication that, in order to benefit from the tradability of banking services, there must be an adequate telecommunications infrastructure.

Unfortunately, this is one of the areas where the vast majority of developing countries has suffered from a relative neglect during the past several decades. Basic telephone networks in most developing countries are unreliable and capacity is far below demand. International telecommunications facilities have been improved in many countries with the introduction of international direct dialling services and more reliable satellite communications. An expansion of such international telecommunications services will, however, have to go hand-in-hand with continued improvements of the domestic telecommunications networks, so that the reliability of communication from local banks and branch offices to an international communications node is ensured.

The need to improve the communications infrastructure involves a number of regulatory and financial considerations. The demand for investments in telecommunications has forced many developing countries to consider the possibility of allowing foreign service providers to engage directly in the provision of telecommunications services to domestic banks and other internationally oriented businesses.[4] In some developing countries, it is possible that this kind of arrangement will have to bypass public monopolies because of the poor quality of the services offered in these networks. This issue is closely connected with the on-going debate on liberalization of telecommunications. For many developing countries, a liberalization of telecommunications serves the dual objectives of forcing the public corporations responsible for post and telecommunications to provide a broader and more efficient range of services and of attracting foreign direct investment (FDI). This component of the infrastructure for the delivery of intermediate or final banking products appears likely to attract increasing foreign investment and the interest of transnational corporations. The challenge for policy makers is to make these two aspects of the policy meet in a mix that ensures both advanced international connections and a broad coverage of telephony services.

5. Regulatory hurdles

The regulatory framework is probably the most important area of potential intervention by policy makers of developing countries. The tradability of a range of banking products generally challenges existing regulatory practices, which tend to be centered on various forms of FDI. For many developing countries, this implies a need to reconsider the framework of policies and regulatory institutions under which domestic and foreign banks operate.

In connection with the efforts to build up capabilities in delivery of tradable services, policy makers in developing countries may wish to consider options for the promotion of exports in the area of banking services. The extent to which technical divisibility, as analyzed in previous chapters, has generated components of the production process or intermediate service products that can be delivered from developing countries, is now fairly large. Nevertheless, the comparative advantages that firms in developing countries share in this regard, for instance on the basis of lower labour costs, appears to be rather limited.

The analysis has established that when the divisibility of a production process increases and intermediate or final products become tradable, they usually depend very little on labour-intensive work processes. In addition, a substantial infrastructure in terms of reliable telecommunications linkages and computer equipment is required for the delivery of such intermediate or final products. This does not, however, rule out the possibilities for firms from developing countries to enter successfully the rapidly growing international market for intermediate or even final products in banking services.

The technical possibilities are expanding. With liberalization of trade in services progressing, the economic and legal barriers to entry into the market are rapidly being eroded. The analysis in this volume indicates, however, that in spite of these emerging opportunities the actual feasibility of building up a competitive capability to deliver services in the banking sector would require two additional features: first, the infrastructure in terms of advanced information and telecommunications technologies must be in place; second, a highly skilled but low-cost labour force must be available.

6. Scenarios for developing countries

The transition to a new period of increased trade in services and the likely consequences of rapid diffusion of new information technologies can be illustrated by alternative future scenarios. These scenarios can be related to the forecasting of "status quo" conditions or forecasts of "rapid change" conditions in relation to regulation and technological change, respectively.

Forecasts of "status quo" conditions envisage that the existing scope of international and national regulations of banking services will continue, and that there is a limited and gradual diffusion of information and telecommunication technologies based systems and networks in the developed countries. This implies, broadly speaking, that a growing gap may emerge between the international banking system and national banking system in developing countries.

Forecasts of "rapid change" envisage, in contrast, the rapid diffusion of information and telecommunication technologies based systems and networks in developing countries. Assuming also that widespread and effective deregulation takes place within international frameworks, including the General Agreement on Trade in Services, a situation is projected where the pressure for technological change and increased competition for markets will compel the vast majority of countries -- including developing countries -- to confront the challenge of transnational banking based on tradable services.

In table VII.2, some likely consequences of the two scenarios are briefly outlined. The consequences are then summarized in terms of three variables: competition in the banking sector, range of banking products and opportunities for off-shore sub-contracting services.

The policies pursued in response to each of these scenarios and in various countries will depend on the specific conditions and objectives of the particular country in question. Both positive and negative aspects emerge from a rapid change scenario in the tradability of service products. More importantly, there are new opportunities to gain from such trends, for developed countries as well as developing countries, which could be exploited through new policy initiatives.

Policy makers may initiate schemes that would encourage domestic firms generally to acquire the necessary capabilities. This could, for instance, involve the setting up of special training courses or the establishment of a computing centre that would be able to undertake some of the electronic data processing that is required for the delivery of tradable banking services. One important option to consider, however, is to facilitate exports of intermediate or final products via the establishment of a special service-oriented export zone. This kind of zone should provide infrastructure facilities for advanced information and telecommunication technologies and could, at the same time, provide an environment that includes special incentives in terms of depreciation for advanced information technology, special administrative regulations that would allow firms in the zone to compete abroad, and a generally liberal environment for domestic firms or joint ventures with foreign firms.

7. The cases of Singapore and Ghana

It is instructive to look at two countries that occupy different positions in the spectrum of developing countries and that have adopted widely different approaches to policies in this area.

Table VII.2. Alternative scenarios for developing countries

Future	Status quo: trade in services restricted	Rapid change: liberalization of trade in services
Status quo: slow diffusion of information and telecommunication technologies	• Traditional range of banking products offered locally. • Few opportunities for off-shore sub-contracting of work routines for foreign banks. • Some opportunities for production of intermediate services in special zones	• Proliferation of transnational banks, based on local affiliates. • More competition between local and transnational banks. • Foreign-owned banks compete on the basis of access to international networks.
Rapid change: widespread diffusion of information and telecommunication technologies	• National banks compete for local markets with information-and-telecommunication-technologies-based banking products.	• Vigorous international competition based on information-and-telecommunication-technologies-based banking products. • New opportunities for off-shore sub-contracting of intermediate services.

(a) Singapore

The Government of Singapore has been very conscious of the need to facilitate the operations of transnational and local service firms. The economic growth that Singapore has experienced during several decades has been primarily based on the growth of the manufacturing sector, but the role of the economy as an entrepôt in regional trade has provided opportunities to attract regional headquarters of major transnational services corporations. The

Government has added further incentives to such firms by pursuing a policy that specifically emphasized the growth of information-oriented firms in Singapore (see box VII.1).

Unlike many other financial centres in the world, Singapore's development was not based on catering mainly to a large home market requiring financial services. Its status as a financial centre has been built on the deliberate cultivation of regional and international financial markets, such as the Asian dollar market and the Euro-dollar markets. In this process, a large number of foreign commercial banks have set up fully-licensed affiliates in the 1970s, and more than 80 offshore banks in the 1980s.[5] The Government has emphasized that a financial centre should be based on the support of a strong domestic economy with a stable currency and minimal inflation. Moreover, Singapore has enjoyed a strategic location where a time-zone advantage bridging Asian and European markets can provide round-the-clock financial services to businesspersons who want to cover their foreign exchange and commodities positions. SWIFT was introduced in Singapore in 1979 and was improved in 1983 by the launching of a new ST200 system which allowed banks to continue adding workstations as the workload of interbank financial transactions increased. The Government has continued to encourage the introduction of computerized systems linked to international financial institutions, such as the Singapore International Monetary Exchange which provide a direct link with the Chicago Monetary Exchange for a round-the-clock financial futures trading system.

The Government of Singapore has thus, as part of its strategy of developing an information-intensive industrial structure in order to expand into future growth areas, placed its

---

Box VII.1. Singapore's information-oriented strategy

"Singapore is staking much of its economic future on telecommunications. With few resources besides its people and infrastructure, Singapore has developed an information-oriented industrial strategy to take advantage of its unique geographical, political, historical and economic position. ...

"As Singapore's standard of living rises, factories are moving to neighbouring countries such as Indonesia, Malaysia and Thailand for low-cost labour. In response, Singapore is striving to attract more information-oriented tenants, in industries such as financial services and computers, and to serve as an Asia-Pacific telecom hub for multinational corporations. ...

"Furthermore, deregulation is lowering telecom rates into and out of Japan. As a result, companies are considering a two-hub approach to Asian communications – locating sites in Japan and Singapore, which are at the opposite ends of the region. Some companies see this as an attractive alternative to the more central Hong Kong.

Several major banks, for example, are making moves "bit by bit," according to a consultant in Singapore."

Source: Communications Week International, 27 May 1991, p. 15.

main emphasis on the establishment of an advanced information and telecommunication infrastructure. In this way, banks that are already operating in Singapore have been able to offer services in the important Asia-Pacific region, while more foreign banks have been encouraged to set up regional offices in Singapore. With a comparatively large number of banks operating in Singapore, the emphasis of banking business has recently been shifting towards offshore markets (box VII.2).

Box VII.2. Growth of offshore markets for banks in Singapore

"Much to the satisfaction of the Monetary Authority of Singapore, activity in the offshore market has continued to grow apace. Average daily turnover in foreign exchange last year was nearly $80 billion, up 30 per cent on the 1989 level. Offshore banking assets rose 16 per cent to $390 billion, and fund management business is growing as the region becomes more wealthy.

According to government figures, offshore loans to non-bank customers grew at a record 45 per cent, reflecting the rapid growth of the regional economy. Assets channelled into the interbank market grew much more slowly, at a rate of just 4.5 per cent."

Source: *Financial Times*, 30 April 1991.

(b) Ghana

The case of Ghana provides an interesting contrast as an example of efforts to devise policies that would improve conditions for the financial services industry which is currently very backward, and which might lead to initiatives to reap benefits from tradability in the longer-term perspective. The banking industry in Ghana is composed of four major domestic-owned banks and two foreign-owned banks. The country is pursuing an Economic Recovery Programme which is aimed at providing an attractive policy environment and infrastructure for rapid economic growth (see box VII.3).

The structural adjustment in which Ghana is engaged involves a strong need for efficient and competitive financial services. Various programmes of assistance are designed to improve the performance of the banking industry, primarily through training and management-rehabilitation efforts. The emerging market for banking services in Ghana provides opportunities for the application of information technology and a more extensive role for tradable service products. Nevertheless, the structure of the Ghanaian banking industry and the strong Government controls that are still largely in existence limit the autonomous decision-making processes of the banks. The national telecommunications infrastructure is only gradually being rehabilitated, and such vitally important components as international links have taken a long time to materialize in practical terms.

Foreign-owned banks such as Barclays Bank and Standard Chartered Bank are moving ahead into the utilization of data transfer much faster than large, domestically-owned banks such as the Ghana Commercial Bank. The most likely result of this tendency is that the primary beneficiaries of tradability would be subsidiaries of foreign banks. The policies of the Government of Ghana have not addressed this problem explicitly, and it seems likely that there will be little initiative in the immediate future to place greater priority on the encouragement of trade in services such as banking.

Box VII.3. The banking industry in Ghana

The Ghanaian banking industry is dominated by four commercial banks. The two largest, Ghana Commercial Bank and Social Security Bank, are both indigenous and controlled by the Government. The other two, Barclays Bank and Standard Chartered Bank, are affiliates of banks based in the United Kingdom, but with a 50-50 share of foreign and domestic investment. These four banks together hold 77 per cent of the total deposit market share. There are also 130 rural banks, controlling 7 per cent of the total savings. In terms of the relatively profitable transactions related to foreign trade, however, Barclays and Standard Chartered appear to hold more than three-quarters of the total amount.

A survey of the use of information technology in the banking industry in Ghana shows almost a third of the computers installed in 1991 were placed in financial institutions. There were 300 personal computers, 11 minicomputers and 6 mainframes, the latter constituting half of the total mainframe installations in Ghana. This shows that information technology has been introduced for some back-office functions in all the major banks. The foreign banks seem to have been most successful in the application of such technology, since they have been able to rely on expertise in their parent companies. Barclays and Standard Chartered Bank have also introduced transfer of data between different branches via the telecommunications network.

Source: M. Falch and K.E. Skouby, *Human Resources, Education and Development in Ghana. A Feasibility Study on the Banking Sector* (Lyngby, Technical University of Denmark, 1991).

8. Options for technical assistance to developing countries

Suggestions for technical assistance to developing countries that arise from the above analysis fall into three categories: (a) directly improving the efficiency and quality of services delivered by domestic banks using information and telecommunication technologies and enhancing the awareness about the implications of tradability; (b) the formulation of new regulatory guidelines that permit local banks to take advantage of the opportunities offered by tradability, but retain a "separation fence" that reduces adverse impacts of turbulent international financial markets; and (c) specific feasibility studies that identify the opportunities for off-shore activities related to specific banking products.

In connection with the first category, technical assistance should aim at providing systems with the qualities mentioned in the discussion of the "suitcase bank" earlier, that is, affordable, easy-to-use-systems which at the same time open up gradually more advanced connections with the international banking community. As an accompanying measure, it is important to raise the understanding of current trends among national policy-makers and, in particular, the management of domestic banks. These actors should be made aware of the risks that exist in terms of allowing a growing gap to emerge between a few banks, primarily those with foreign investment or cooperation that offer a wide range of tradable services on the one hand, and a stagnating domestically oriented formal and informal banking sector serving the majority of local customers with a limited range of services on the other.

A natural follow-up activity of the provision of systems of the above kind is technical assistance to domestic banks aimed at increasing their capacity to develop and market competitive services. On the one hand, this could take the form of training that would assist the banks in broadening their product range and improving the capabilities of staff to tailor their products to local markets. On the other hand, assistance could be provided to raise the technological level of both the retail and corporate service delivery of domestic banks, for instance through a limited number of demonstration projects. Both training programmes should build on the system provided.

In connection with the second category, the most important assistance would relate to streamlining the national regulatory framework in harmony with the emerging, liberalized multilateral rules proposed under the General Agreement on Trade Services. This assistance could also extend to the formulation and effective implementation of regulations that consider the necessity of minimum sizes of markets to generate capacities leading to the active promotion of regional cooperation arrangements. Finally, such assistance could go hand in hand with the improvement of regulations so as to shield the banking industry without isolating it.

In the third category, one possibility is to undertake follow-up studies of banking products that still have a substantial component of labour-intensive routines or other routines that can be carried out in developing countries. But even more important are studies that concretely identify the pre-requisites in terms of information and telecommunication technologies infrastructure and human resources that are needed in a particular country to exploit the emerging opportunities for off-shore facilities management. This is important, particularly since the competition for such activities will be extremely intense in the near future. A related area of assistance would be to support workshops with participants directly interested in the estab-

Table VII.3. Options for assistance to developing countries

Category of activity	Technical assistance options
Efficiency and quality raising	• Provision of affordable and easy-to-use information and telecommunication technologies-based systems for banking. • Awareness-raising seminars concerning tradability for government policy-makers and management in domestic banks. • Training provided to assist domestic banks in broadening product ranges and improving delivery of services.
Regulatory guidelines	• Assistance in streamlining the national regulatory framework with the emerging, liberalized multilateral rules. • Implementation of national regulations promoting regional cooperation on the use and development of information and telecommunication technologies-based banking technology. • Improvement of regulations protecting the national banking sector without isolating it.
Export opportunities	• Identification of the pre-requisites for exports of banking services in terms of information and telecommunication technologies infrastructure and human resources. • Feasibility studies identifying banking services that require a substantial component of routines that can be undertaken in a developing country. • Workshops to establish off-shore centres and/or export-oriented zones.

lishment of off-shore centres or export-oriented zones for transnational banking.

The options for assistance outlined briefly above have been summarized under the three categories of different activities related to policy objectives in table VII.3 below. It should be noted that the options outlined in the table are meant as illustrative examples of a more general nature, and that other possibilities can be envisaged for individual countries, depending on their existing infrastructure and capabilities.

C. Policy implications for developed countries and cooperation with developing countries

For banks in the developed countries, the increased tradability of banking services offers a wide range of challenges and benefits. The experience indicates that information and telecommunication technologies based service products have become crucial to national competitiveness. Banking products that exploit the opportunities for trade in services clearly constitute important competitive assets in an international perspective, and will dominate the future markets for banks in all developed countries.

As discussed in chapter V, the potential for the delivery of services across borders has reduced the need to establish foreign affiliates. In some cases, technological progress has changed the activities of United States banks and has contributed to the closure of existing affiliates of United States banks in Europe. In addition, the possibility of shifting major processing tasks to other locations -- e.g., to computer centres in the home countries of major transnational banks -- has reduced the need for a physical presence of United States banks in Europe. In other words, the growing tradability of banking services has already influenced the structure of the banking sector in developed countries and the mode of operation for overseas subsidiaries of major transnational banks.

In this section, however, the focus of the discussion is on policy implications for Governments and banks in developed countries, of tradability of banking services for the operations of transnational banks in developing countries. There are three interrelated issues concerning tradability for banking services that

can lead to benefits for both developing and developed countries. One issue concerns the ways in which transnational banks would benefit from co-operation with banks or specialized banking-service firms in developing countries, including the potential for sub-contracting some of their intermediate production processes to firms in developing countries. The second issue concerns the infrastructure that is needed internationally and locally for transnational banks to be active in developing countries and the potential for delivery of final banking products in these countries. The third issue concerns the important questions of international regulation and liberalization of trade in services. There are reasons to believe that this last issue will continue to be the most influential one in determining the ways in which tradability will offer mutual benefits to developed and developing countries. But one should not loose sight of the practical, technical requirements fostered by the shift to tradable products.

1. Subcontracting

The analysis in chapters III and V of this study has shown that, although there are technical possibilities and there is an economic potential to sub-contract intermediate service products or components of the production process in banks to firms in developing countries, in reality the incentive to move such tasks to developing countries are apparently few at present. One problem is that most of the labour-intensive routines that exist in the production of banking-service products are dependent on specialized skills and/or knowledge of local conditions. Another is that the cost structure of the vast majority of tradable services is dominated by investments in advanced computer facilities, telecommunications and dedicated software applications. Labour costs are frequently marginal in services that have become tradable. A third factor is no doubt that an international market for traded banking services is not yet established due to regulations and traditions. Traditionally, many banks in developed countries are reluctant to acquire intermediate services from firms in developing countries due to trust and safety issues. Most banks are concerned that the security of their systems and privacy considerations of customers may be jeopardized in the process of out-sourcing some components of the production process, particularly components that involve detailed knowledge of the financial situation of the customer.

The reasons for reluctance on part of the banks in developed countries are furthermore motivated by a general fear of security problems that are not particularly related to developing countries. Nevertheless, a general impression is that, if the production of intermediate products takes place in special export zones, or if it is part of an alliance or another form of long-term collaboration, these problems of trust and security become less important.

2. Infrastructure and delivery of banking products

One of the main concerns of policy makers in developed countries is likely to be associated with questions related to information and telecommunication technologies infrastructure in developing countries and its linkages with international networks. An appropriate and reliable information and telecommunication technologies infrastructure is necessary for the delivery of final banking services in developing countries and the procurement of, for example, intermediate services from these countries.

The demand for services from developing countries will probably not, on its own, constitute a significant market that would justify major private investments by transnational banks in an information and telecommunication technologies infrastructure for a developing country. In most cases it is likely that such investments by foreign banks would be motivated by other forms of trade, e.g., the possibility of sub-contracting the delivery of intermediate service products that require investment in new physical facilities for information processing and communication. For policy makers in developed countries, it would therefore be more natural to consider various possibilities of using international development assistance and finance to develop more advanced information and telecommunication technologies infrastructure in developing countries. This kind of investment could be seen as a means to encourage transnational banks to become active in markets in developing countries, which are otherwise regarded as marginal areas of business.

However, the development of satellites may, as discussed above in chapter IV, change this situation. It might become economically feasible to establish a satellite-based connection using V-SAT technology between developed countries and a developing country just for banking-business purposes.

3. Regulatory frameworks

The third area of concern is the issue of regulation. This issue covers several aspects. One aspect is the need to facilitate trade in services under new forms of cooperation between developed and developing countries. Another aspect concerns the necessity of introducing a new framework of regulation at the international level which provides adequate supervision of financial transactions and the communication of data between different countries. A third aspect concerns the coordination of national legislation related to both domestic and foreign investment in services to ensure the best possible opportunities for realizing the tradability of services, respecting the problem of ensuring the building of domestic capabilities. Experience shows that this demands a certain period of time and size of market.

Policy makers in developed countries have already given considerable attention to this issue under the Uruguay Round of Multilateral Trade Negotiations, but there are a number of other measures that may complement the provisions of the General Agreement on Trade in Services. Among these are measures to streamline the regulation of transborder data flows between developed countries, which may provide useful precedents for similar regulation in developing countries.

Another kind of relevant measure involves the creation of special facilities that would enable banks from developing countries to participate in regional networks; such facilities may also provide very useful opportunities for banks -- or bank-related service providers -- from a single developing country to develop services and capabilities on a scale that is necessary to survive in the global competition which is likely to emerge in the long run.

Notes

1   Information obtained from GATT Secretariat.

2   See UNCTC, *Transnational Service Corporations and Developing Countries: Impact and Policy Issues*, UNCTC Current Studies No. 10 (United Nations publication, Sales No.89.11.A.14).

3   See Knud Erik Skouby, "Banks and development of technology: The role of the banking sector in Sub-Saharan Africa", paper presented at a regional symposium on savings and credit for development in Africa, Abidjan, 27-30 April 1992, p. 8.

4   For a discussion of recent development with respect to FDI in telecommunications in developing and developed countries, see UNCTAD Programme on Transnational Corporations, *World Investment Report 1993: Transnational Corporations and Integrated International Production* (United Nations publication, Sales No. E.93. II. A.14), pp. 82-83.

5   See Tan Chwee Huat, *Financial Markets and Institutions in Singapore* (Singapore, Singapore University Press, 1987).

Chapter VIII
CONCLUDING SUMMARY

The purpose of the present volume has been to analyze the potential opportunities and impacts of increased tradability of banking services. The concept of tradability of services used in this volume, namely, the ability to deliver service products at arm's length across national borders, derives from the fact that the application of new technologies of information processing and telecommunications are augmenting the potential of various services to be transported almost instantaneously to other areas of the world for additional processing or simply for final use. The core of the volume is a detailed study of the production and delivery of a full range of modern banking products, analyzing the technical aspects of tradability, that is, the divisibility of production processes and the transportability of product components and final products in both retail and corporate banking.

A. Main issues

The main issues that are associated with increased tradability of banking services include the following:

- Which factors are increasing the tradability of services, and how have they affected the development of modern banking?

- What are the technological, economic and regulatory barriers that impede the process of delivering banking services abroad? What is the role of the expansion of international dedicated networks for banking services in the reduction of such barriers?

- How does increased tradability affect the structure of transnational banking, in particular with reference to the choice between foreign direct investment and direct trade?

- What are the implications of the tradability of banking-service products for developing and developed countries? More specifically, what advantages and disadvantages emerge from the new opportunities offered by increased tradability?

- What policy measures should be considered in order to exploit the new opportunities for, and to reduce potentially negative impacts of, the tradability of banking services?

B. Tradability of banking products

The discussion of the product categories examined in chapter III and annex I shows that the creation and delivery of a wide range of modern banking products are presently based on computerized routines. The process of what may be termed telematization is accelerating rapidly, and affects virtually every product category in modern banks. In fact, with the significant exception of products that involve the physical transportation of material objects, such as cash, or some qualitative aspects of risk assessment in relation to credit intermediation, banking services in advanced developed countries rely overwhelmingly on computerized routines. The transportability of these services is high; in many cases the processing of bank transactions takes place at locations far removed from the point of entry. This transportability, or the technical aspect of tradability, has been exploited by some financial institutions in the form of sharing centralized computer facilities across borders, and has led to a number of out-sourcing arrangements (for example, facilities management in developed countries). All these indications point to the extent to which banking has been positioned in the forefront with regard to the application of information technology and telecommunications.

A more detailed product-by-product examination also reveals that the process of increasing technical tradability has affected bank products differently during various periods. Within the corporate banking sector, for instance, service products such as foreign exchange transactions, futures, options and securities were among the first to be traded on an international market, partly because the customers were already internationalized to a large degree. Comprising relatively few transactions and usually involving large sums of capital raised in major financial markets, these corporate bank products were offered as high value financial instruments through elaborate processes of credit rating, etc. . New technologies have added facilities of wider geographical scope to the search for profitable deals in the provision of such financial service products, but have hardly changed the core procedures for their production or delivery.

In contrast, retail banking products have tended to comprise a large number of transactions that involve minor sums of money and are primarily offered on domestic markets. These products are now being rapidly telematized and thus are technically able to be offered at arm's length on an international market, since the addition of further transactions for such products requires only marginal capacity increments in the computer centres that serve the new customers. Given a growing rate of diffusion of electronics payment cards and terminal equipment related to electronic funds transfer (the so-called EFTPoS terminals) and the expansion of telecommunications links, banks will be increasingly able to offer retail services in markets that extend across national borders. It is important to note, however, that there is little evidence yet of this process taking place on a major scale, suggesting that the influence of other factors such as regulatory barriers and the importance of trust between banks and their customers remain highly significant as determinants of actual market potential.

Finally, the analysis has indicated that, for the majority of product categories, increased tradability relies significantly on heavy capital investment such as advanced mainframe computer processing and telecommunications facilities, while the role of labour inputs is severely reduced. Whatever remains of labour-intensive transactions tends to be either routine work located at the counter, or non-routine work that involves highly qualified tasks with major responsibilities, such as credit ratings of customers. Therefore, the dominant trend has been to move the bulk of back-office transactions to places where these facilities are available and reliable, which in most cases have been situated in the developed countries.

In tables VIII.1 and VIII.2 below, banking services characterized by good transportability -- and thus the technical preconditions for tradability -- are presented. Table VIII.1 shows the products for which one or several work components are technically transportable and for which possibilities for out-sourcing the production of these components exist in principle. The table also indicates the main characteristics of the work processes that enter into the production of these components, relying on either "simple" manual labour, electronic processing and/or skilled labour.

Table VIII.2 shows final banking products that are usually available from major banks in developed countries. The table indicates the transportability of such final products -- which are thus technically tradable. It also contains an assessment of the extent of current trade in such final products actually taking place. Table VIII.2 also includes a column that contains an assessment of the availability of certain banking products in developing countries in sub-Saharan Africa (excluding the South African Republic). This information provides an indication of the potential for delivery of banking products from abroad. It also shows the types of existing services from domestic banks that are likely to be affected by the tradability of banking services.

C. Barriers to tradability

The lack of actual trade for a majority of transportable banking-service products derives from a number of factors. A closer look at the decisions taken by major banks suggests that impediments are associated primarily with regulatory barriers, language problems and the uncertain economic viability of trade as a substitute for foreign direct investment. In addition, there remain some impediments that are imposed by the lack of standardization in major networks, such as the slow diffusion of electronic data interchange standards in many countries. Finally, concerns with the security of transactions undertaken abroad have affected decisions to maintain remote processing within firms or national borders.

Barriers for tradability are being reduced via the gradual expansion of international user networks for the banking industry, such as the computerized SWIFT network for interbank financial transactions set up in 1974. A number of other dedicated networks set up to serve global financial transactions, such as Reuters, have contributed in fundamental ways to meeting the advanced communications and information needs of the industry. Another, increasingly important, kind of network relates to the communication between banks and their customers, e.g., via public telecommunications utilities.

Such networks have only recently begun to emerge to serve retail banking on a larger scale, for instance in linking EFTPoS terminals with banks; the constraints to their expansion and simplification probably constitute one of the major hurdles that need to be overcome in the near future. The proliferation of these networks, and the potential benefits that appear to be

Table VIII.1. The transportability of intermediate banking products

Product	Transportable intermediate products	Character of production process
Retail banking		
Cheque	Bookkeeping	Manual and electronic
	Clearing	Manual and electronic
Debit cards	Credit rating	Skilled
	Clearing	Electronic
Credit cards	Credit rating	Skilled
	Clearing	Electronic
Pension scheme savings	Custodial service	Skilled
Bills	Credit rating	Skilled
Mortgage deed	Issuing and recording	Manual
Housing loan	Credit rating	Skilled
Consumer loan	Credit rating	Skilled
Corporate banking		
Bank draft	Bookkeeping	Manual and electronic
	Clearing	Manual and electronic
Direct debit	Bookkeeping	Manual and electronic
	Clearing	Manual and electronic
Debit collecting	Document processing	Manual
Letter of credit	Document processing	Manual
	Bank transfer	Electronic
Futures	Credit rating	Skilled
Guarantee	Credit rating	Skilled
Financial loan	Credit rating	Skilled
	Interest calculation	Electronics
	Document processing	Manual
Export credit loan	Credit rating	Skilled
	Interest calculation	Electronic

Source: Based on tables III.12 and III.13.

Table VIII.2. The transportability of final banking products, actual trade, and availability in sub-Saharan countries

Final product	Transportability	Actual trade	Offered in sub-Saharan Africa
Retail banking			
Debit cards	Good	Yes	No
Credit cards	Very good	Yes	Occasionally
EFTPoS	Very good	No	No
Bank transfer	Very good	Yes	Widely
Homebanking	Very good	Some	No
Prepayment card	Fair	No	Occasionally
Current account	Good	No	Widely
Savings account	Good	Yes	Widely
Housing loan	Fair	No	Widely
Consumer loan	Fair	No	Widely
Corporate banking			
Bank draft	Good	Yes	Widely
Direct debit	Good	Yes	No
Homebanking	Very good	Yes	No
EDI	Very good	Yes	No
Forward contract	Good	Yes	No
Futures	Good	Yes	No
Options	Good	Yes	No
Guarantee	Good	Yes	Widely
Financial loan	Good	No	Widely
Loan for procurement of equity	Good	No	Widely
Financial leasing	Good	Yes	No

Source: Based on tables III.12, III.13 and VII.1.

derived from access to them, comprise a particular challenge to developing countries which must seriously consider the need for substantial improvements of their telecommunications infrastructures.

Progress achieved under the Uruguay Round of Multinational Trade Negotiations, in which the framework for a more liberalized regulatory regime relating to trade in services has emerged, is also significant for the likely reduction of barriers to tradability. It should be noted, however, that international telecommunication tariffs tend to remain considerably more expensive than domestic tariffs. In many developing countries, this gap in tariff structure will probably continue, or even widen, due to the importance of income from international calls for local post and telegraph administrations and the high rate of inflation in many economies.

D. Impact of tradability

A key issue is the kind of impact increased tradability will have on the structure of international transactions in banking services. The results of a survey conducted for this volume, addressed to a selected group of experts from banks in North America, Europe and Japan, indicate that tradability of services has been utilized both in a defensive strategy, signalling partial withdrawal from foreign markets by banks that have been affected by the financial crisis, and in an offensive competitive strategy to expand the reach of banks that are experiencing a growth phase. The choice of strategy appears to be determined by the character of the banks' environment rather than by the technological opportunities offered by new networks.

In addition, the survey indicated that, in many situations, foreign direct investment and trade in banking services do not become alternative modes of delivery of service products, but will tend to complement each other in an overall effort to deliver products abroad. For this reason, the fear that a reduction of the amount of foreign direct investment in services in developing countries will result from the opening of their markets for trade may be exaggerated. Growing markets tend to foster additional efforts to extend the range of banking services offered, and this can lead to a larger degree of presence in terms of investment in local affiliates or alliances between foreign and local banks. In fact, alliances or "correspondent banking" agreements between banks operating in different markets have been an increasingly important way to facilitate the delivery of services abroad, particularly for middle-sized banks that have entered international markets in recent years.

A systematic analysis of the potential benefits and disadvantages of increased tradability for developing and developed countries, respectively, reveals that the most important benefits lie in the improvement of the level and quality of services offered. For developing countries in particular, the main advantage accruing from tradability lies in the possibilities of a more extensive access to international credit and the improvement of the quality of banking services locally due to competitive pressures arising from a wider access to alternative suppliers of services.

Given the current trends in telematization and enhanced tradability of services in the banking industry, the potential for off-shore banking operations -- that is, firms in developing countries offering to undertake components of the production process for various banking services -- seems unlikely to expand. As mentioned earlier, the labour-intensive transactions associated with banking products tend to be reduced with increased tradability, while access to capital-intensive facilities plays an increasingly important role. Some labour-intensive routines that are related to the processing of paper-based accounts co-exist with telematized processing; although they are likely to be phased out gradually, the scale of such work processes will remain significant within the foreseeable future. A good example is the processing of credit-card claims, which continues to employ paper receipts for clearing simultaneously with EFTPoS-based transactions. Another example, relating to corporate banking, is the processing of letters of credit, which still functions on the basis of documents.

Nevertheless, such activities are in the process of being substituted by telematized routines, and out-sourcing of these activities does not seem likely to form a growth area in the future. The implication for developing countries generally is that the possibilities for offering cheap labour in relation to the remote processing of bank transactions will remain marginal. On the other hand, countries that emphasize the creation of a reliable and advanced information and telecommunications technology infrastructure will probably be able to expand their financial sectors gradually in a way that provides opportunities for offering off-shore processing facilities, at least within a regional framework. In other words, countries with reliable and advanced information and telecommunications technology infrastructure and with competitive assets in terms of highly skilled computer operators and system engineers may be able to exploit the opportunities that can arise for offering

various kinds of facilities management worldwide in the future.

This volume has confirmed that tradability exists for a range of banking products and the evidence suggests that tradability will also occur in a range of other information-related service industries. Statistical data based on the United States experience presented in chapter VI show that trade in services has indeed increased during the 1980s. Although a definite trend in the distribution of trade vs. FDI in United States exports of services could not be identified, it is evident that international transactions in services are growing rapidly.

However, the present volume has also indicated that both technical tradability and current trade of service products depend, to a large degree, on the nature of the production process and the final product. Regulatory barriers and cultural factors such as language and trust have also reduced the actual amount of trade taking place. In order to assess tradability and barriers to actual trade in other service industries such as accounting or computer software, it would therefore be necessary to rely on detailed investigations of products, structure of the industries involved and strategies for internationalization similar to those which have been carried out in the present study.

E. Policy implications

The policy implications arising from the foregoing analysis are complex. The technical potential for tradability associated with the majority of modern banking products has apparently not been exploited on account of factors that relate to economic, regulatory and cultural barriers over which Governments have little control. For instance, economic recession has reduced the scope for the expansion of banks, and has turned the attention of a large segment of the financial sector in developed countries towards strategies of survival. Accordingly, banks look for cost reductions in connection to back-office transactions. In this area, the telematization process has progressed very far, as a result of which many transactions are undertaken on the basis of access to networks and advanced mainframe computer facilities. In addition, banks appear to emphasize the marketing of new products in their home countries for rather long periods before venturing into international markets.

The opportunities for benefiting from tradability seem to fall into two categories, namely, the development of *enhanced local financial services* and the selective promotion of *regional financial centres*. Enhanced local financial services are likely to result from liberalization of the regulatory regime, which raises competition and encourages banks in developing countries to offer more and better services. This does not necessarily imply the total dismantling of regulation in the domestic banking industry, and there is likely to be a need to maintain what has been called a regulatory "separation fence" which shelters certain domestic financial activities from other, primarily international, transactions that are governed by less stringent regulations. The case of Singapore shows that the objective of attracting international financial services can be combined with the maintenance of prudential regulation at the domestic level. The improvement of local financial services appears significantly dependent on the expansion of the information and telecommunications technology infrastructure, and it becomes increasingly important to provide such infrastructure to the local services sector.

The product-by-product analysis has not, however, provided unambiguous indications of specific products or product categories that might be particularly suited to off-shore production in developing countries, that is, where there is a high level of divisibility and where developing countries have comparative advantages in relation to, e.g., labour inputs. Rather, the analysis suggests that the benefits that may be expected from increased tradability will become available to centres where the necessary information and telecommunciations technology infrastructure has been created, and where the labour force is qualified to maintain this infrastructure at high levels of reliability and security. Governments will thus have to consider several models in which to provide such infrastructure. One option, which is the model largely adopted by Singapore, is to raise the level of telecommunications facilities in the domestic economy generally, based on a strategy of creating an "intelligent island". The other option would be to establish limited zones within which the necessary information and telecommunications technology facilities and manpower resources are made available, and emphasize the growth of international or regional services.

F. Technical assistance options

Suggestions for technical assistance to developing countries that arise from the above analysis fall into three categories:

- Supplying easy-to-use software-systems and enhancing the awareness and preparedness of the domestic banking sector in developing countries *vis-à-vis* international banks.

- The formulation of new regulatory guidelines which permit local banks to take advantage of the opportunities offered by tradability, but retain a "separation fence" from international financial markets.

- Workshops involving interested banking representatives from developed countries and developing countries to identify the specific opportunities for off-shore activities related to specific bank products.

In connection with the first category, technical assistance should aim at providing systems with the qualities mentioned earlier in the discussion of the "suitcase bank", that is affordable, easy-to-use-systems, which at the same time allow a gradual, more advanced connection, with the international banking community. As an accompanying measure, it is important to raise the understanding of current trends among local policy-makers and, in particular, the managements of domestic banks. These actors should be made aware of the risks that exist in terms of allowing a growing gap between a few banks, primarily those with FDI that offer a wide range of tradable services on the one hand, and a stagnating domestically oriented formal and informal banking sector serving the majority of local customers with a limited range of services on the other.

In connection with the second category, the most important form of assistance would relate to streamlining national regulatory frameworks and harmonizing them with the emerging, liberalized international rules. The formulation and effective implementation of policies to promote regional cooperation that generates the necessary incentives for increases in productivity as well as the improvement and expansion of services, is also important. A facilitation of international transactions should go hand in hand with a better management of regulations that shield the domestic banking sector from fluctuations and crises in international markets without isolating it from the pressures of international competition.

In the third category, the most immediately rewarding aspect seems to be assistance to support workshops with participants from banks in developed and developing countries directly interested in the establishment of off-shore centres, export-oriented zones or export-oriented cooperation projects for transnational banking.

In the longer run, it is important to conduct studies that concretely identify the prerequisites in terms of information and telecommunications technology infrastructure and human resources that are needed in a particular country to exploit the emerging opportunities for off-shore facilities management. This is particularly important since the competition for such activities is likely to be very intense in the near future.

Annex 1

BANKING SERVICES AND THEIR TRADABILITY: A PRODUCT-WISE DESCRIPTION AND ANALYSIS

Contents

A.I. INTRODUCTION

A.I.1. The structure of the annex

This annex describes the nature of banking service products with the purpose of identifying possibilities for tradability of the products. These are divided into homogeneous groups, and the tradability and the divisibility of each product is examined.

An important question to consider before analyzing the products, is: What is a banking product? The question seems simple at first, but a precise definition is not easy to provide. There are two ways of answering the question: From the customer's and from the bank's point of view. A payment can be handled for example, as an electronic payment or as a paper-based payment. In both cases, the customer experiences the "same" service, but the two types of payments are different, and represent two different banking products, which fulfil the same function.

The definition of banking products in this annex is based on the bank's point of view, and the products will be categorized, whenever it is possible, on the basis of the technical performance and not of the demands they fulfil.

The annex is divided into two parts, dealing with retail and corporate products respectively. The reason for this division is that the behaviour of the respective users/consumers is quite different in many respects regarding the use of technology, the amounts traded, etc.

It is difficult to make an exact distinction between what is corporate and what is retail that has global validity. The most precise definition of *corporate* is perhaps *non-retail*. But the definitions of both retail (private) and corporate differ from country to country. These facts should not, however, influence the analysis or the conclusions, because the important point is the awareness of the difference in the need as well as in the demand in general.

The definition of *corporate* is slightly different from what is normally used in the economic literature. It should be noted that the term corporate throughout this annex covers both "interbanking" and "inter-company banking". Furthermore it is very important to note that the grouping of the products in some respects is disputable. This is primarily because the division of the products is based on a benchmark which is not unambiguous. This means that a product which is placed as a corporate product, in some situations, can be used by retail users and vice versa.

Each part of the discussion is further divided into sections dealing with the main groups of retail and corporate banking services (see table A1.1). A list of products is provided in table A1.2.

Products are further divided into negotiable and non-negotiable where relevant. Negotiability refers to the ability for trading a banking product between individuals. For example, a loan usually can not be traded between persons, while bonds (which are part of a loan) usually can be traded. Negotiability will, ceteris paribus, have a positive influence on tradability, first because there exists a price-setting procedure, and second because these kinds of products usually will consist of more working processes than the non-negotiable products (offering a greater scope for divisibility). For example, bonds are issued and then traded, while loans are issued without trading afterwards.

The descriptions are static, which means that potential future developments are left out of the present discussion. This is primarily because the gap between the products described here, and the products used in developing countries is very large, and discussing future development will not make much difference to the conclusions. Such a discussion would, however, be extremely relevant, as far as analysis of individual countries' situation is concerned.

A.I.2. Explanation of the tables

The tables in sections A.II and A.III of this annex are divided into eight columns. The contents of each column are explained below:

No.:
Each product is given a unique number, which is listed in the first column.

Product:
The name(s) of each product, which is (are) listed is (are) not necessarily the only name(s) -- the names in the tables must be seen as

examples among many different commercial names. The commercial names differ from country to country, bank to bank, etc.

Description:
There is a very short description of the functions of the product. The text in this column is concentrated on the basics of the products - e.g., what is the purpose of the product?

Tradability:
The technical aspect of tradability of each product is described with special reference to the possibility of isolating one or more parts of the process in producing the banking product and its/their tradability.

Divisibility:
The divisibility of the products is described by mapping the working process and breaking it up into smaller parts. A part of the process that is followed by another is indicated by an arrow. The routines which are carried out by using EDP are especially relevant, because the degree of divisibility is highly dependent on the technology used in the production of the products.

The columns headed "technology" and "endowments" do not contain text, but codes -- written as letters and numbers. The codes refer to the technology used in the production of the service, and the prerequisite conditions or general endowments of a country/area, in which the products are to be traded/used. The analysis focuses on technology and general endowments as follows:

Technology:
The required technology for using the product is described in terms of a code. The technology-code reflects the software and hardware required, as shown below.

Software

Hardware		1	2	3
	A			
	B			
	C			

The software availability aspect of technology is indicated by the following codes:

1: manual routines or "no" software used.

2: standard software.

3: special software.

The nature of the hardware (including some parts of the infrastructure) which is used for producing the product is indicated by the following letters:

A: non-EDP based hardware used (e.g., calculators).

B: personal-computer environment.

C: mainframe environment.

These codes only give an indication of the state-of-the-art technology which is used for producing a certain product or service. It may be possible to use other kinds of technology to produce a certain product. For example, there will be, ceteris paribus, more manual routines in producing a certain product or service in a developing country, than in producing the same type of product or service in a developed country.

The requirements with respect to general endowments are described by dividing them into three levels:

Table A1.1. A classification of the products examined

Type of service	Transactions-of-payments services	Liquidity management	Financing	Deposits

Retail
Negotiable
	Cheque (2)	Forward contract (5, 24)	Bills (6)
			Mortgage
			  deed (7, 27)
				Short deposit (11)
				Time deposit retail (12)
				Pension scheme
				  savings (13)

Non-negotiable	Cash dispensing/ handling (1) Payment card (3) Bank transfer (4)		Credit card (8) Consumer loan (9) Housing loan (10)	

Corporate
Negotiable
	Bank draft (14)	Options (22)
		Futures (23)
			Bills (26)
			Mortgage deed (7, 27)
				Current
				  account (35)
				Time deposit
				  corporate (36)
				Wholesale deposit (37)

Non-negotiable	SWIFT (15)
	Letter of credit (16)
	
	Reuter (17)
	Globex (18)
	
	Dealing 2000 (19)
	EDI (20)
	Direct debit (21)
		Forward
		  contract (5, 24)
		SWAP (25)
			Lending against security
			  to bills (28)
			Financial loan (29)
			Loan for equity (30)
			
			Leasing (31)
			Mortgage loan (32)
			Guarantee (33)
			Export credit (34)	

Note: Figures in parentheses refer to the number assigned to the products in the tables in sections A.II and A. III below; reflecting the order in which the products are discussed below.

E Endowments:
The endowment-code is indicated by the following codes:

I: poor standards (e.g., those in many developing countries).

II: endowments of a middle standard.

III: high standards (e.g., OECD-standards) of infrastructure and general endowments.

The rating is only meant to indicate broadly the level of the prerequisite socio-economic conditions that a country/area must fulfil to be able to use the different products. There will be many situations in which countries/areas with identical codes will have some conditions which differ. The consequence might be an ambiguous use of the codes, and it would be possible for instance for two similarly coded countries/areas to have different possibilities for using a product. In one country/area it can prove impossible to use a certain product, while it could be attractive in another country/area - despite the fact that the countries have the same code.

Table A1.2. List of products examined

Cash handling/dsipensing (1)
Cheque (2)
Payment card (3)
Bank transfer (4)
Forward contract (5, 24)
Bills (6, 26)
Mortgage deed (7, 27)
Credit card (8)
Consumer loan (9)
Housing loan (10)
Short deposit (11)
Time deposit (12, 36)
Pension scheme savings (13)
Bank draft (14)
SWIFT. (15)
Letter of credit (16)
Reuters (17)
Globex (18)
Dealing 2000 (19)
EDI (20)
Direct debit (21)
Options (22)
Futures (23)
SWAP (25)
Lending against security to bills (28)
Financial loan (29)
Loan for equity (30)
Leasing (31)
Mortgage loan (32)
Guarantee (33)
Export credit (34)
Current account (35)
Fixed term deposit(37)

Note: Figures in parentheses refer to the number assigned to the product in the tables in sections A.II and A.III below, reflecting the order in which the products are discussed.

The endowment-code is intended to help the reader obtain a realistic picture of the group of countries that will be able to use the banking products examined. The general endowments considered are typically measured as an aggregate of several variables, e.g., GDP per capita, rate of infant mortality, etc.

The last column lists the related products, if any. The references are given both by the names or abridgements of the names of the related products and by the numbers assigned to the related products in the discussion in this annex.

In addition to the above items indicated in the various columns of the tables that follow, each product is described with respect to diffusion and the possibilities for using the products through comments provided at the bottom of each table. The focus here is on the prospects for tradability of the products in/by countries with limited technical and infrastructure endowments. Thus, it is assumed that the developed countries are able to use all available banking products.

A.II. RETAIL BANKING PRODUCTS

A.II.1. Transactions-of-payments services

			Transactions-of-payments services - retail				
No.	Product	Description	Tradability	Divisibility	Technology	Endow-ments	Related products
1.	Cash handling/ dispensing	Banknotes and coins are usually issued exclusively by the central bank or the monetary authority. They are, however, handled/dispensed by commercial and other banks.	Cash dispensing is done at the counter. It is also done through self-service at ATMs, making the product tradable to some extent.	Notes and coins are dispensed at the counter (manual procedure in the bank). The tasks of establishing, maintaining and filling ATMs can be divided from the bank.	A1	I	Cheque (2) Payment cards (3)

Comments on diffusion and use of cash handling/dispensing (1)

Cash handling/dispensing at the counter can be done with the existing technology in developing countries. The possibility for redrawing cash from an ATM requires a higher level of technology, and for this reason ATMs can not be used with the existing technology in many developing countries

			Transactions-of-payments services - retail				
No.	Product	Description	Tradability	Divisibility	Technology	Endow-ments	Related products
2.	Cheque Check Draft	Cheques are claims which private persons and companies are able to issue to each other. Cheques are usually drawn on commercial banks which can be domestic as well as foreign banks. Cheques are usually cleared regularly between banks who have mutual claims. The credit rating of a cheque must never exceed that of the bank on which it is drawn.	Acceptance of cheques will usually depend on the knowledge of and/or confidence in the debtor, and the bank on which the cheque is drawn. This requires an exhaustive knowledge, which is usually obtained by credit rating and special local knowledge of the specific debtor. It is required to compare the signature on the cheque with the approved signature from the bank on which the cheque is drawn. Cheque clearing is usually done by telex, electronic clearing (EDP-network) or (very seldom) by mailing the cheque to the bank from which it is drawn. Tradability is very poor as regards issuing and redeeming, while bookkeeping and clearing offer good possibilities for tradability.	The cheque is issued by a bank (manual routine). ⇒ Debtor fills in the cheque (manual routine). ⇒ Creditor accepts the cheque as payment by controlling the creditworthiness (manual routine and use of databases). ⇒ The cheque is redeemed by creditor and written on the books 1) of the issuing bank or 2) of another bank (EDP-based bookkeeping). If 2, then the cheque is cleared and then written on the books afterwards (Use of electronic network or telex)	A3	II	Bank draft (14) Bills (28) Cash handling/ dispensing (1)

Description of diffusion and use of cheques (2)

Cheques, which are paper based, are primarily used for transaction purposes.

The possibilities for using cheques with use of the existing technology in developing countries are relatively good as far as issue and transfer of cheques is concerned. But rapid cheque clearing requires relatively solid technical endowments in modern banking. Taking both aspects into account, the possibilities for using cheques are reckoned to be good.

Transactions-of-payments services - retail							
No.	Product	Description	Tradability	Divisibility	Technology	Endow- ments	Related products
3.	Payment card	The only purpose of a payment card is payment, in contrast to a credit card. The payment card is a perfect substitute for a cheque: "The electronic cheque". It is possible to use the payment card for three purposes: • Cash money in the bank (the card issuing bank or another bank). • Cash money in automatic teller machines. • Pay for goods and services in shops.	Acceptance of payments by payment card will normally depend on the knowledge of and/or confidence in the bank on which the amount is drawn. This requires an exhaustive knowledge, which is usually obtained by credit rating and special knowledge of the specific debtor. The card-issuing bank needs to check information concerning the card: ex codes, validity, etc. Clearing of card payments is done by telex, electronic (EDP-network) or by sending the receipt. Tradability is relatively good, as the card issuing bank has not necessarily to be a "local" bank. Issuing and redeeming can be undertaken in one place, while bookkeeping and clearing can be executed in another location.	The card is issued, which requires knowledge about the prospective card holders' creditworthiness (manual routine and use of databases) ⇒ Card issuing (manual routine) ⇒ Payments or cash withdrawals (manual routine or electronic data transfer) ⇒ The withdrawal is redeemed by creditor and entered on the books 1) of the card issuing bank, or 2) of another bank (EDP-based bookkeeping) If 2) then the payment is cleared and entered on the books afterwards (Use of electronic network or telex)	B3	II	Credit card (8) Cheque (2)

Comments on diffusion and use of the payment card (3)

It is possible to use payment cards in both well-equipped and relatively poor countries (in terms of the technical endowments of the country). Electronic payments require a very well-developed infrastructure, whereas paper-based use of payment cards requires much less. Clearing the payment card transactions requires relatively solid technical endowments in modern banking.

The possibilities for using payment cards are considered to be relatively good. The wider use of payment cards depends, in principle, on the paper-based solution, although the electronic solution affects the efficiency.

			Transactions-of-payments services - retail				
No.	Product	Description	Tradability	Divisibility	Technology	Endow-ments	Related products
4.	Bank transfer Credit transfer	The bank transfer can transfer money and advice from debtor to creditor, domestic as well as international (see SWIFT (15)). A bank transfer can be executed from a computer work station by the debtor, or from the bank on behalf of the debtor.	Acceptance of a bank transfer will usually require knowledge of and/or confidence in the transferring bank. This requires an exhaustive knowledge, which usually is obtained by credit rating and special local knowledge of the specific bank. A bank transfer is an electronic transfer, which offers very good tradability possibilities.	Debtor orders a bank transfer by means of • telephone, telex or another non-EDP based communication (manual routine) ⇒ or, • via a computer work station (EDP based routine) ⇒ An amount of money and an advice is sent to another bank - the debtor's bank (EDP based routine)	2B	II	Payment cards (3) Cheques (2)

Description of diffusion and use of the bank transfer (4)

Bank transfers are carried out as electronic information between banks, and it is possible to use bank transfers only in technically well-endowed countries.

A.II.2. Liquidity management

No.	Product	Description	Tradability	Divisibility	Technology	Endow-ments	Related products
		Liquidity management - retail - negotiable					
5.	Forward contract	The forward contract is a contract which offers the buyer and the seller of foreign exchange or securities the opportunity for fixing the price or the exchange rate, thereby securing the value of an amount of foreign currency or the underlying asset.

A bank is usually the intermediate between seller and buyer, and the involved parties thereby have mutual claims on the bank and not on each other.

The buyer and seller do not have to buy or sell the assets until the day of execution. This means, ceteris paribus, less liquidity requirements. | The forward contract requires the acceptance of the person or the company which/who is going to be the counterpart in the contract. This requires an exhaustive knowledge, which usually is obtained by credit rating and special local knowledge of the person or the company.

After the contract is entered, the contract is stocked in the bank, and the contract is usually made up at the day of maturity.

Extension is, however, possible.

Tradability is good after the contract is entered. | Enquiry from the buyer or the seller (manual routine). ⇒

The enquiry is evaluated and the contract is entered (manual routine). ⇒

The contract is made up after eventual extensions (EDP-based routine). | C3 | III | Options (22)

Futures (22) |

Description of diffusion and use of the forward contract (5, 24)

A forward contract is a document which in principle is paper based, but obtaining the information in the forward contract usually requires a relatively high technological level. It is relatively uncomplicated to get the necessary information on request by telefax, telex etc.

A.II.3. Financing

Financing - retail - negotiable							
No.	Product	Description	Tradability	Divisibility	Technology	Endow-ments	Related products
6.	Bills	Bills are a common type of negotiable outstanding debts. Bills are primarily used for money lending, as far as retail banking is concerned. The bill is a negotiable loan, and has therefore two sides: The drawer is the creditor and the drawee the debtor. The debtor is required to pay the amount of the bill at the day of maturity to the owner of the bill. The bill is a loan type which makes it possible, in case of a default for the creditor to acquire the debtor's assets immediately without going to court. Discounting the bill in a bank or by a banker makes it possible for the drawer to redeem the amount of the bill before maturity. The drawer of the bill is hereby changed.	The drawer of a bill is usually a bank or a banker. The acceptance of bills will normally depend on the knowledge of and/or confidence in debtor. This requires an exhaustive knowledge, which usually is obtained by credit rating. It is possible for the drawee to get a guarantee from a bank or a banker for payment at the terms of the bill. The cost (price) of the bill is calculated and paid up front. The tradability possibilities are rather poor.	The creditworthiness of drawee is rated (manual routine). $\Rightarrow$ The bill is issued by the drawer (manual routine). $\Rightarrow$ Payment from the drawee at the maturity of the bill (manual routine).	B1	I-II	Consumer loan (9) Financial loan (29)

Comments on diffusion and use of bills (6, 26)

Bills are documents which in principle are paper based, but the information enclosed requires, in general, a high technological level. It is easy to get the required information on request by telefax, telex etc.

Trading transactions require relatively solid technical endowments in modern banking.

			Financing - retail - negotiable				
No.	Product	Description	Tradability	Divisibility	Technology	Endow-ments	Related products
7.	Mortgage deed	Mortgage deeds are issued as security for loans. The pledge of the deed is written on the document, but it is only executed in case of default of the loan. The mortgage deed is a negotiable security - the holder of the mortgage deed has the right to fulfil the terms of the deed in case of a default.	The mortgage deed places the control over an asset (or part of an asset) in case of default, in the hands of the owner of the mortgage deed. The mortgage deed is usually recorded according to the Land Registration Act of the country in question. The acceptance of deed as security for a loan will normally depend on the knowledge of and/or confidence in the debtor and in the estimated value of the asset in question. This requires an exhaustive knowledge of value and the tradability of the asset, which usually is obtained by valuing the asset and special local knowledge of the specific situation. It is possible for the owner of the deed to sell the deed in the market, and this offers the issuing party the possibility to buy it back. The mortgage deed is frequently guaranteed by a bank. The tradability is rather poor.	Enquiry from the owner of an asset to borrow an amount of money (manual routine). ⇒ To fulfil the enquiry it is required to issue a mortgage deed. The mortgage deed is issued, and (usually) recorded in a register to secure the pledge of the borrower (EDP-based routine).	A1	I	Housing loan (10) Guarantee (33)

Comments on diffusion and use of the morgage deed (7, 27)

Mortgage deeds are documents which are paper based. The information in a mortgage deed requires a relatively high technological level, but it is comparatively easy to get the required information on request by telefax, telex etc.

Trading transactions require relatively solid technical endowments in modern banking.

Financing - retail - non-negotiable							
No.	Product	Description	Tradability	Divisibility	Technology	Endow-ments	Related products
8.	Credit card	The purpose of a credit card is to allow both credit and payment, in contrast to a payment card which simply allows payment. The credit card is used for two purposes: • Cash money in automatic teller machines. • Pay for goods and service in shops.	Acceptance of payments by credit card will normally depend on the knowledge of and/or confidence in the bank on which the amount is drawn. This requires an exhaustive knowledge, which is usually obtained by credit rating and special knowledge of the specific debtor.	The card is issued, which requires knowledge about the coming card holders creditworthiness (manual routine and use of databases). ⇒ Card issuing (manual routine). ⇒ Payments or cash withdrawals (manual routine or electronic data transfer). ⇒	B 2	III	Payment card (3) Consumer loan (9)

Comments on diffusion and use of the credit card (8)

A credit card is a combination of a credit facility (like consumer loans) and a payment card.

Using credit cards as payment cards is possible in well equipped countries (EDP-based) as well as in areas with relatively poor technical endowments (paper based). But clearing the credit card transactions requires relatively solid technical endowments in modern banking.

Electronic payments require a very well developed infrastructure, whereas paper based use of credit cards requires much less.

The possibilities for using credit cards are reckoned to be relatively good, primarily because the use of a payment card in principle depends on the paper based solution.

Financing - retail - non-negotiable							
No.	Product	Description	Tradability	Divisibility	Technology	Endow-ments	Related products
9.	Consumer loan	A consumer loan involves lending to private individuals. It does not set limits for the borrowers' possibilities to set the avails.	Acceptance and the price (interest) of a loan will normally depend on the knowledge of and/or confidence in the customer/borrower. It requires an exhaustive knowledge of the borrower, which usually is obtained by credit rating. Tradability is rather poor as far as the valuing of the credit-worthiness is concerned, while the interest calculation, advice etc. offer bigger possibilities for tradability.	The creditworthiness of borrower is rated (manual routine). $\Rightarrow$ The loan document is issued of the bank (manual routine). $\Rightarrow$ The avails are paid (manual routine). $\Rightarrow$ The loan is amortized, and the terms for paying, interest calculation, advice etc. are set according to the loan document or the contract (EDP-based routine).	C3	I	Creditcards (8)

Comments on diffusion and use of the consumer loan (9)

Bank loans (including all kinds of loans) include two major working assignments, namely, rating of the creditworthiness, and accounting, calculations etc. during the period of amortization. The first is a purely manual routine, while the second involves (or can involve) the use of electronic devices.

The possibilities for using bank loans are however considered to be relatively good, first of all because the use of bank loans primarily depends on a paper-based solution, while the electronic solution is a matter of efficiency.

On the other hand, lending will often require a personal (face to face) contact between the banker and the customer. This requires a relatively close geographical location, which for example could imply many branches. Branches and personal contact can, however, to a certain extent be replaced by long distance contact through telephone, telefax etc.

			Financing - retail - non-negotiable				
No.	Product	Description	Tradability	Divisibility	Technology	Endow-ments	Related products
10.	Housing loan	Housing loans require the borrower to place the avails in real estate. The borrower will normally deposit a mortgage deed, as security for the loan.	Acceptance and the price (interest) of a loan will normally depend on the knowledge of and/or confidence in the customer/borrower. It requires an exhaustive knowledge of the borrower, which usually is obtained by credit rating. Tradability is rather poor as far as the valuing of the creditworthiness is concerned, while the interest calculation, advice etc. offer bigger possibilities for tradability.	The creditworthiness of borrower is rated (manual routine). $\Rightarrow$ The loan document is issued by the bank (manual routine). $\Rightarrow$ The avails are paid out by the bank (manual routine). $\Rightarrow$ The loan is amortized, and the terms for repaying, interest calculation, advice etc. is set according to the loan document or the contract (EDP-based routine).	C3	I	Consumer loan (9)

Comments on diffusion and use of the housing loan (10)

Bank loans (including all kinds of loans) include two major working assignments, namely, rating of the creditworthiness, and accounting, calculations etc. during the period of amortization. The first is a purely manual routine, while the second involves (or can involve) the use of electronic devices.

The possibilities for using bank loans are, however, reckoned to be relatively good, because the use of bank loans primarily depends on a paper-based solution, while the electronic solution is a matter of efficiency.

On the other hand, lending will often require a personal (face to face) contact between the banker and the customer. This requires a relatively close geographical location, which for example could imply many branches. Branches and personal contact can though to a certain extent be replaced by long distance contact such as telephone, telefax etc.

A.II.4. Deposits

			Deposits - retail				
No.	Product	Description	Tradability	Divisibility	Technology	Endow-ments	Related products
11.	Short deposit	A short deposit is a bank account which offers the depositor the right to withdraw the amount at very short (or no) terms of notice. The interest rate on short deposits are very low - in some countries/banks, short deposits are not interest-bearing at all.	Deposits require an acceptance of the price (interest), terms and the stability of the bank (the financial sector in the country). This will normally depend on the confidence in the monetary policy of the country (e.g., inflation risk). The tradability is rather poor due to the restrictions imposed by the Government, the creditworthiness of the bank and the stability of the financial system in general. But interest calculation, advice etc. offer larger possibilities for trade.	A bank account is opened (manual routine or EDP-based routine). $\Rightarrow$ An amount is deposited to the bank (manual routine). $\Rightarrow$ Interest is assigned to the account, advice is sent out etc. (EDP-based routine). $\Rightarrow$	B3	I-II	Time deposit (36)

Comments on diffusion and use of the short deposit (11)

All deposits include in principle one major working assignment which is accounting, calculations etc. This assignment involves (or can involve) use of electronic devices.

The possibilities for using deposits are reckoned to be relatively good, first of all because the use of bank deposits primarily depends on a paper-based solution, while the electronic solution is a matter of efficiency.

Deposits - retail							
No.	Product	Description	Tradability	Divisibility	Technology	Endow-ments	Related products
12.	Time deposit	Time deposits are bank accounts which limit the depositors' possibilities to withdraw the deposited amount in respect of time. The terms of notice will typically be 1-6 months. The interest rate on time deposits usually depends on the maturity of the deposit.	Deposits require an acceptance of the price (interest), terms and the stability of the bank (the financial sector in the country). This will normally depend on the confidence in the monetary policy of the country (e.g., inflation risk). Tradability is rather poor due to government restrictions, the creditworthiness of the bank and the stability of the financial system in general. But interest calculation, advice etc. offer greater possibilities for trade.	A bank account is opened (manual routine or EDP-based routine). ⇒ An amount is deposited at the bank (manual routine). ⇒ The deposit interest is calculated, advice is sent out etc. (EDP-based routine).	B3	I-II	Short deposit(11)

Comments on diffusion and use of the time deposit (12)

Deposits include in principle one major working assignment which is accounting, calculations etc. This assignment involves (or can involve) the use of electronic devices.

The possibilities for using deposits are reckoned to be relatively good, because the use of bank deposits primarily depends on a paper-based solution, while the electronic solution is a matter of efficiency.

Deposits - retail							
No.	Product	Description	Tradability	Divisibility	Technology	Endow-ments	Related products
13.	Pension scheme savings	Pension scheme savings are deposits or a portfolio of securities with the purpose of saving for pension. The terms of this type of savings will typically be 10-50 years. The risk aversion is typically very low, and an average interest which secures the real value of the savings is required - but not much more.	Deposits require an acceptance of the price (interest), terms and the stability of the bank (the financial sector in the country). This will normally depend on the confidence in the monetary policy of the country (e.g., inflation risk). The tradability prospects are rather poor due to restrictions imposed by the Government, the credit-worthiness of the bank and the stability of the financial system in general. But interest calculation, advice etc. offer greater scope for trade.	An account is opened (manual routine or EDP-based routine). ⇒ An amount is deposited at the bank, with the purpose of eventually buying securities (manual routine). ⇒ The deposit interest is calculated, advice is sent out etc. (EDP-based routine).	B3	II	

Comments on diffusion and use of pension scheme savings (13)

Pension scheme savings are, in principle, nothing but long-term deposits, which include one major working assignment, i.e. accounting, calculations etc. This assignment involves (or can involve) the use of electronic devices.

The possibilities for using deposits are, however, reckoned to be relatively good, because the use of bank deposits primarily depends on a paper-based solution, while the electronic solution is a matter of efficiency.

A.III. Corporate banking products

A.III.1. Transactions-of-payments services

		Transactions-of-payments services - corporate					
No.	Product	Description	Tradability	Divisibility	Technology	Endow-ments	Related products
14.	Bank draft	Bank drafts are claims which private persons and companies are able to buy and use as payments. Bank drafts are issued by commercial banks which can be domestic as well as foreign banks. Bank drafts are usually cleared regularly between banks that have mutual claims. • The credit rating of a bank draft must never exceed that of the bank which has issued the draft.	Acceptance of bank drafts will usually depend on the knowledge of and/or confidence in the bank which has issued the draft. This requires an exhaustive knowledge of the bank in question, which usually is obtained by credit rating and special local knowledge of the specific bank. Clearing is usually done by telex, electronic clearing (EDP-network) or (very seldom) by mailing rescripts.	The bank draft is issued (manual routine). ⇒ Creditor accepts the bank draft as payment by controlling the creditworthiness (manual routine and use of databases). ⇒ The tradability is good. The draft is redeemed by creditor and written on the books 1) of the issuing bank or 2) of another bank (EDP-based bookkeeping).	A1	I	Cheque (2) Bank transfer (4)

Comments on diffusion and use of the bank draft (14)

Bank drafts are paper-based banking products, primarily used for transaction purposes.

To issue and transfer bank drafts requires limited endowments, but their clearing, on the contrary requires relatively solid technical endowments in modern banking.

Transactions-of-payments services - corporate							
No.	Product	Description	Tradability	Divisibility	Technology	Endow- ments	Related products
15.	SWIFT	The Society for Worldwide Interbank Financial Telecommunication (SWIFT) is the oldest and biggest of the international financial networks. It links more than 3,000 institutions in 72 countries including all of the world's major financial centres. It has two principal functions: processing of messages and transmission. These functions allow banks to automate their data transmission procedures and eliminate problems of language and interpretation.	SWIFT must be regarded as primarily a service which makes it possible for other banking products to become internationally tradable.	A customer enquires at the bank for making a message or a payment to a business partner/private person in another country (manual routine). ⇒ The bank sends a message through the SWIFT network (EDP-based routine). ⇒ The receiver replies or confirms the message through the SWIFT network (EDP-based routine).	C3	I-II	Bank transfer (4) EDI (20)

Comments on diffusion and use of SWIFT (15)

SWIFT provides electronic transfer of information between banks, domestic as well as international. Consequently, the requirements as to the technical endowments needs are relatively high.

			Transactions-of-payments services - corporate				
No.	Product	Description	Tradability	Divisibility	Technology	Endow-ments	Related products
16.	Letter of credit (L/C) Documentary credit (D/C)	A letter of credit is a guarantee from a bank to benefit a third party, when certain documents are presented at the bank. The documents in question are specified in the contract. The letter of credit is: 1. A payment service: It links seller and buyer. 2. A credit service: The payment is handled before the goods are exchanged. 3. A guarantee service: The bank guarantees the payment. A letter of credit serves two purposes: import and export. The first guarantees the buyer while the second guarantees the seller. An import letter of credit will become an export letter of credit, just seen from the buyer's point of view. The bank (not the seller) bears the credit risk, if the buyers' payment is defaulted.	Acceptance and the price of a L/C will normally depend on the knowledge of and/or confidence in the third party and his bank (when exporting). It requires an exhaustive knowledge of the bank, which usually is obtained by credit rating. The tradability is rather good as far as the valuing of the creditworthiness is concerned, and the interest calculation, advice etc. offer even bigger possibilities for tradability.	EXPORT: An exporter wants to secure the payments for his goods, and enquires at the bank (manual routine). ⇒ Buyer's bank writes a L/C and sends it to the bank of the seller (manual routine). ⇒ Buyer's bank sends the documents to seller's bank (manual routine). ⇒ The seller get the L/C from his bank (manual routine). ⇒ Sellers sends the goods and hands over the bill of lading to his bank (manual routine).⇒ Seller is benefited by his bank (EDP-based routine).⇒ Buyer sends an amount to sellers bank (EDP-based routine).⇒ The L/C is closed.	A1	I-II	Guarantee (33)

Comments on diffusion and use of the letter of credit (16)

A letter of credit is a document which is paper based, but the information in the letter of credit requires a relatively high technology. However, it is relatively easy to get the needed information on request by telefax, telex etc.

		Transactions-of-payments services - corporate					
No.	Product	Description	Tradability	Divisibility	Technology	Endow-ments	Related products
17.	Reuters	Reuters is one of the most important providers of financial networks. Although, Reuters is much more than a network provider, the network is an indispensable part of its services. It has been estimated that approximately 30 per cent of the world market transactions in foreign exchange is traded via Reuters.	Reuters must be regarded as primarily a service which makes it possible for other banking products to become internationally tradeable.	A customer enquires at the bank for making a message or a getting information to be able to trade with a business partner in another country (manual routine).⇒ The bank sends a message through or gets information from the Reuters network (EDP-based routine).⇒ The exchange of information will be used for trading (manual routine).	C3	I-II	SWIFT (15) L/C

Comments on diffusion and use of Reuters (17)

Reuters supplies banks and other financial institutions with electronic information. This requires a high level of technology.

			Transactions-of-payments services - corporate				
No.	Product	Description	Tradability	Divisibility	Technology	Endow-ments	Related products
18.	Globex	Globex is a service which is seen as the world's biggest marketplace for futures and options. It has been launched in cooperation by the Chicago Board of Trade, Chicago Mercantile Exchange, the New York Mercantile Exchange, MATIF in Paris and Sydney Futures. World trade in futures and options will be included in the central computer with the same priorities and rights.	Globex must be regarded as primarily a service which makes it possible for other banking products to become internationally tradable.	A customer enquires at the bank for making a message or a getting information to be able to trade with a business partner in another country (manual routine).⇒ The bank sends a message through or gets information from the Globex network (EDP-based routine).⇒ The exchange of information will be used for trading (manual routine).	C3	I-II	SWIFT (15)

Comments on diffusion and use of Globex (18)

Globex supplies banks and other financial institutions with electronic information. This requires a high level of technology.

Transactions-of-payments services - corporate							
No.	Product	Description	Tradability	Divisibility	Technology	Endow-ments	Related products
19.	Dealing 2000	An automated trading system under introduction for foreign exchange dealers. This service will show the dealers an updated screen with the best available rates for any of foreign exchange.	Dealing 2000 must be regarded as primarily a service which makes it possible for other banking products to become internationally tradeable.	A customer enquires at the bank for making a message or a getting information to be able to trade with a business partner in another country (manual routine). $\Rightarrow$ The bank sends a message through or get information from the Dealing 2000 network (EDP-based routine). $\Rightarrow$ The exchange of information will be used for trading (manual routine).	C3	I-II	SWIFT (15)

Comments on diffusion and use of Dealing 2000 (19)

Dealing 2000 supplies banks and other financial institutions with electronic information. This requires a high level of technology.

No.	Product	Description	Tradability	Divisibility	Technology	Endow-ments	Related products
		Transactions-of-payments services - corporate					
20.	Payments according to electronic data inter-change (EDI)	EDI is trade information where all paper is substituted with electronic data flows. In basic manuals and training materials for modern banking payment transactions and credit intermediation constitute the fundamental services. Electronic data interchange is a new type of payment service delivered by banks. Technology constitutes the means by which the banks may deliver tradable services via public or dedicated networks. It must be noted that the payment is the only "banking" product which is connected to EDI. All other information such as invoice, orders etc. are trade documents.	Acceptance of a bank transfer will usually require knowledge of and/or confidence in the transferring bank. This requires an exhaustive knowledge, which usually is obtained by credit rating and special local knowledge of the specific bank. A bank transfer is an electronic transfer, which offers very good possibilities for trade.	A debtor orders a bank transfer by • telephone, telex or another non-EDP-based communication (manual routine) ⇒ or, • via a computer work station (EDP based routine). ⇒ An amount of money and an advice are sent to another bank - the debtor's bank (EDP based routine).	C3	III	Bank transfer (4)

Comments on diffusion and use of EDI (20)

The non-bank service (or part) of EDI, as well as the part which involves banks (the payments), is based on very sophisticated electronic equipment, and requires a high level of technology.

			Transactions-of-payments services - corporate				
No.	Product	Description	Tradability	Divisibility	Technology	Endow-ments	Related products
21.	Direct debit	Direct debit is the transfer of money, by order of creditor, from a debtor's bank account to a creditor's bank account. Direct debit can be domestic as well as international (note SWIFT). Direct debit can be executed from a computer work station by the debtor, or from the bank on behalf of the debtor.	Acceptance of direct debit will usually require very good relations between buyer and seller, and knowledge of and/or confidence in the transferring bank. This requires an exhaustive knowledge, which usually is obtained by credit rating and special local knowledge of the specific bank. Direct debit is an electronic transfer, which offers very good possibilities for trade.	The creditor orders a direct debit (bank transfer) by means of • telephone, telex or another non-EDP based communication (manual routine). ⇒ or, • via a computer work station (EDP based routine). ⇒ An amount is drawn on the debtor's account and an advice is sent to the debtor (EDP based routine).	C3	III	Bank transfer (4)

Comments on diffusion and use of direct debit (21)

Direct debits are automatic transfers of money from debtors' bank to creditors' bank. Direct debit is more or less equivalent to bank transfers, which are electronic transfers of information between banks. It only possible to use direct debit in technically well-equipped countries.

A.III.2. Liquidity management

No.	Product	Description	Tradability	Divisibility	Technology	Endow-ments	Related products
		Liquidity management - corporate - negotiable					
22.	Options	An option is a contract between two parties - the issuing party and the buying party. The option offers the holder the right, but not the obligation, to buy (call) or sell (put) an asset at a given time, to a given price and in a given quantity. The buying party pays a premium for the option. It is possible to buy options with different underlying assets, e.g., securities, raw material or currency An option can be traded.	Options are negotiable securities which require a market. It is necessary to have a guarantee for the creditworthiness of the issuing party. The tradability is good as far as the market is concerned. But in respect to the credit rating the tradability is limited.	The creditworthiness of issuing party is rated (manual routine). $\Rightarrow$ The option is issued (manual routine). $\Rightarrow$ The option is sold/bought (manual routine). $\Rightarrow$ If the buying party uses the option the difference between the current price and the price according to the option is paid out.	C3	III	Forward contract (5, 24) Futures (23)

Comments on diffusion and use of options (22)

Options are documents which in principle are paper-based, but the information enclosed requires, in general, a high technology level. It is easy to get the necessary information on request by telefax, telex etc.

Trading transactions in options require relatively solid technical endowments in modern banking.

			Liquidity management - corporate - negotiable				
No.	Product	Description	Tradability	Divisibility	Technology	Endow-ments	Related products
23.	Futures	A futures contract is similar to a forward contract except that changes in the contract price are settled daily. It is a standard contract between two parties --the issuing party and the buying party. The future offers the holder the obligation, to buy or sell an assets at a given time, to a given price and in a given quantity. It is possible to buy or sell futures with many different underlying assets, e.g., securities, raw material or currency. Futures are standard negotiable forward contracts.	Futures are negotiable securities which require a market. It is necessary to know the creditworthiness of the issuing as well as the buying party. The issuing party is usually a clearing houses. Tradability is good as far as the market is concerned. But in respect to the credit rating the tradability is limited.	The creditworthiness of the issuing party is rated (manual routine). ⇒ The futures are issued (manual routine). ⇒ The futures are sold/bought (manual routine). ⇒ At maturity the buying party pays out the difference between the current price and the price according to the futures.	C3	III	Forward contract (5, 24) Futures (23)

Comments on diffusion and use of futures (23)

Futures are documents which in principle are paper-based, but the information enclosed requires, in general, a high level of technology. It is easy to get the necessary information on request by telefax, telex etc.

Trading transactions require relatively solid technical endowments in modern banking.

			Liquidity management - corporate - non-negotiable				
No.	Product	Description	Tradability	Divisibility	Technology	Endow-ments	Related products
24.	Forward contract	The forward contract is a contract which offers the buyer and the seller of foreign exchange or securities the possibility for fixing the price or the exchange rate, and thereby securing the value of an amount of foreign currency or a number of securities. A bank is usually the intermediary between seller and buyer, and the involved parties have hereby mutually claims on the bank and not on each other. The buyer and seller do not have to buy or sell the assets until the day of execution. This means, ceteris paribus, less liquidity requirements at a given time.	The forward contract requires the acceptance of the person or the company which/who is going to be the counterpart in the contract. This requires an exhaustive knowledge, which usually is obtained by credit rating and special local knowledge of the person or the company. After the contract is entered, the contract is stored in the bank, and the contract is usually completed at the day of maturity. Extension is however possible. The tradability is good after the contract is entered.	Enquiry from the buyer or the seller (manual routine). $\Rightarrow$ The enquiry is evaluated and the contract is entered (manual routine). $\Rightarrow$ The contract is fulfilled eventually after extensions (EDP-based routine). $\Rightarrow$	C3	III	Option (22) Futures (23)

Comments on diffusion and use of the forward contract (5, 24)

A forward contract is a document which in principle is paper-based, but the information in the forward contract usually requires a relatively high level of technology. But it is relatively easy to get the necessary information on request by telefax, telex, etc.

		Liquidity management - corporate - non-negotiable					
No.	Product	Description	Tradability	Divisibility	Technology	Endow-ments	Related products
25.	SWAP	In a SWAP, one class of securities is exchanged for another in a deal that involves no cash. The most important feature is that with exchange offers there is no simultaneous change in the asset structure of the firm. A SWAP is a banking product or banking transaction, which is used for hedging/taking interest or currency risks. There are two kinds of SWAPS: • Interest SWAP • Currency SWAP A SWAP contract is similar to two or more mutual forward contracts, except that the SWAP contract is settled once and for all. It is not a standard contract between two parties.	A SWAP is a contract which leaves no possibilities for trade.	The creditworthiness of the two parties are mutually rated (manual routine). ⇒ The SWAP is issued (manual routine). ⇒ The SWAP is rolled over according to the contract which can cause a cash flow, and at maturity one of the two parts pays out the difference between the current price and the price according to the contract (EDP-based routine).	B2	III	Forward contract (5, 24)

Comments on diffusion and use of the SWAP (25)

A SWAP contract is, in principle, a series of forward contracts, which are paper-based. Although the information in the SWAP contract requires well-developed technological endowments, it should be noted that it is relatively uncomplicated to get the necessary information on request by telefax, telex etc.

III.3. Financing

			Financing - corporate - negotiable				
No.	Product	Description	Tradability	Divisibility	Technology	Endow-ments	Related products
26.	Bills	Bills are a common type of negotiable outstanding debts. Bills are primarily used for money lending and payments, as far as corporate banking is concerned. The bill is a negotiable loan, and has therefore two sides: The drawer is the creditor and the drawee the debtor. The debtor is required to pay the amount of the bill at the day of maturity to the owner of the bill. The bill is a loan type which makes it possible, in case of a default, for the creditor to distrain upon the debtor's asset, immediately, without going to court. Discounting the bill in a bank or by a banker makes it possible for the drawer to redeem the amount of the bill before maturity. The drawer of the bill is thereby changed.	The drawer of a bill is usually a bank or a banker, but bills are regularly used as payment/credit with creditor as drawer. The acceptance of bills will normally depend on the knowledge of and/or confidence in debtor. This requires an exhaustive knowledge, which usually is obtained by credit rating and special - local - knowledge of the specific debtor. It is possible for the drawee to get a guarantee from a bank or a banker for payment at the terms of the bill. The cost (price) of the bill is calculated and paid up front. The tradability is rather poor.	The creditworthiness of drawee is rated (manual routine). ⇒ The bill is issued of the drawer (manual routine). ⇒ Payment from the drawee at the maturity of the bill (manual routine). ⇒	B1	I-II	Consumer loan (9) Financial loan (29)

Comments on diffusion and use of bills (6, 26)

Bills are documents which in principle are paper-based, but the information enclosed requires, in general, a high technological level. It is easy to get the required information on request by telefax, telex etc.

Trading transactions require relatively solid technical endowments in modern banking.

Financing - corporate - negotiable							
No.	Product	Description	Tradability	Divisibility	Technology	Endow-ments	Related products
27.	Mortgage bond Mortgage deed	Mortgage deeds are issued as security for loans. The pledge of the deed is written on the document, but it is only executed in case of default of the loan. The mortgage deed is a negotiable security -- the holder of the mortgage deed has the right to fulfil the terms of the deed in case of a default.	The mortgage deed places the control over an asset (or part of an asset) in case of default, in the hands of the owner of the mortgage deed. The mortgage deed is usually recorded according to the Land Registration Act of the country. The acceptance of a deed as security for a loan will normally depend on the knowledge of and/or confidence in debtor and in the estimated value of the asset in question. This requires an exhaustive knowledge of the value and the tradability of the asset, which usually is obtained by valuing the asset and special local knowledge of the specific situation. It is possible for the owner of the deed to sell the deed in the market, and this offers the issuing party the possibility to buy it back. The mortgage deed is frequently guaranteed by a bank or banker.	Enquiry from the owner of an asset to borrow an amount of money (manual routine). ⇒ To fulfil the enquiry, it is required to issue a mortgage deed. The mortgage deed is issued, and (usually) recorded in a register to secure the pledge of the borrower (EDP-based routine).	A1	I	Housing loan (10) Guarantee (33)

Comments on diffusion and use of the mortgage deed (7, 27)

Mortgage deeds are documents which are paper-based. Although the information in a mortgage deed requires a relatively high technological level, it is comparatively simple to get the required information on request by telefax, telex etc.

Trading transactions require relatively solid technical endowments in modern banking.

			Financing - corporate - non-negotiable				
No.	Product	Description	Tradability	Divisibility	Technology	Endowments	Related products
28.	Money lending against security to bills Bill discounting	Lending against security to bills fulfil companies' requirements for liquidating the capital which is not available as bills. It includes: • Credit against bills deposited in the bank (lending against security to at portfolio of bills). • Discounting of single bills.	Lending against security to bills requires an exhaustive knowledge of the accounts receivable (of the trade debtors). This is usually obtained by credit rating, which is a very important part of this kind of banking service. Depositing of the bills will actually be done by handing over the physical document to the bank. The tradability of this banking product is rather small.	The bill is issued (manual routine). $\Rightarrow$ The bill is given to the bank (manual routine). $\Rightarrow$ Credit rating in the bank (manual work). $\Rightarrow$ The size of the loan is calculated on the basis of the credit rating (manual routine and use of data-bases). $\Rightarrow$ The loan is issued (data processing).	B2	II-III	Financial loan (29)

Comments on diffusion and use of lending against security to bills (28)

Bank loans (including all kinds of loans) include two major working assignments: rating of the creditworthiness of the borrower, and accounting, calculations etc. during the period of amortization. The first is a purely manual routine, while the second involves (or can involve) the use of electronic devices.

The possibilities for using banking loans are however reckoned to be relatively good, because the use of bank loans primarily depends on paper-based procedures, while the use of electronic procedures is a matter of efficiency.

On the other hand, lending will often require a personal (face-to-face) contact between the banker and the customer. This requires a relatively close geographical location, which for example could imply many branches. Branches and personal contact can though, to a certain extent be replaced by long distance contact through telephone, telefax etc.

			Financing - corporate - non-negotiable				
No.	Product	Description	Tradability	Divisibility	Technology	Endow-ments	Related products
29.	Financial loan	Financial loans are usually money lending with security to a portfolio of securities.	Acceptance and the price (interest) of a loan will normally depend on the risk associated with the security portfolio, and knowledge of and/or confidence in the customer/borrower. It requires exhaustive knowledge of the borrower. The tradability is rather poor as far as the valuing of the creditworthiness is concerned, while the interest calculation, advice etc. offers larger trade prospects.	The creditworthiness of the borrower is rated (manual routine). ⇒ The loan document is issued by the bank (manual routine). ⇒ The securities are bought and deposited in the bank (manual routine or EDP-based routine). ⇒ The loan is amortized, and the terms for repaying, interest calculation, advice etc. are set according to the loan document or the contract (EDP-based routine).	C2	III	Money lending against security bills (28)

Comments on diffusion and use of the financial loan (29)

Bank loans (including all kinds of loans) include two major working assignments: rating of the creditworthiness, and accounting, calculations etc. during the period to amortization. The first is a purely manual routine, while the second involves (or can involve) the use of electronic devices.

The possibilities for using bank loans are however, reckoned to be relatively good, because the use of bank loans primarily depends on paper-based procedures, while the use of electronic procedures is a matter of efficiency.

On the other hand, lending will often require a personal (face-to-face) contact between the banker and the customer. This requires a relative closely geographical location, which for example could imply many branches. Branches and personal contact can, to a certain extent, be replaced by long distance contact through telephone, telefax etc.

Financing - corporate - non-negotiable							
No.	Product	Description	Tradability	Divisibility	Technology	Endow-ments	Related products
30.	Loan for procure-ment of equity	A loan for procurement of equity can be guaranteed by a non-governmental organization, joint ventures or regular bank loans. Foreign aid programmers use these kinds of loans usually for projects in developing countries. As far as the developed part of the world is concerned the terms will be similar to other kinds of loans.	Acceptance and the price (interest) of a loan will normally depend on the knowledge of and/or confidence in the company or the projects. It requires an exhaustive knowledge of the company or the project. The tradability is rather poor as far as the valuing of the creditworthiness is concerned, while the interest calculation, advice etc. offer bigger possibilities for trade.	The creditworthiness of borrower is rated (manual routine). $\Rightarrow$ The loan document is issued by the bank (manual routine). $\Rightarrow$ The avails are paid out by the bank (manual routine). $\Rightarrow$ The loan is amortized, and the terms for repaying, interest calculation, advice etc. are set according to the loan document or the contract (EDP-based routine). $\Rightarrow$	B2	I-III	Financial loan (29) Mortgage loan (32)

Comments on diffusion and use of the loan for equity (30)

Bank loans (including all kinds of loans) include two major working assignments: rating of the creditworthiness, and accounting, calculations etc. during the period of amortization. The first is a purely manual routine, while the second involves (or can involve) the use of electronic devices.

The possibilities for using bank loans are however, reckoned to be relatively good, because the use of bank loans primarily depends on paper-based procedure, while the use of electronic procedures is a matter of efficiency.

On the other hand, lending will often require a personal (face-to-face) contact between the banker and the customer. This requires a relatively close geographical location, which for example could imply many branches. Branches and personal contact can, however, to a certain extent be replaced by long distance contact through telephone, telefax etc.

No.	Product	Description	Tradability	Divisibility	Technology	Endow-ments	Related products
			Financing - corporate - non-negotiable				
31.	Leasing	Leasing agreements or leasing contracts offer companies alternatives to buying assets such as • Operating equipment • Production facilities Leasing agreements are special ways to finance assets, which make it possible for companies to use equipment or plants on rental provisions. Leasing exists in two different forms: 1) Leasing agreements which are confined to financial involvement between the leasing company and the commercial company. The leasing company does not anticipate operating the assets (maintenance etc.). 2) Leasing agreements where the leasing company participates in operating the asset.	Leasing agreements which are confined to financial involvement are in many respects similar to loans. The tradability is very limited. There is no tradability for leasing agreements which involve operating the asset. It should be noted, also, that this leasing form is not a "pure" banking product.	The creditworthiness of company is rated (manual routine). ⇒ A leasing contract is issued (manual routine). ⇒ Payment due to the leasing contract (manual routine).	B2	III	Loan for equity (30) Financial loan (29)

Comments on diffusion and use of leasing (31)

Leasing is equivalent to bank loans with security in assets. There are two major working assignments: rating of the creditworthiness, and accounting, calculations etc. during the period of amortization. The first is a purely manual routine, while the second involves (or can involve) the use of electronic devices.

The possibilities for using bank loans are however, reckoned to be relatively good, first of all because the use of banking loans primarily depends on paper-based procedure, while the use of electronic procedures is a matter of efficiency.

On the other hand, lending will often require a personal (face-to-face) contact between the banker and the customer. This requires a relatively close geographical location, which for example could imply many branches. Branches and personal contact can, to a certain extent be replaced by "long distance" contacts through telephone, telefax etc.

			Financing - corporate - non-negotiable				
No.	Product	Description	Tradability	Divisibility	Technology	Endow-ments	Related products
32.	Building loan Real estate financing Intermediate loan Mortgage loan	A mortgage loan is money lending with security to real estate, and it is given for two purposes: • Building new real estate. • Rebuilding existing real estate.	Acceptance and the price (interest) of a loan will normally depend on the knowledge of and/or confidence in the customer/borrower. It requires an exhaustive knowledge of the borrower. The tradability is rather poor as far as the valuing of the creditworthiness is concerned, while the interest calculation, advice etc. offer greater possibilities for trade.	The creditworthiness of borrower is rated (manual routine). ⇒ The loan document is issued by the bank (manual routine). ⇒ The avails are paid out by the bank (manual routine). ⇒ The loan is amortized, and the terms of repayment, interest calculation, advice etc. are set according to the loan document or the contract (EDP-based routine).	A1	I	Housing loan (10) Financial loan (29)

Comments on diffusion and use of the mortgage loan (32)

Banking loans (including all kinds of loans) include two major working assignments: rating of the creditworthiness, and accounting, calculations etc. during the period of amortization. The first is a purely manual routine, while the second involves (or can involve) the use of electronic devices.

The possibilities for using bank loans are however, reckoned to be relatively good, because the use of bank loans primarily depends on paper-based procedures, while the use of electronic procedures are a matter of efficiency.

On the other hand, lending will often require a personal (face-to-face) contact between the banker and the customer. This requires a relative close geographical location, which for example could imply many branches. Branches and personal contact can, though, to a certain extent be replaced by long distance contact through telephone, telefax etc.

No.	Product	Description	Tradability	Divisibility	Technology	Endow-ments	Related products
		Financing - corporate - non-negotiable					
33.	Guaran-tees	Guarantees are contracts which serve as securities for loans. The creditor of a loan is hereby guaranteed that the required amount is paid out due to the contract. The guarantor of a loan is, in case of a default, required to fulfil debtors requirements. A guarantee can cover the entire loan or part of a loan.	Acceptance and the price of a guarantee will normally depend on the knowledge of and/or confidence in the customer/ borrower. It requires an exhaustive knowledge of the borrower. The tradability is rather good, though valuing of the credit-worthiness causes limitations.	The creditworthiness of borrower is rated (manual routine). $\Rightarrow$ The guarantee is of the bank (manual routine). $\Rightarrow$ The loan will be repaid by guarantor, but **only** in case of default (manual routine).	A1	I	Mortgage deed (7, 27)

Comments on diffusion and use of the guarantee (33)

Guarantees involve, in principle, two major working assignments: rating of the creditworthiness, and issuing a document.

			Financing - corporate - non-negotiable				
No.	Product	Description	Tradability	Divisibility	Technology	Endow-ments	Related products
34.	Export credit loan	Credit with security in export orders	Acceptance and the price (interest) of a loan will normally depend on the knowledge of and/or confidence in the customer. It requires an exhaustive knowledge of the borrower. The tradability is rather poor as far as the valuing of the creditworthiness is concerned, while the interest calculation etc. offer bigger possibilities for trade.	The creditworthiness of borrower is rated (manual routine). $\Rightarrow$ The loan document is issued of the bank (manual routine). $\Rightarrow$ The avails are paid out by the bank (manual routine). $\Rightarrow$ The loan is amortized, and the terms for repayment, interest calculation, advice etc. are set according to the loan document or the contract (EDP-based routine).	B2	II-III	L/C (16)

Comments on diffusion and use of the export credit (34)

Bank loans (including all kinds of loans) include two major working assignments: rating of the creditworthiness, and accounting, calculations etc. during the period of amortization. The first is a purely manual routine, while the second involves (or can involve) the use of electronic devices.

The possibilities for using bank loans are, however, reckoned to be relatively good, because the use of banking loans primarily depends on paper-based solution procedure, while the electronic procedure is a matter of efficiency.

On the other hand, lending will often require a personal (face-to-face) contact between the banker and the customer. This requires a relatively close geographical location, which for example could imply many branches. Branches and personal contact can, however, to a certain extent be replaced by long distance contact through telephone, telefax etc.

A.III.4. Deposits

			Deposits - corporate				
No.	**Product**	**Description**	**Tradability**	**Divisibility**	**Technology**	**Endow-ments**	**Related products**
35.	Current account Checking account	Current accounts are bank accounts which do not limit the depositors possibilities to withdraw the deposited amount in respect to time. The current account is typically used for day-to-day business transactions. The interest rate on current accounts will usually be very low or even zero, depending on the monetary policy of the specific countries. But the market interest, the market power (negotiation between the bank and the company) and maturity of the deposit is decisive for the interest.	Deposits require an acceptance of the price (interest), terms and the stability of the bank (the financial sector in the country). This will normally depend on the confidence in the monetary policy of the country (e.g., inflation risk). The tradability is rather poor due to the restrictions imposed by the government, the creditworthiness of the bank and the stability of the financial system in general. But interest calculation, advice etc. offer greater possibilities for trade.	A bank account is opened (manual routine or EDP-based routine). ⇒ An amount is deposited to the bank (manual routine). ⇒ The deposit interest is calculated, advice is sent out etc. (EDP-based routine).	B3	I-II	Short deposit (11) Time deposit (36)

Comments on diffusion and use of the current account (35)

Deposits involve, in principle, one major working assignment which is accounting, calculations etc. This assignment involves (or can involve) use of electronic devises.

The possibilities for using deposits are, however, reckoned to be relatively good, because the use of deposits primarily depends on paper-based procedures, while the use of electronic procedure is a matter of efficiency.

			Deposits - corporate				
No.	Product	Description	Tradability	Divisibility	Technology	Endow-ments	Related products
36.	Time deposit	Time deposits are bank accounts which limit the depositors' possibilities to withdraw the deposited amount in respect to time. The terms of notice will typically be 1-6 months. The interest rate on time deposits will usually depend on the market interest, the market power (negotiation between the bank and the company) and maturity of the deposit. Time deposit can, in most countries, be placed abroad and/or in foreign currency.	Deposits requires an acceptance of the price (interest), terms and the stability of the bank (the financial sector in the country). This will normally depend on the confidence in the monetary policy of the country (e.g., inflation risk). The tradability is rather poor due to the restrictions imposed by the government, the creditworthiness of the bank and the stability of the financial system in general. But interest calculation, advice etc. offer greater prospects for trade.	A bank account is opened (manual routine or EDP-based routine). $\Rightarrow$ An amount is deposited to the bank (manual routine). The deposit interest is calculated, advice is sent out etc. (EDP-based routine).	B3	I-II	Short deposit (11)

Comments on diffusion and use of the time deposit (36)

Deposits involve in principle one major working assignment, which is accounting, calculations etc. This assignment involves (or can involve) the use of electronic devices.

The possibilities for using deposits are, however, reckoned to be relatively good, because the use of deposits primarily depends on paper-based procedures, while the use of electronic procedure is a matter of efficiency.

Deposits - corporate							
No.	Product	Description	Tradability	Divisibility	Technology	Endow-ments	Related products
37.	Fixed term deposit Wholesale deposit	Wholesale deposits are deposits which are fixed in respect to time. The terms of notice will typically be 1-6 months. The interest rate on wholesale deposits will usually depend on the market interest. Wholesale deposits are usually very big amounts and in most countries deposits could be in foreign currency.	Wholesale deposits require stability of the bank and the financial sector in the country. This will normally depend on the confidence in the monetary policy of the country (e.g. inflation risk). The tradability is rather good.	A bank account is opened (manual routine or EDP-based routine). ⇒ An amount is deposited to the bank (manual routine).	B3	II-III	Short deposit (11) Time deposit (36)

Comments on diffusion and use of fixed term deposit (37)

Deposits involve, in principle, one major working assignment, which is accounting, calculations etc. This assignment involves (or can involve) the use of electronic devices.

The possibilities for using deposits are reckoned to be relatively good, because the use of deposits primarily depends on paper-based procedures, while the use of electronic procedure is a matter of efficiency.

TELEMATIZATION OF BANKING: RESULTS OF A QUESTIONNAIRE SURVEY

INTRODUCTION

With the purpose of strengthening the analysis of the effects of increased technical tradability of banking services on the current and future organization of international banking operations, with special emphasis on the consequences of increased tradability on foreign direct investment (FDI) and/or trade, the research team drew up a questionnaire addressed to experts in the field of telematization of the banking industry. The aim of the questionnaire was to throw light on the general trends in the telematization of banking and their implications. Questions were not related to facts in specific banks. The survey was conducted in the summer of 1992.

The questionnaire was sent to 20 banks/banking experts and answers from the following 15 respondents from eight home countries were received[1]:

ABN-AMRO Bank	Netherlands
Chemical Bank	United States
DuWayne Peterson	United States
Commerzbank	Germany
Crédit Lyonnais	France
Dai-Ichi Kangyo Bank	Japan
Fuji Bank	Japan
Sakura Bank	Japan
Tokai Bank	Japan
Den Danske Bank	Denmark
Multimedia Skills	United Kingdom
National Westminster	United Kingdom
Royal Bank of Canada	Canada
Paribas	France
Unibank	Denmark

RESULTS OF THE SURVEY

Presentation and discussion of responses
The questions posed in the survey and the responses to each of them are presented and discussed below.

1. Has the number of affiliates of banks (including subsidiaries and co-ownership arrangements) increased or decreased in the last 10 years -- excluding the effects of mergers?

Responses to the question are tabulated below:

	Increased	Decreased	No change
In home country	9	5	1
Abroad	10	5	0
In developing countries	9	3	2

Although this is a question related to events in the past, answers from respondents were not identical,[2] reflecting the different home countries of respondents. According to the Japanese experts, the number of affiliates has increased both in the home countries of the banks and abroad, including also developing host countries. In contrast, North American experts held that the number of affiliates abroad, including in developing countries, had decreased, while the development in the home country was more uncertain. Answers from European experts pointed in different directions. On the whole, the tendency was for experts from the larger countries to believe that the number of affiliates in the home country has increased, while experts from smaller countries were of the opposite opinion. The same tendency was apparent in relation to trends in the number of affiliates abroad: experts from larger countries reported an increase, while experts from smaller countries reported a decrease. With reference to developing countries, there is a general agreement that the number of foreign affiliates in those countries has increased.

The main conclusions that can be drawn from these answers are that they reflect developments in different geographical areas and that new information and communication technologies (which must be assumed to be at a similar stages of development in Japan, United States of America and Europe) are not the only determining elements in the development of the affiliate structures of banks. Furthermore, one may conclude that Japanese banks have apparently been expanding their international network, while American banks have been reducing their international network. European banks have mostly been expanding internationally.

2. *Will the number of affiliates of banks increase or decrease in the next 5-10 years -- excluding the effects of mergers?*

Responses to the questions are tabulated below:

	Increase	Decrease	No chanege
In home country	8	6	1
Abroad	7	5	3
In developing countries	10	2	2

This question is related to future developments and the answers reflect even greater uncertainty than those to question 1. There was no agreement among respondents as to whether the number of affiliates will increase or decrease in home countries and abroad. But there was a clear majority in favour of the opinion that the number of affiliates in developing countries will increase.

As in the case of the answers to the first question, the answers to a great extent differed according to the nationality of respondents. Japanese banking experts believed that the number of affiliates will increase in relation to all three categories: in the home country, developed countries abroad and in developing host countries. Responses from both American and European experts were more uncertain, although there was a tendency among European experts to believe that the number of affiliates in home countries will decrease and that the number of affiliates in developing countries will increase. Japanese banking experts are apparently not only in a position to look back on an expanding network of Japanese banks. They are also confident that this development will continue in the future. American and European experts, on the other hand, are more cautious. There was a general tendency among the latter to foresee a concentration on the home markets and an expansion to a certain extent on the foreign markets.

3. What are the most important reasons for establishing affiliates abroad?

Responses to the questions are tabulated below:

Reason	Corporate	Retail
Better service to international customers	15	0
Gaining market shares abroad	7	3
Strategic positioning	10	3
Service can not be delivered there any other way	4	3
Other (which?)	4	0

From the responses to this question, it is apparent that affiliates in foreign countries mostly are established for the purpose of servicing international corporate customers. There were only few answers regarding retail banking. In the case of United States banks, Citibank (which is not included in this survey) is the only one doing retail business outside the United States. However, many former colonies host affiliates of banks from the former colonial powers.

All respondents agreed that better service to international corporate customers is an import-ant reason for establishing affiliates abroad. Two thirds of the respondents expressed the view that strategic positioning was an important motive, while only half of the respondents believed that gaining market shares abroad was an important factor.

Apart from the reasons mentioned in the questionnaire, some respondents listed additional reasons including:

- Establishment of critical mass as an international bank;
- geographic expansion;
- execution of activities that are not allowed in home country, as in the case of Japanese banks in the securities market in London;
- presence for the purpose of assessing profitable opportunities.

4. What are the most important reasons for closing affiliates abroad?

Responses to the questions are tabulated below:

Reason	Corporate	Retail
Mergers between banks with affiliates in the same countries	6	2
Not profitable	12	7
Foreign customers can be provided services from head offices by means of telecommunications	5	0
Cooperation with foreign banks	5	0
Other (which?)	1	0

As in the case of the third question, answers to the fourth question reflect the fact that banks seldom are involved in retail banking in foreign countries. Less than a third of the total responses related to retail banking.

Four fifths of the respondents were of the view that the category "not profitable" is an important reason for closing affiliates. It is obvious that affiliates will be closed if not profitable, unless the dominating reason for establishment is of a strategic character. The intention of the question was to assess **whether** foreign affiliates were or were not profitable. But it is not clear how exactly the respondents understood the question.

The conclusion in relation to the category "foreign customers can be serviced from abroad from head office by means of telecommunications" is much clearer. Only one third of respondents provide this response, clearly underlining either the lack of importance attached by many banking experts attach to information and communication technologies in relation to the international organization of banking operations, at least thus far.

The two categories "mergers between banks with affiliates in same country" and "cooperation with foreign banks" were also indicated by one third of the respondents.

The expansion of Japanese banks is reflected in the fact that the only category indicated in the answers from the Japanese experts was "not profitable". The difference in answers between the Japanese banks and the North American and European respondents suggests that mergers, cooperation or telecommunications-based services are not necessarily elements of an expansionist strategy but to a greater extent defensive measures to curb a difficult situation.

5. *"In the future, affiliates will increasingly report directly to the head of office, eliminating intermediary regional or country headquarters as a result of telecommunications": True or false?*

Responses:

True: 12   **False:** 4

The predominant response was that this statement is true. Three fourths of respondents gave this answer, and there were no marked differences among respondents from different countries. The conclusion suggested is that although the number of foreign affiliates of banks may increase, intermediary regional or country headquarters are likely to be of diminished importance.

One respondent pointed out that whether the statement is true or not depended on the type of activity in question. With respect to the processing of data, the above-mentioned statement was true. However, it did not apply to managerial questions. This answer underlines the necessity of being specific in relation to different kinds of services and production processes when analyzing developments in the division of labour and the organizational structure.

6. *The two extremes in servicing customers abroad are crossborder trade and foreign direct investment (FDI), including branches, subsidiaries or co-ownership. Will crossborder trade gain in importance as compared to FDI? Or will intermediate solutions (such as correspondent relationships with foreign banks) be preferred?*

Responses to the question are tabulated below:

Item	Corporate banking	Retail banking
Crossborder trade will prevail	6	1
Foreign direct investment will prevail	10	8
Intermediate solutions (which?)	2	2

The predominant response was that foreign direct investment would prevail. This was the case both with respect to retail banking and corporate banking. Some of the respondents, however, were of the view that cross-border trade would prevail in corporate banking.

One of the banking experts, contrary to most of the other respondents, was of the view that cross-border trade would prevail in retail banking and FDI would prevail in corporate banking. The background for this answer must be the fact that debit cards can be used internationally to a much greater extent than they are at present. This phenomenon, which will expand in the coming years, should not be overlooked by focusing entirely on corporate banking.

Another respondent drew attention to the fact that the answer to the question to a large extent depended on the kind of banking service under consideration. Some services that *can* be provided through cross-border delivery would be provided through that mode of delivery. For other services that cannot be provided at arm's length across borders, FDI will prevail where profitable, while intermediate solutions may be applied where FDI was not profitable.

7. Will new information and telecommunication technologies affect the "choice" between trade and FDI?

Responses:

Yes: 6   **No:** 9

In response to this question, a majority of three fifths of the respondents answered that new information and telecommunication technologies would not affect the "choice" between trade and FDI. This result may seem somewhat surprising, but it probably reflects the opinion of most experts that technology is only one element, and perhaps a minor one, in explaining changes in international banking operations.

The Japanese experts unanimously agreed that new information and telecommunication technologies do not affect the "choice" between trade and FDI. The experts from North American banks, on the other hand, unanimously stated that the answer was affirmative. This raises the question as to whether American banks are more telematized than Japanese banks, which is not very plausible. The explanation probably lies, as already mentioned, in the expansive strategy of Japanese banks in which technology is only a minor determinant. One respondent drew attention to the fact that retail banking under all circumstances generally requires local presence, while another respondent emphasized that banks, via leased lines, may do their computer processing in the home country, once again drawing attention to data processing as an important area for transborder processing and hence trade.

8. *Will the relationship between head offices and affiliates (whether local or foreign) tend towards centralization or decentralization in the production of services as a consequence of new information and telecommunications technologies?*

Responses to the questions are tabulated below:

Item	Corporate	Retail
Centralization	10	3
Decentralization	5	9

Two thirds of the respondents believed that the relationship between head offices and affiliates would tend towards centralization in corporate banking, while decentralization was the prospect in retail banking. The opinion of the majority of experts is apparently that new information and telecommunication technology will allow banks to centralize their corporate business and at the same time decentralize their retail business.

Some of the respondents, however, did not agree with this assessment. One of them expressed a diametrically opposite opinion, namely, that corporate banking will become decentralized and retail banking centralized. The reason for this disagreement may be a different assessment of the consequences of the new information and telecommunication technology for corporate and retail banking, but it may also have to do with the interpretation of the question. It is not clear whether the question is related to the processing of data or the delivery of banking services, which once again underlines the need to be specific in relation to different kinds of services and production processes.

9. *What are the most important determinants of the "choice" between trade and FDI?*

Responses to the questions are tabulated below:

Determinants	Corporate	Retail
Technology	5	2
Economic aspects (e.g., transaction costs)	10	3
Political/judicial aspects (e.g., authorization)	5	4
Cultural aspects (e.g., trust)	4	7

According to the respondents, the most important determinants of the "choice" between foreign direct investment and trade in corporate banking were the economic aspects. They were indicated by two thirds of the respondents, while technology, regulatory or political/judicial aspects and cultural aspects were indicated by only one third.

In retail banking, according to half of the respondents, cultural aspects were the most important, underlining the importance of trust between banks and retail customers and locally based knowledge about retail customers.

It is important to note that although, as discussed in the main text, technological developments create the possibility for cross-border trade in services, technology was not considered by banking experts to be the most important determinant in the "choice" between FDI and trade. Economic aspects were considered more important in corporate banking and cultural aspects in retail banking.

Interestingly, in line with their answers to the other questions, none of the banking experts from Japan indicated technology as an important determinant of the choice between trade and FDI. Only economic and cultural aspects were indicated as important.

10. With the new information and tele-communications technologies and the greater possibilities for splitting up the production process of financial services, do you see any potentials for independent foreign firms or affiliates of transnational corporations abroad to take part in and share in the production process of financial services (outsourcing)?

Responses:

Yes: 10   **No:** 1   **Not sure:** 4

Two thirds of the experts indicated that they saw potential for independent foreign firms or affiliates of transnational corporations abroad to take part in and share in the production process of financial services by transnational/foreign banks. Only one respondent did not see this potential.

Some of the respondents added that in the future banks will, to a greater extent, concentrate on "pure" banking services and leave out information technology services. The latter services, such as back-office processing of data, may become outsourced, while the banks focus on services that are value-added. One of the respondents mentioned mortgage processing which might be executed by non-financial corporations with sufficient computer power such as, for example, the Ford Motor Company.

Two respondents mentioned that IVANS are already taking part in shares of the production process of financial services. GEISCO, e.g., does not only provide data-processing support for foreign affiliates; they also provide cash management services, e.g. CHEMLINK, for a num-

ber of banks. One respondent expressed the view that the most important development in relation to this question has to do with transnational corporations performing "internal banking" or operating directly on international financial markets.

11. What are the main constraints for such a development (as mentioned in question 10)?

Answers to this question by the respondents can be grouped in the following categories:

- One category relates to the loss of control over the whole of the production process when outsourcing parts of the production chain. One respondent mentioned the risk of losing the strategic ability for manoeuvering.

- Another category is concerned with banking regulations both in the home country and in the host country. The Canadian Banking Law of 1980 was cited as an example. That law prohibits foreign banks from processing their Canadian transactions outside Canada.

- A third category relates to the qualifications of local labour. Some respondents mentioned that lack of adequately educated labour power in terms of financial and technological know-how may be a constraint on localization of production.

- Finally, one respondent mentioned a number of key considerations: costs, reliability, security and confidentiality.

A few respondents made some further comments. One expert stated that telecommunications transaction costs are still too high and that this hindered the tradability of banking services. Another expert expressed the view that credit remained the major banking product and that this was based on local knowledge concerning customers. Tradability of banking products will generally be limited to advanced products such as derivatives and swaps. Retail banking will remain a domestic business.

Conclusions

The general results of the questionnaire survey may be summarized as follows:

- There is no uniform global trend with respect to foreign direct investment and/or trade in banking services. Japanese banks are expanding their international networks, while American banks are reducing theirs.

- There is a general agreement, however, that the number of affiliates of transnational banks will increase in host developing countries in the coming years.

- The difference in developments in Japan, United States and Europe underlines the opinion of the majority of respondents who believe that technology is not as important as economic factors (in corporate banking) and cultural factors (in retail banking) in considering the international organization of banking operations.

- The internationalization of banking services is predominantly related to corporate customers. This is the case both with respect to FDI and with respect to cross-border trade.

- It is not possible from the survey to give an answer to the question as to whether cross-border trade in corporate banking will gain in importance compared with foreign direct investment. But in retail banking, foreign direct investment is clearly considered to be more important.

- The most important reason for establishing affiliates abroad providing corporate banking services is the possibility for improving services to corporate customers expanding internationally.

- A majority of respondents to the questionnaire do not believe that information and telecommunication technologies will affect the "choice" between foreign direct investment and trade. This is entirely in line with the assessment that technology is not the most important determinant in the international organization of banking operations. But it does not correspond very well with the answers to more specific questions concerning future organizational structures in the banking industry.

- With respect to the above, a clear majority of the respondents, for instance, believe that affiliates will increasingly report directly to head offices as a result of telecommunications, eliminating regional or country headquarters.

- Furthermore, information and telecommunications technologies will allow centralization in corporate banking and decentralization in retail banking, according to a majority of respondents.

- Last but not least, a clear majority of respondents believe that the new information and telecommunications technologies and the greater possibility for splitting up the production process of financial services entail potentials for independent firms or affiliates of transnational corporations abroad to take part in and share in the production process of financial services.

● The responses suggest that on a more general level, technology is apparently not considered to be the most decisive factor in the future internationalization of banking services, but in more specific areas, technology is considered important. Thus, in considering the tradability of banking services and its consequences for the organizational structure of banks, it is important to be specific concerning different services and production processes. The general opinion among the respondents was that the biggest potentials for outsourcing in the banking industry, as a consequence of new information and telecommunication technologies, lay in back-office processing.

Notes

1   It is recognized that this small sample of banks/banking experts does not allow for generalizations on the basis of statistical analysis. Answers to the questionnaire only give a qualitative indication of the opinions of banking experts. All the same, the number of respondents indicating answers in relation to the different questions are enumerated in the discussion of the results. The sums are often higher than 15, as respondents had the possibility to choose more than one alternative where appropriate.

2   There is an element of estimation in the responses as regards the condition: " excluding the effects of mergers".

Select list of publications of the UNCTAD Programme on Transnational Corporations

A. Individual studies

Environmental Management in Transnational Corporations: Report on the Benchmark Corporate Environment Survey. 278 p. Sales No. E.94.II.A.2. $29.95.

Accounting, Valuation and Privatization. 190 p. Sales No. E.94.II.A.3. $25.

Management Consulting: A Survey of the Industry and Its Largest Firms. 100 p. Sales No. E.93.II.A.17. $25.

Transnational Corporations: A Selective Bibliography, 1991-1992. 736 p. Sales No. E.93.II.A.16. $75. (English/French.)

Small and Medium-sized Transnational Corporations: Role, Impact and Policy Implications. 242 p. Sales No. E.93.II.A.15. $35.

World Investment Report 1993: Transnational Corporations and Integrated International Production. An Executive Summary. 31 p. ST/CTC/159. Free-of-charge.

World Investment Report 1993: Transnational Corporations and Integrated International Production. 290 p. Sales No. E.93.II.A.14. $45.

Foreign Investment and Trade Linkages in Developing Countries. 108 p. Sales No. E.93.II.A.12. $18.

World Investment Directory 1992. Volume III: Developed Countries. 532 p. Sales No. E.93.II.A.9. $75.

Transnational Corporations from Developing Countries: Impact on Their Home Countries. 116 p. Sales No. E.93.II.A.8. $15.

Debt-Equity Swaps and Development. 150 p. Sales No. E.93.II.A.7. $35.

From the Common Market to EC 92: Regional Economic Integration in the European Community and Transnational Corporations. 134 p. Sales No. E.93.II.A.2. $25.

World Investment Directory 1992. Volume II: Central and Eastern Europe. 432 p. Sales No. E.93.II.A.1. $65. (Joint publication with ECE.)

The East-West Business Directory 1991/1992. 570 p. Sales No. E.92.II.A.20. $65.

World Investment Report 1992: Transnational Corporations as Engines of Growth: An Executive Summary. 30 p. Sales No. E.92.II.A.24.

World Investment Report 1992: Transnational Corporations as Engines of Growth. 356 p. Sales No. E.92.II.A.19. $45.

World Investment Directory 1992. Volume I: Asia and the Pacific. 356 p. Sales No. E.92.II.A.11. $65.

Climate Change and Transnational Corporations: Analysis and Trends. 110 p. Sales No. E.92.II.A.7. $16.50.

Foreign Direct Investment and Transfer of Technology in India. 150 p. Sales No. E.92.II.A.3. $20.

The Determinants of Foreign Direct Investment: A Survey of the Evidence. 84 p. Sales No. E.92.II.A.2. $12.50

The Impact of Trade-Related Investment Measures on Trade and Development: Theory, Evidence and Policy Implications. 108 p. Sales No. E.91.II.A.19. $17.50. (Joint publication with UNCTAD.)

Transnational Corporations and Industrial Hazards Disclosure. 98 p. Sales No. E.91.II.A.18. $17.50.

Transnational Business Information: A Manual of Needs and Sources. 216 p. Sales No. E.91.II.A.13. $45.

World Investment Report 1991: The Triad in Foreign Direct Investment. 108 p. Sales No.E.91.II.A.12. $25.

Transnational Corporations: A Selective Bibliography, 1988-1990. 618 p. Sales No.E.91.II.A.10. $65. (English/French.)

Transnational Corporations in South Africa: A List of Companies with Investments and Disinvestments. 282 p. Sales No. E.91.II.A.9. $50.00.

University Curriculum on Transnational Corporations *

      Vol.   I   *Economic Development.* 188 p. Sales No. E.91.II.A.5. $20.00.

      Vol.   II   *International Business.* 156 p. Sales No. E.91.II.A.6. $20.00.

      Vol.   III *International Law.* 180 p. Sales No. E.91.II.A.7. $20.00.

      * The Set: Sales No. E.91.II.A.8. $50.00.

Directory of the World's Largest Service Companies: Series I. 834 p. ISSN 1014-8507. (Joint publication, UNCTC/Moody's Investors Service, Inc.) $99.

The Challenge of Free Economic Zones in Central and Eastern Europe. 444 p. Sales No. E.90.II.A.27. $75.

Accountancy Development in Africa: Challenge of the 1990s. 206 p. Sales No. E.91.II.A.2. $25. (Also available in French.)

Transnational Banks and the International Debt Crisis. 157 p. Sales No. E.90.II.A.19. $22.50.

Transborder Data Flows and Mexico: A Technical Paper. 194 p. Sales No. E.90.II.A.17. $27.50.

Debt Equity Conversions: A Guide For Decision-Makers. 150 p. Sales No. E.90.II.A.22. $27.50.

Transnational Corporations and Manufacturing Exports from Developing Countries.
124 p. Sales No. E.90.II.A.21. $25.

Transnational Corporations in the Transfer of New and Emerging Technologies to Developing Countries. 141 p. Sales No. E.90.II.A.20. $27.50.

Transnational Corporations, Services and the Uruguay Round. 252 p. Sales No. E.90.II.A.11. $28.50.

The Uruguay Round: Services in the World Economy, 220 p., ISBN 0-8213-1374-6. (Joint publication, UNCTC/World Bank.) $13.50.

Transnational Corporations in the Plastics Industry. 167 p. Sales No. E.90.II.A.1. $20.

Objectives and Concepts Underlying Financial Statements. 32 p. Sales No. E.89.II.A.18. $8.

Services and Development: The Role of Foreign Direct Investment and Trade. 187 p. Sales No. E.89.II.A.17. $20.

Transnational Corporations in South Africa and Namibia: A Selective Bibliography. 98 p. Sales No. E.89.II.A.13. $12.

Transnational Corporations in the Construction and Design Engineering Industry. 60 p. Sales No. E.89.II.A.6. $9.

Foreign Direct Investment and Transnational Corporations in Services. 229 p. Sales No. E.89.II.A.1. $26.

Data Goods and Data Services in the Socialist Countries of Eastern Europe. 103 p. Sales No. E.88.II.A.20. $13.50.

Conclusions on Accounting and Reporting by Transnational Corporations: The Inter-governmental Working Group of Experts on International Standards of Accounting and Reporting. 58 p. Sales No. E.88.II.A.18. $7.50. (Also available in Arabic, Chinese, French, Russian, Spanish.)

Transnational Corporations in World Development: Trends and Prospects. 628 p. Sales No. E.88.II.A.7. $56. (Also available in Arabic, Chinese, French, Russian, Spanish.)

Executive Summary. Transnational Corporations in World Development: Trends and Prospects. 66 p. Sales No. E.88.II.A.15. $3.

Transnational Corporations: A Selective Bibliography, 1983-1987.

    Vol.   I   441 p. Sales No. E.88.II.A.9. $45.

    Vol.   II   463 p. Sales No. E.88.II.A.10. $49.

Joint Ventures as a Form of International Economic Co-operation: Background Documents of the High-Level Seminar Organized by the United Nations Centre on Transnational Corporations in Co-operation with the USSR State Foreign Economic Com-

mission and the USSR State Committee on Science and Technology, 10 March 1988, Moscow. 210 p. Sales No. E.88.II.A.12. $21.

International Income Taxation and Developing Countries. 108 p. Sales No. E.88.II.A.6. $13.50.

Transnational Corporations in Biotechnology. 136 p. Sales No. E.88.II.A.4. $17.

Foreign Direct Investment in the People's Republic of China: Report of the Round-Table Organized by the United Nations Centre on Transnational Corporations in Co-operation with the Ministry of Foreign Economic Relations and Trade, People's Republic of China, Beijing, 25 and 26 May 1987. 115 p. Sales No. E.88.II.A.3. $15.50.

Bilateral Investment Treaties. 194 p. Sales No. E.88.II.A.1. $20.

UNCTC Bibliography, 1974-1987. 83 p. Sales No. 87.II.A.23. $12.

Licence Agreements in Developing Countries. 108 p. Sales No. E.87.II.A.21. $13.50.

Consolidated List of Products Whose Consumption and/or Sale Have Been Banned, Withdrawn, Severely Restricted or Not Approved by Governments, Second Issue (UNCTC in collaboration with FAO, WHO, ILO and other relevant intergovernmental organizations). 655 p. Sales No. E.87.IV.1. $60.

Transnational Corporations and Non-fuel Primary Commodities in Developing Countries. 89 p. Sales No. E.87.II.A.17. $10.

Transnational Corporations in the Man-made Fibre, Textile and Clothing Industries. 154 p. Sales No. E.87.II.A.11. $19.

Transnational Corporations and Technology Transfer: Effects and Policy Issues. 77 p. Sales No. E.87.II.A.4. $11.

Analysis of Engineering and Technical Consultancy Contracts. 517 p. Sales No. E.86.II.A.4. $45.

Transnational Corporations in the International Semiconductor Industry. 471 p. Sales No. E.86.II.A.1. $41.

Trends and Issues in Foreign Direct Investment and Related Flows. 96 p. Sales No. E.85.II.A.15. $11.

Environmental Aspects of the Activities of Transnational Corporations: A Survey. 114 p. Sales No. E.85.II.A.11. $12.50.

Transnational Corporations and International Trade: Selected Issues. 93 p. Sales No. E.85.II.A.4. $11.

B. Serial publications

UNCTC Current Studies, Series A

No. 1. Patrick Robinson, *The Question of a Reference to International Law in the United Nations Code of Conduct on Transnational Corporations.* 22 p. Sales No. E.86.II.A.5. $4.

No. 2. Detlev Vagts, *The Question of a Reference to International Obligations in the United Nations Code of Conduct on Transnational Corporations: A Different View.* 17 p. Sales No. E.86.II.A.11. $4.

No. 3. *Foreign Direct Investment in Latin America: Recent Trends, Prospects and Policy Issues.* 28 p. Sales No. E.86.II.A.14. $5.

No. 4. *The United Nations Code of Conduct on Transnational Corporations.* 80 p. Sales No. E.86.II.A.15. $9.50.

(Also published by Graham & Trotman, London/Dordrecht/Boston. $31.50)

No. 5. *Transnational Corporations and the Electronics Industries of ASEAN Economies.* 55 p. Sales No. E.87.II.A.13. $7.50.

No. 6. *Technology Acquisition under Alternative Arrangements with Transnational Corporations: Selected Industrial Case Studies in Thailand.* 55 p. Sales No. E.87.II.A.14. $7.50.

No. 7. *Foreign Direct Investment, the Service Sector and International Banking.* 71 p. Sales No. E.87.II.A.15. $9.

(Also published by Graham & Trotman, London/Dordrecht/Boston. $25).

No. 8. *The Process of Transnationalization and Transnational Mergers.* 91 p. Sales No. E.89.II.A.4. $12.

No. 9. *Transnational Corporations and the Growth of Services: Some Conceptual and Theoretical Issues.* 96 p. Sales No. E.89.II.A.5. $12.

No. 10. *Transnational Service Corporations and Developing Countries: Impact and Policy Issues.* 50 p. Sales No. E.89.II.A.14. $7.50.

No. 11. *Transnational Corporations and International Economic Relations: Recent Developments and Selected Issues.* 50 p. Sales No. E.89.II.A.15. $7.50

No. 12. *New Approaches to Best-practice Manufacturing: The Role of Transnational Corporations and Implications for Developing Countries.* 76 p. Sales No. E.90.II.A.13. $12.50.

No. 13. *Key Concepts in International Investment Arrangements and Their Relevance to Negotiations on International Transactions in Services.* 66 p. Sales No. E.90.II.A.3. $9.

No. 14. *The Role of Free Economic Zones in the USSR and Eastern Europe.* 84 p. Sales No. E.90.II.A.5. $10.

No. 15.   *Economic Integration and Transnational Corporations in the 1990s: Europe 1992, North America and Developing Countries.* 52 p. Sales No. E.90.II.A.14. $12.50.

No. 16.   *The New Code Environment.* 54 p. Sales No. E.90.II.A.7. $7.50.

No. 17.   *Government Policies and Foreign Direct Investment.* 68 p. Sales No. E.91.II.A.20. $12.50.

No. 18.   *Foreign Direct Investment and Industrial Restructuring in Mexico.* 114 p. Sales No. E.92.II.A.9. $12.

No. 19.   *New Issues in the Uruguay Round of Multilateral Trade Negotiations.* 52 p. Sales No. E.90.II.A.15. $12.50.

No. 20.   *Foreign Direct Investment, Debt and Home Country Policies.* 50 p. Sales No. E.90.II.A.16. $12.

No. 22.   *Transnational Banks and the External Indebtedness of Developing Countries: Impact of Regulatory Changes.* 48 p. Sales No. E.92.II.A.10. $12.

No. 23.   *The Transnationalization of Service Industries: An Empirical Analysis of the Determinants of Foreign Direct Investment by Transnational Service Corporations.* 62 p. Sales No. E.93.II.A.3. $15.00.

No. 24.   *Intellectual Property Rights and Foreign Direct Investment.* 108 p. Sales No. E.93.II.A.10. $20.

No. 25.   *International Tradability in Insurance Services.* 54 p. Sales No. E.93.II.A.11. $20.

No. 26.   *Explaining and Forecasting Regional Flows of Foreign Direct Investment.* 58 p. Sales No. E.94.II.A.5. $25.

UNCTC Advisory Studies, Series B

No. 1.   *Natural Gas Clauses in Petroleum Arrangements.* 54 p. Sales No. E.87.II.A.3. $8.

No. 2.   *Arrangements Between Joint Venture Partners in Developing Countries.* 43 p. Sales No. E.87.II.A.5. $6.

No. 3.   *Financial and Fiscal Aspects of Petroleum Exploitation.* 43 p. Sales No. E.87.II.A.10. $6.

No. 4.   *International Debt Rescheduling: Substantive Issues and Techniques.* 91 p. Sales No. E.89.II.A.10. $10.

No. 5.   *Negotiating International Hotel Chain Management Agreements.* 60 p. Sales No. E.90.II.A.8. $9.

No. 6.   *Curricula for Accounting Education for East-West Joint Ventures in Centrally Planned Economies.* 86 p. Sales No. E.90.II.A.2. $10.

No. 7.   *Joint Venture Accounting in the USSR: Direction for Change.* 46 p. Sales No. E.90.II.A.26. $12.

No. 10.   *Formulation and Implementation of Foreign Investment Policies: Selected Key Issues.* 84 p. Sales No. E.92.II.A.21. $12.

The United Nations Library on Transnational Corporations:

    Set A (Boxed set of 4 volumes. ISBN 0-415-08554-3. £350):

    Volume One: *The Theory of Transnational Corporations.* 464 p.

Volume Two: *Transnational Corporations: A Historical Perspective.* 464 p.

Volume Three: *Transnational Corporations and Economic Development.* 448 p.

Volume Four: *Transnational Corporations and Business Strategy.* 416 p.

    Set B (Boxed set of 4 volumes. ISBN 0-415-08555-1. £350):

Volume Five: *International Financial Management.* 400 p.

Volume Six: *Organization of Transnational Corporations.* 400 p.

Volume Seven: *Governments and Transnational Corporations.* 352 p.

Volume Eight: *Transnational Corporations and International Trade and Payments.* 320 p.

    Set C (Boxed set of 4 volumes. ISBN 0-415-08556-X. £350):

Volume Nine: *Transnational Corporations and Regional Economic Integration.* 331 p.

Volume Ten: *Transnational Corporations and the Exploitation of Natural Resources.* 397 p.

Volume Eleven: *Transnational Corporations and Industrialization.* 425 p.

Volume Twelve: *Transnational Corporations in Services.* 437 p.

    Set D (Boxed set of 4 volumes. ISBN 0-415-08557-8. £350):

Volume Thirteen: *Cooperative Forms of Transnational Corporation Activity.*

Volume Fourteen: *Transnational Corporations: Transfer Pricing and Taxation.*

Volume Fifteen: *Transnational Corporations: Market Structure and Industrial Performance.*

Volume Sixteen: *Transnational Corporations and Human Resources.*

    Set E (Boxed set of 4 volumes. ISBN 0-415-08558-6. £350):

Volume Seventeen: *Transnational Corporations and Innovatory Activities.*

Volume Eighteen: *Transnational Corporations and Technology Transfer to Developing Countries.*

Volume Nineteen: *Transnational Corporations and National Law.*

Volume Twenty: *Transnational Corporations: The International Legal Framework.*

International Accounting and Reporting Issues:

1984 Review. 122 p. Sales No. E.85.II.A.2. $13.50.

1985 Review. 141 p. Sales No. E.85.II.A.13. $15.

1986 Review. 158 p. Sales No. E.86.II.A.16. $15.

1987 Review. 140 p. Sales No. E.88.II.A.8. $17.

(Also published by Graham & Trotman, London/Dordrecht/Boston. $65).

1988 Review. 95 p. Sales No. E.88.II.A.3. $12.

1989 Review. 152 p. Sales No.E.90.II.A.4. $12.

1990 Review. 254 p. Sales No. E.91.II.A.3. $25.

1991 Review. 244 p. Sales No. E.92.II.A.8. $25.

1992 Review. 328 p. Sales No. E.93.II.A.6. $25.

National Legislation and Regulations Relating to Transnational Corporations:

Vol. I (Part One) 302 p. Sales No. E.78.II.A.3. $16.

Vol. I (Part Two - Supplement) 114 p. Sales No. E.80.II.A.5. $9.

Vol.II 338 p. Sales No. E.83.II.A.7. $33.

Vol.III 345 p. Sales No. E.83.II.A.15. $33.

Vol.IV 241 p. Sales No. E.85.II.A.14. $23.

Vol.V 246 p. Sales No. E.86.II.A.3. $23.

Vol.VI 322 p. Sales No. E.87.II.A.6. $45.

Vol.VII 320 p. Sales No. E.89.II.A.9. $36.

Transnational Corporations in South Africa and Namibia: United Nations Public Hearings:

Reports of the Panel of Eminent Persons and of the Secretary-General. 242 p. Sales No. E.86.II.A.6. $65.

* *Verbatim Records.* 300 p. Sales No. E.86.II.A.7.

Statements and Submissions. 518 p. Sales No. E.86.II.A.8. $54.

Policy Instruments and Statements. 444 p. Sales No. E.86.II.A.9.

Four-volume set — $200.

   * May not be purchased separately.

Transnational Corporations in South Africa: Second United Nations Public Hearings, 1989

Report of the Panel of Eminent Persons, Background Documentation. 162 p. Sales No. E.90.II.A.6. $19.

Statements and Submission. 209 p. Sales No. E.90.II.A.20. $21.

Transnational Corporations (formerly *The CTC Reporter*).

Published three times a year. Annual subscription price: $35; individual issues $15.

Transnationals, a quarterly newsletter, is available free of charge.

United Nations publications may be obtained from bookstores and distributors throughout the world. Please consult your bookstore or write to:

United Nations Publications

Sales Section	OR	Sales Section
Room DC2-0853		United Nations Office at Geneva
United Nations Secretariat		Palais des Nations
New York, N.Y. 10017		CH-1211 Geneva 10
U.S.A.		Switzerland
Tel: (1-212) 963-8302 or (800) 253-9646		Tel: (41-22) 917-1234
Fax: (1-212) 963-3489		Fax: (41-22) 917-0123

All prices are quoted in United States dollars.

For further information on the work of the UNCTAD Programme on Transnational Corporations, please address enquiries to:

United Nations Conference on Trade and Development
Programme on Transnational Corporations
Palais des Nations, Room E-8006
CH-1211 Geneva 10

Switzerland
Telephone: (41-22) 907-5707
Telefax: (41-22) 907-0194
Telex: UNCTNC 661062

QUESTIONNAIRE

The tradability of banking services: Impact and implications

In order to improve the quality and relevance of the work of the UNCTAD Programme on Transnational Corporations, it would be useful to receive the views of readers on this and other similar publications. It would therefore be greatly appreciated if you could complete the following questionnaire and return to:

Readership Survey
UNCTAD Programme on Transnational Corporations
United Nations Office in Geneva
Palais des Nations
Room E-9008
CH-1211 Geneva 10
Switzerland

1. Name and address of respondent (optional):

_____

_____

_____

2. Which of the following best describes your area of work?

Government	❑	Public enterprise	❑
Private enterprise	❑	Academic or research institution	❑
International organization	❑	Media	❑
Non-profit organization	❑	Other (specify) _____	

3. In which country do you work? _____

_____

4. What is your assessment of the contents of this publication?

Excellent ☐   Adequate ☐

Good ☐   Poor ☐

5. How useful is this publication to your work?

Very useful ☐   Of some use ☐   Irrelevant ☐

6. Please indicate the three things you liked best about this publication:

_____

_____

_____

7. Please indicate the three things you liked least about this publication:

_____

_____

_____

8. If you have read more than the present publication of the UNCTAD Division on Transnational Corporations and Investment, what is your overall assessment of them?

Consistently good ☐   Usually good, but with some exceptions ☐

Generally mediocre ☐   Poor ☐

9. On the average, how useful are these publications to you in your work?

Very useful   ☐   Of some use   ☐   Irrelevant   ☐

10. Are you a regular recipient of *Transnational Corporations* (formerly *The CTC Reporter*), the Programme's tri-annual publication which reports on the Programme's and related work?

Yes   ☐   No   ☐

If not, please check here if you would like to receive a sample
copy sent to the name and address you have given above   ☐